THE ORAONS OF CHOTA NAGPUR

THE ORAONS OF CHOTA NAGPUR

BY

SARAT CHANDRA ROY

GYAN

ISBN : 978-81-212-1838-2 (HB)

First Published, 1915

Published, 2018

Published by

Gyan Publishing House
5, Ansari Road
Daryaganj, New Delhi-110002
Phone: 011-47034999, 9811692060
www.gyanbooks.com
E-mail: books@gyanbooks.com

Printed at: G. Print Process, Delhi.

List of Illustrations.

PREFACE.

The present work is the result of fifteen years' intimate acquaintance with the Orāons, including three years' special enquiries about their customs and usages.

The Orāons are spread over such a large tract of the Chōtā Nāgpur plateau that local variations of the customs recorded in this book necessarily occur. And as with advancing civilization old customs, habits, ideas and beliefs are now in a process of transformation, decay or disappearance, all the customs and usages described here can hardly be found together in any one village at this day.

Should the present work be favourably received by the public, it is proposed to follow it up by another volume giving an account of the religious and magico-religious system, the domestic ceremonies and usages and the language and folklore of the Orāons so as to complete our picture of the tribe.

The great importance for administrative purposes of the study of the ethnology of such backward tribes as the Orāons has been referred to by Dr. Haddon in the Introduction which he has so very kindly written for this work and for which I cannot adequately express my gratitude to him. As for the scientific interest of such a study, the observations made elsewhere by the same eminent authority with reference to the Cochin tribes apply with equal force to the Orāons: "These backward jungle-folk have a peculiar interest for ethnologists as they appear to retain many of the customs and beliefs which we may well suppose characterised mankind in very ancient times; they are ethnological survivals which bear the same relation to Anthropology as that borne to Zoology by those generalised or persistent types dating from geological antiquity in various groups of animals that rejoice the heart of the Zoologist."

I take this opportunity of recording my most respectful gratitude to His Honour Sir Charles Stuart Bayley, K.C.S.I., I.S.O., Lieutenant-Governor of Bihār and Orissā, for kind words of encouragement during the preparation of this work. To the Hon'ble Mr. E. A. Gait, C.S.I., C.I.E., I.C.S., Member, Executive Council, Bihar and Orissa, my debt of gratitude is incalculable. To him I owe my initiation into the study of Anthropology as a science, and his never-failing kindness and words of encouragement and advice have throughout cheered and guided me in my labours. Finally, I have to thank the Rev. P. T. Martin, B.A. (Cantab.) for the trouble he has kindly taken in revising the proofs of certain parts of the book.

RANCHI,
The 1st June, 1915.

S. C. ROY.

CONTENTS

INTRODUCTION.

Mr. Saratchandra Roy in 1912 published a a valuable book entitled "The Mundas and Their Country," and now he has placed ethnologists further in his debt by the present volume on the Oraons. More than half of the earlier work was taken up by an account of the ancient and recent history of the people; fortunately for the student the early history of the Oraons is not so complicated and the author is able to give an adequate account of their traditional history and migrations in one chapter.

As in so many other instances, the name by which these people are called is not their name for themselves, which is Kurukh, but the term Oraon has now become their official appellation. All authorities are agreed that the Oraons are a Dravidian people who immigrated on to the plateau of Chota Nagpur. Mr. Gait says that according to their traditions they came from the Carnatic up the Narbada river and settled in Bihar on the banks of the Son, and he adds that their language is "more closely allied to Canarese than to any other Dravidian language spoken in the south of India" ("Census of India 1901" VI. pt I (1903), p. 328).

It is quite evident from a perusal of the ethnographical data presented with such praiseworthy detail in this book that the culture of the Oraons is of complex origin, as their history would lead one to expect. One problem for future research is to dissect out, as it were, the various elements which are associated together and thus to reconstruct the cultural history of the people; at the same time the traditional and recorded history and the racial affinities of the people must be taken into account. Fortunately Mr. Roy has provided very full and most valuable data for the two most important tribes of one portion of Chota Nagpur, but a study of the kind suggested will necessitate research not only among the neighbouring tribes but among peoples farther afield.

We have a suggestive indication of the early condition of the Oraons before they set out on their wanderings if, as our author believes, they formed part of the Vanara army that helped the Aryan hero Rama Chandra in defeating the non-Aryan king Rawana of Lanka. They appear, according to this identification, to have lived in caves and fought with sticks and stones; even at the present day the Oraons still use about half-a-dozen varieties of sticks in their hunting excursions. They fed largely on wild plants and roots, were addicted to drink, and took great delight in singing to the sound of the *mandal* which is still their favourite musical instrument. "A few references in the Ramayana would seem to show that even the physiological conditions of paternity were not yet understood by this people" (p. 26). Ramachandra not only called his allies "friends" and "brethren" but also "monkeys" (*vanara*); for this term he must have had a good reason. It certainly was not a term of contempt, as the Vanaras are spoken of as "amiable-looking" and "good fellows." The author's suggestion is that various monkeys were the totems of the leading sections of the Dravidian hill-men of Rama Chandra's army and to this day there are monkey-totems amongst the Oraons of Chota Nagpur and the flesh of the monkey is tabu to all Oraons (p.22). The conclusion is drawn that "the totem was derived from the mother's side, descent being matrilineal in those days and paternity imperfectly understood" (p.23).

In the course of their wanderings from South India the Oraons practised agriculture and cattle-breeding and learnt the use of metal implements, but before they settled in the valley of the Son in what is now the Shahabad district in Bihar they seem to have preferred cattle to all else. This was the area of their economic and social characterisation. Driven thence by the Cheros, perhaps on the downfall of the Gupta dynasty, they migrated to the north-west portion of the plateau of Chota Nagpur, where they lived in tolerable amity with the Mundas; on becoming predominant, however, they crowded out the Mundas, who retreated to the southern and eastern parts of the plateau. The plateau was "the area originally of their consolidation and subsequently of disintegration and degradation" (p.51), and here they haye been subject to various cultural influences, among which that of the Mundas has probably been most potent though Hinduism and quite recently Christianity have not been without effect.

One of the most interesting suggestions offered by Mr, Roy is that there was formerly a system of marriage between grand-parents and grand-children and other relatives belonging to these generations. (pp. 352-355). This form of marriage has recently received much attention from Dr. Rivers ("History of Melanesian Society," II. 1914) ,who says: "The evidence for the existence of marriage with the grand-daughter of the brother at the present time [in Melanesia] is less definite, but there is a clear tradition of its occurrence in the past and it is said still to be practised....Such a marriage regulation is not unique, but is actually in vogue at the present time (or at the time Howitt's record was made) among the Dieri of Australia. Not only does a Dieri man sometimes marry the granddaughter of his elder brother, but there are certain modes of speech in use among the people which resemble closely the way in which terms of relationship are used in Pentecost......There is a Dieri saying 'those who are *Noa* to each other are also *Nadada* to each other,' and this is equivalent to saying that the maternal grandfather and his daughter's daughter are potential consorts. Thus, not only does the marriage in question still take place among the Dieri, but 'there is a clear recognition that relatives belonging to generations twice removed from one another are naturally husband and wife (p. 47). Rivers also points out that "the nature of the dual organisation with matrilineal descent makes it clear that if a man is to marry a woman of a generation younger than his own, he will be limited in his choice to two groups of relatives; viz., women having the status of his daughters and those having the status of his daughter's daughters, for other women ... will be of the same moiety as himself." He believes that marriage with a granddaughter, as an organised practice, had its origin in a state of society in which the elders had in some way acquired so predominant a position in the community that they were able to monopolise all the young women, those of each moiety becoming as a matter of course the wives of the elders of the other moiety. The obvious consequence of such a condition is that, as young men grow up, they will find the young women who would naturally have been their wives already appropriated by the old men. Their only chance of obtaining wives will be that women will be given to them who have already been the wives of their elders. In such a society a man could only give wives to his sons' sons and to his sisters' sons, thus bringing about the two forms of marriage, the existence of which has either been demonstrated or inferred in Melanesia, viz., marriage with the wife of the mother's brother and marriage with the wife of the father's father. Rivers also points out that cross-cousin marriage arose as a modification of the marriage with the wife of the mother's brother (pp. 58-61).

Rivers holds that in all places where we have evidence of the existence of marriage with the wives of the father's father and mother's brother we may conclude that the dual organisation with matrilineal descent was the older form of social organisation and that other forms, such as totemism, are later, as is also cross-cousin marriage. Among the Dieri of Australia the dual organisation with matrilineal descent and a totemic system exist side by side (p. 84). The Orāons have travelled beyond this stage of culture as totemic descent is patrilineal and no trace has been discovered as yet of the dual organisation; but accepting the hypothesis of Rivers we may assume that these two missing institutions were once characteristic of the Orāons and formed the basis of Dravidian society. Among the Nayārs, it will be remembered, there are mother-right kinship groups (*taravad*) which are strictly exogamous, but the dual organisation is unrecorded, so far as I am aware. The two divisions of the Todas, the Teivaliol and Tartharol, are endogamous and each is divided into a number of exogamous septs resembling the *gotras* of a caste (W.H.R. Rivers, "The Todas", 1906, p. 679), whereas the two divisions in a dual organisation are exogamous.

Totemism is patrilineal and exogamous and has most of the features of the typical totemism of Australia, but descent from or relationship with the totem does not seem to occur, totem badges are not employed, and there are no ceremonies in connection with the totem. Mr. Roy makes the suggestion that the animal effigies, which serve as the emblems of certain villages at the Jātrā and to which offerings are made, probably "represent the totems of the first Orāon settlers of the village and were in process of evolution into totem-deities when further progress in that direction was arrested" (pp. 340-341). Every village, however, has its distinctive flag to which similar offerings are made; the flag appears to have replaced the animal effigy. Although the totem clan has remained the basis of the social structure of the Oraons the Parha confederacy has supplanted the old totem-clan as the political unit (p. 344).

A very important institution of the Oraons is the bachelors' dormitory concerning which we now have adequate information for the first time. It is correctly described as "a very archaic form of economic, social, and religious organization" (p. 211). According to the tradition of the Oraons it was "brought by their ancestors from their ancient home on the Rohtas plateau to their present home" (p. 212). The boys living in the house are grouped into three age grades, as are also the girls in their dormitory (p. 261). Theoretically the perfect freedom which is allowed between these young people does not exist between members of the same clan, but the practice is very different. Marriage, however, between members of the same clan, *gotra*, is strictly prohibited, and it is not considered desirable for the boy and girl to belong to the same village even though they be members of different clans (p. 247). Risley ("Tribes and

Castes of Bengal", II., 1891, p. 140) points out that the bachelors' dormitory is not confined to the Orāons, but is met with among the Juangs, the Hill Bhuiyahs of Keonjhur and Bonai. and the Jhumia Maghs of the Chittagong Hill tracts. It also occurs among the Mundas, but among them it is only in certain localities that it forms an institution exactly like that of the Oraons ("Mundas", p. 385). The bachelors' house is found in Assam among the Abors, Ao Nagas, and Mikirs, and occurs sporadically in Indonesia, New Guinea, and Melanesia.

Renewed attention is now being paid to the distribution and significance of stone monuments, a subject on which my friend Mr. W. J. Perry is about to publish some interesting conclusions based on his researches in the ethnological literature of the Indonesian area. The use of stones among the Oraon appears to be limited to the following instances: Chandi, who is represented by stones (pp. 225, 228, 240), is the chief deity of the hunting stage of primitive Oraon culture, who through appropriate rites may be made to impart sufficient strength to the procreative powers of young men to enable them to increase indefinitely the number of huntsmen in the tribe (p. 239). Dalton says that Chanda or Chandi is the god or goddess of the chase and is always invoked preparatory to starting on great hunting expeditions.

Any rock or stone serves to represent this deity. Stone slabs on which spectators sit generally occur at one end of the *akhra*, or dancing ground (p. 274), which is a circular plot of ground, often a circular earthen platform (p. 289). The bride and bridegroom during the *sindurdan* portion of the marriage ceremony stand on a curry-stone. Sling-stones are employed (pp. 238, 283), and according to tradition the Orāons erected a stone fort when on the Rohtas plateau (p. 35).

The Mundas have funeral ceremonies which closely resemble those of the Oraons but they bury the ashes under a large stone slab supported on four small pieces of stone placed at the four corners ("The Mundas and their Country", p. 466). The large stone slabs may also lie flat on the ground (l. c., p. 387). "The village-*sāsan*, or burial ground, with the rude stone slabs (*sasan-diriko*) that guard the mortal remains of the ancestors (*haram-horoko*) of the village-family, is to this day a favourite meeting-ground of the once almighty Panch [or council of the village elders]". (l. c., p. 122, and cf. plate, p. 40). It is well known that the Khasis of Assam erect very numerous stone monuments of various kinds, including monoliths analogous to those of the Mundas, and it is significant that the Munda (like all the other languages of Chota Nagpur, except Oraon) and Khasi languages belong to the Austric family of languages. The most obvious explanation is that the Orāons have borrowed their funeral customs, along with(in some places)* the flat stone grave-slabs, and the stone seats of the *akhra* (l. c., p. 387), from the Mundas. The various kinds of dolmens which occur scattered throughout the Deccan, so far as we know, were put up by Dravidian-speaking peoples. The grave-slabs of Chota Nagpur and of the Khasi hills, on the other hand, are erected by Austric-speaking peoples.

* In such places they speak Mundari and follow many Mundari customs. In some Oraon villages, however, the charred bones of the cremated corpse of an Oraon dying between the Sarhul ceremony (in March-April) and the next annual har-bori (bone-drowning)ceremony in Pous(December) when they are consigned to their final resting-place at the appointed 'Kundi' in some stream or water-channel, are temporarily deposited in a small earthen jug underneath upright stone-slabs (called 'pulkhi') planted, one for each Khunt or Sept, close to the village site. In the hot months and in the rains these 'pulkhi' stones are in a few villages thatched over with straw, and on every suitable occasion (such as the Eating of the New upland Rice in Bhado or the Eating of bread at the Karam festival) offerings of food are made before these stones. Generally, however, the corpse of an Oraon dying between the Sarhul and the annual har-bori ceremony lies temporarily buried in the village 'Masan', and the 'Pulkhi' stones are mere memorial stones set up by well-to-do Oraons in memory of some of their deceased old relatives.—S.C.R.

To an early cultural stage unquestionably belong the remarkable magico-religious observances of the seasonal hunts. The spring hunt is generally confined to the lads while residing in the bachelors' dormitories, whereas the summer hunt which is the most important, is undertaken by the men at large; archaic features connected therewith are the tabu on metal coins, strict sexual continence, tabu on edible domestic animals, and the behaviour of women like men when the men are out hunting (pp. 231-233).

Presumably of a later phase is the cult of local spirits whose haunts were disturbed during the process of clearing the jungles. These spirits as also certain ancestor-spirits were called *khunt-bhut* or sept-spirits (p. 107).

The seasonal occupations are reflected in appropriate seasonal dances and songs. After the harvesting of the low-land rice in November and December tho merry season of plenty and comparative leisure from work in the fields is ushered in by the "great marriage" of the dead. This ceremony at which the calcined bones are deposited in their final resting place in the 'kundi,' "is continued with the marriage of the living, and is ended with the marriage of Nature with God—of Mother Earth herself with the Sun-god" (p. 277). Until this union has been celebrated theOraon may neither use nor even gather new vegetable roots, fruits, or flowers of the season, nor may he manure his fields (p. 279). A sun-god is at the head of the pantheon of most, perhaps all, the Munda-speaking tribes of Chota Nagpur, and the Santals at all events in addition to a recognition of the vague supreme sun-god offered human sacrifices to a mountain god. The cultural relations of the various forms of religious belief and practice are of considerable importance and deserve careful study.

There are so many interesting features in the ethnography of the Oraons that it is difficulty to know which to select for special mention. Those to which reference has been made may be taken as samples of the wealth of material provided for ethnologists by Mr. Roy.

Finally, the sections on Later History (pp. 36-51) and Economic Condition (pp. 202-209) very clearly bring out the great importance of the study of anthropology for administrative purposes. The lot of the Orāons would have been far happier if there had been less ignorance concerning the origin and history of local land tenure.

CAMBRIDGE, A. C. HADDON.
March 25, 1915.

THE ORĀONS.

CHAPTER I

—:0:—

Origin and History.

The secluded Plateau of Chōtā Nāgpur forms one of the principal centres, in India, of aboriginal and semi-aboriginal tribes. Among the purely aboriginal tribes of the Plateau, the Orāons appear to occupy the first rank in intelligence and social progress as they stand foremost in numerical strength. Before they had entered the country, they appear to have passed beyond the savage or hunter state and the nomadic or herdsman state, and reached the settled agricultural stage of social culture. In fact, the Orāons claim the honour of having introduced the use of the regular plough into the Chōtā Nāgpur Plateau. The topographical situation of the Plateau, rising as it does to a great elevation above the adjoining Districts, from which the approach lies through precipitous forest-covered hill-passes or ghāts, has, however, helped in the preservation amongst this people, of many a 'survival' of the hunting and pastoral stages of culture. And even their religious and socio-religious usages and ceremonies connected with agriculture are the outcome of a very early stage of development.

i POPULATION.

Number.

Of the various castes and tribes inhabiting the Chōtā Nāgpur Plateau, the Orāons, as we have said, are the most numerous. They are indeed a very prolific people. In one decade (1901-1911), their number appears to have increased by over 25 *per cent.* At the census of 1901, the total number of Orāons was 614,501. At the census of 1911, the total number of Orāons, including Christian converts, was found to be 864,152. Of the non-Christian Orāons, 373,095 were males and 378,888 females. As many as 157,414 Orāons returned themselves as Hindus, whereas 594,569 were entered as pure Animists. Christian Orāons number 112,738 in the Province of Bihar and Orissa. Of these Orāon converts, 88, 647 live in the Rānchi district (Chōtā Nāgpur Plateau), 7,340 in the Palāmau district of Chōtā Nāgpur, 443 in the Singbhūm district of Chōtā Nāgpur, 16,251 in the Orissa States. In the Darjeeling district, there were 125 Christian Orāons in 1911.*

For statistics see Appendix.

The Orāons now living in Bengal and Assam, as also the majority of those now living in the Bhāgalpūr Division of Bihār are immigrants, principally from the Chōtā Nāgpur Plateau. They went as labourers to those parts, where many of them have now settled down.

ii Tribal Names.

Kurukh. The Orāons in their own language call themselves Kūṛukhs. The origin of this national name of the Orāons is sometimes traced to one of their mythical hero-kings called Kaṛakh. To this personage tradition ascribes the origin of the ancient name Karuṣ-deś, which roughly comprised what is now the district of Shāhābād,—a former home of the Orāons. Dr. Francis Buchanan* (afterwards Buchanan Hamilton) tells us,—"Another Daitya† named Karakh, of those remote times, is said to have had possession of the country between the Son and Karmanasa, which was then called Karukh-Des. Few traces however remain of this personage, and sometime afterwards a new

* *Eastern India*, Vol. 1, 405. Dr. Buchanan's account was prepared between the years 1807 and 1816, under the orders of the Government of India, and edited by Montgomery Martin (London 1838).

† 'Daitya' is a generic name applied to the barbaric aboriginals.

name, Kikat,* was applied to the country. It is by many alleged that the whole of Kikata in more modern times took the name of Magadha, from the Mags, who settled in its eastern parts.'†

Although the name of the country as Kaṛūkh-deś is now lost, the memory of their palmy days under their ancient king Kaṛakh was not perhaps forgotten by the Orāons when they entered Chōtā Nāgpūr. The name Kūṛukh was probably derived originally from some now obsolete Dravidian root‡ meaning, 'man', and it may well have been given to the mythical king Kaṛakh just in the same way as the name Adam was given to the Hebrew progenitor of mankind.§

* The name 'Kikata' is however found even in the *Rig-veda.*

† The identification of the Kūṛūkhs with the Karuṣ people was also suggested by Rev. F. A. Grignard in the *Anthropos* Vol. IV, (1909). But it is difficult to agree with Father Grignard in his identification of the 'Kūṛūkhs' with the 'Rākṣasas of Samṣkrit literature. The Rākṣasas in the Epics are described as a remarkably tall race, whereas the Orāon's stature is below the average. Moreover, in Orāon folklore, and even in their story of the genesis of the human race and of the *bhuts (Vide Appendix)*, we hear of the Rākṣasas as their enemies.

‡ I am indebted for this suggestion to Mr. E. A. Gait. Compare the name 'Manu' given to the Hindu progenitor of mankind (*manava*).

§ It may be noted that Korkai (now a village on the Tam-

But the term, has also a close resemblance to the Saṁṣkrit root *Kṛṣ*, to plough. The Orāons usually transform the nasal ṣ (ष) sound of other tongues into the kh sound of their own. Whether the name of king Kaṛūkh and his country Kaṛūkh-deṣ had a Saṁṣkritic origin or not, the resemblance of the name with Krsak or krṣāṇ,* ploughman (from *kṛṣ*, to plough), was too obvious to be ignored. And this similarity of names may not improbably have helped the Orāons in their adoption or retention of the name Kūṛukh. When, centuries ago, they entered the Chōtā Nāgpur Plateau, these tribesmen of ancient King Kaṛakh, and kinsmen of the Canārese of the ancient Pāndya kingdom of Koṛkai, found the country occupied by tribes ruder than themselves. Most of those tribes, such as the Kōṛwās and the Birhōṛs had till then been either hunters or herdsmen; and even those tribes, such as the

braparni river in Tinnevelly) was, long before the Christian Era, the name of the capital town of the Pandya kingdom of the Carnatic (Karnataka) which is, properly speaking, the land of the Kanarese. And Kanarese or Canarese, we are told, is closely related to the Orāon or Kūṛūkh tongue. Vide *Encyclopædia Britannica* (11th Edn.) Vol. V, p. 361, and Vincent Smith's *Early History of India* (2nd Edn, 1908, Claredon Press, Oxford) 173.

* The ṇ (ण) sound and the nasal ṛ (ष) sounds are interchangeable, and 'Krsāṇ' or 'Krisaṇ' is easily transformed into 'Kṛkhar' or 'Kṛūkhar' (= Orāons)

Mundās, who had taken to agriculture, as yet employed but a very rudimentary method of tilling the soil, perhaps with a pointed stick. Some of them indeed are, to this day, partial to the *jhuming* or dāhō system of tillage.*

No wonder, therefore, that the Orāons on their arrival amongst such peoples should have prided themselves on their superior equipment for the race of life, as also on their tradition of former rule in the Karūṣa country, and assumed or emphasised the distinguishing tribal name of the 'Kūṛukhar',— or 'Kūṛukh',† a name which, as we have seen, had historic associations for them. They had also before them a historic precedent for such an assumption,by a whole people, of the proud name of the 'ploughmen'. For, even so, from the Vedic period onwards, did the invading Aryans call themselves tillers, *Kṛṣṭayah*, (plural of *kristi*)‡ in contradistinction to the then non-cultivating natives of the soil. And similarly did the Indian Aryans apply the name of 'Yavana Krṣ' to their own cultivating kinsmen, the Iranians, whom they had left behind them in what is now Persia. As Messrs. Macdonald and Keith show, from the Rigveda onwards, terms (such as *kṛṣṭaya*, and *cārṣanya*)

* Dalton's *Ethnology of Bengal*, (1872), 264.

† Kūṛkhar is the plural form of 'Kūṛkhas,' an Orāon.

‡ Morgan and Keith's *Vedic Index*, 183.

meaning 'ploughmen' are employed to denote 'people', and used interchangeably with such words as 'janāh' ,(people) and 'manuṣāh' (men).* And the 'five peoples' described in the Vedas, the Brāhmanas, and the Saṁhitās, variously as the *panca krṣtaya*,† *panca kṣitya*, *panca carṣaṇya*, *panca janah*, and *panca manuṣah*, have been taken by old Hindu commentators like Śayana to refer to the four Aryan castes and the Niṣāda non-Aryans.‡ It may be noted that the Kūṛukhs of the Sarangaṛh tributary state in Orissa are now partly known as Dhāngaṛs and partly as Kiṣāns (literally, cultivators) ; and the latter name is also applied to the Orāons in certain other localities, such as in parts of the Sambalpur District, as well as in the Bamra, Rairkhol, and Pal-Lahera States in Orissa.§ Thus, then, it may appear probable that the Orāons of Chōtā Nāgpur came to call themselves the Kūṛukhs in the double sense of the tribesmen of the traditional hero-king Kaṛūkh, and also in the sense of a tribe of agriculturists,—Kriṣāṇ or Kūṛkhar.¶

* Ib., 183.

† The ṇ (ण) sound coming after ṣ (ष) is generally transformed into the 't' sound in Sanskrit.

‡ Macdonnel and Keith's *Vedic Index of Names and Subjects*, Vol. I, 181 ff. (John Murray, London, 1912).

§ Grierson, *Linguistic Survey of India*, IV, 430, 436; *Bengal Census Rep.* 1911, pt. 1. 394, 395.

¶ Krūkhar or Kūṛukhar is the plural form of Kūṛukh, an

Dhangars, Kodas, Modis. Although agriculture is now the normal occupation of the Orāons of Chōtā Nāgpur, needy people of the tribe occasionally work for other people on wages. Ordinarily, it is unmarried young men whose services as labourers are thus available. And an unmarried Orāon is called 'jōnkh' in the Orāon language, and 'Dhāngaṛ' in local Hindi.* Thus, both the words 'dhāngar' and 'jōnkh' gradually came to acquire

Orāon. Other derivations that have been or may be suggested are the following:—(1) Col. Dalton's informant would derive the name from *Konkan* which, according to his informant was the cradle of the race.—Dalton's *Ethnology*, 245. (2) Rev. Dr. F. Hahn is of opinion that the word Kūrukh may be identified with the Kolarian *horo*, man, or may be derived from the Dravidian-Scythian word '*Kuruk*,' a cry-er; *Kurukh Grammar*, Introd. (3) Dr. Grierson suggests though doubtfully, that the name Kūṛukh may be connected with Dravidian *Karugu*, an eagle, and be the name of a totemistic clan. *Linguistic Survey* Vol. IV, 406. (4) It may be noted that (i) in the Orāon language, *Kurugnā* (root, *Kurug*) means to enclose, to fence in (as a field), and *Kurgi*, or Kurkhi means a 'fencing' or 'enclosure' and may not improbably have some connection with the name 'kurukh'; (ii) *Kurias* in Orāon, means 'to beat; and '*Kurus*' is 'one who beats; and (iii) in Samskrit 'Kriṣṇa' (black) and 'Kṛṣṇa-twach' (black-skinned) are epithets frequently applied to the non-Aryan aboriginals by the early Aryan immigrants into India.

* Thus, the dormitory for bachelors in Orāon villages is called a *Jonkh Erpa*, and also a *Dhangar-basa*.

the secondary signification of labourers or servants. As such Orāon labourers were almost the only people of the tribe with whom foreigners first came in contact, the name Dhāngaṛ came to be applied to the tribe as a whole. In the early notices of Chōtā Nāgpur by European writers we generally find the tribe called by that name. Thus, Walter Hamilton in his 'Description of Hindostan' (1820), writes,—"The Khetauri, the Koeri, and the Dhanggar, are still the principal inhabitants of Chota Nagpur. The Dhanggar are still impure, as probably unconverted Mlechchas."* Again, in his 'East India Gazetteer,† under the heading 'Chota Nagpur', the same writer says,—"The Dhanggar are still unconverted Mlechchas or barbarians. This territory contains a large population of Cole and Lurka Cole." A more recent writer, Col. Dalton,‡ observes, "The Kurukh or Oraons of Chota Nagpur are the people best known in many parts of India as 'Dhangars'." But it is not only the Chōtā Nāgpur Orāon who is called by that name, but his fellow-tribesmen

* *A Geographical, Statistical, and Historical Description of Hindostan*, Vol. 1, p. 288 (London, John Murray, 1820).

† *East India Gazetteer* (2nd Edn. London, 1828) Vol. 1, 415, 416.

‡ *Ethnology of Bengal* (1872) p. 245. Col. Dalton derives the name from 'dang' or 'dhang,' a hill, and takes the name to mean a 'hill-man.' It may be noted, however, that in the Kūṛukh language, 'dhāng' means 'sense.'

living in parts of the Shāhābād, Chāmpāran, and Bhāgalpūr districts of Bihār, and in some of the Tributary states of Orissā, are also called Dhāngars, and their language, which is the same as Kūṛukh, is described as Dhāngari.*

In the Orissa States, although they are sometimes called (Dhāngars) by their neighbours, the Orāons describe themselves as 'Kiṣāṇs', cultivators, or 'Koṛās', diggers; they are also known as 'Dhāngar-kodās.'†

A number of Orāons now living in the eastern parts of the Rānchi district and in the adjoining district of Mānbhum are known as Mōdis and sometimes as Kōṛās. The name Mōdi, like the name Kōṛā,—has reference to their skill in working in earth such as raising embankments, mud-walls, *etc.*

In this way, different occupations followed by the Orāons in different localities have secured them from their neighbours different names, and have in some cases created and, in others, as in the case of the Mōdis, are on the way to creating different subsections of the same tribe amongst whom intermarriage is no longer permitted.

Male.

Their traditions as well as philological and cultural evidences show that the Orāons of Chōta Nāgpur and

* Grierson, *Linguistic Survey*, IV. 410.

† *Census Report, Bengal, Bihar and Orissa*, 1911, pt. 1, 394.

the *Ma-ler* of the Rajmahal Hills are two divisions of what was once a single tribe. While the Orāons still formed one tribe with the ancestors of the Mālér and the Māl Pāhāriās of the Rājmahal Hills, and all lived together in the Karūṣ-deś and followed the same occupation, the name by which the whole tribe was known would appear to have been the *Mālé*,—another name meaning 'man'.* In his *Indika*, the Greek historian Megasthenes (*circa*, 300 B.C.) gives the following account of the peoples occupying the country 'from the seaboard to the south-east up to the Ganges' which separates the present Shāhābād and Patnā districts from North Bihār. "The tribes called Calingæ are nearest the sea, and higher up are the *Mandei* and the *Malli* in whose country is Mount Mallus, the boundary of all that district being the Ganges."† This Malli tribe of Megasthenes probably included the ancestors of the present Mālés of the Rājmahal hills and those of the Orāons of Chōtā Nāgpūr. At the present

* Dalton's *Ethnology*, p. 303. In Orāon, the word 'mal' now means a wrestler, fighter, hero; and its plural from is *malar*; 'āl' means 'man; and its plural form is 'ālar' (men). Dr. Grierson would derive the name from the common Dravidian, *mala*, mountain.

† *Ancient India, as described by Megasthenes and Arian*, by J.W. McCrindle pp. 134-135. (Trubner & Co., London, 1877).

day, this name is retained only by the branch of the tribe, that migrated to the Rājmahal Hills. 'All other tribes they call Galer'.* *Galer* is apparently the plural form of *Gal.* Whether this name 'Gal' is a variant of the term *Kol* or not, the Hindu neighbours of the remnant of the tribe that was left behind in Bihār appear to have applied the name of 'Kol' to the whole tribe, as also to people of the Mundā race. And this name, which appears to have originally meant simply 'man', as the name 'Mālé' means to this day, gradually acquired the opprobrious signification of 'pigs' or 'pig-eaters'.† And at this day it is not only the remnant of the Kūṛukh tribe still lingering in or about their old home in Rohtāsgarh and elsewhere in Bihār but even the Chōtā Nāgpur Orāons who are not infrequently called 'Kōls.

Oraon. But if the name 'Kōl' was applied indiscriminately by their later Hindu neighbours to the Kūṛukhs as well as to their neighbours of the Mūndā race, a more distinctive name soon came to be presented to the former by the imaginative Hindu. When the Hindu immigrants into Chōtā Nāgpur found

* Dr. Buchanan's 'Eastern India,' II,125 (London, 1838)

† Cf. the expression '*kola-biddhwangsinah*', slayers of pigs, in *Chandi*, 1.5.

themselves in the midst of a large array of aboriginal tribes and a veritable babel of tongues, amongst which their unpractised eyes and ears could detect little or no difference, the one circumtance about the Kŭṛukhs that no people living amongst them could long overlook was the rapidity with which they multiplied.*

The Hindu's imagination found in Hindu legendary lore what it considered a fitting likeness, and naturally compared these Kŭṛukhs to the progeny of the legendary monster-king Rāwana of Rāmāyana fame.† For, popular tradition represents king Rāwana as having been blessed with one-hundred-thousand sons and one-hundred-and-twenty-five-thousand grandsons. And the Kŭṛukhs with what appeared to the Hindu their monstrously impure habits, and their extraordinary prolificness

* The *Census Report* of 1911 shows that in one decade the Orāons have increased by 25 *per cent.*

† Rev. Dr. F. Hahn (*Kurukh Grammar*, Introduction) agrees in holding that the name Orāon was coined by the Hindus; but he supposes that its base is *orgora*, hawk which is the name of a totemistic sept of the Orāons. Dr. Grierson compares the name with *Kaikadi Urapai*, man; Burgandi, *urapo*, man, *Urang*, men, and goes on to observe 'the Hindus say that the word *Oraon* is simply the Indo-Aryan *Uran*, spendthrift, the name being an allusion to the alleged thriftless character of the people to whom it is applied.'

came to be called, as they are often called to this day, *Rionī pūt* or the progeny of Rāwana.* The name Rāwan, pronounced, as some people do, with an arrested 'O' sound at the beginning gave us the present form'O-rāwan' or Orāon. It is worthy of note that the Orāons, as I have already said, never use this name in their own tongue, but always call themselves the Kūṛukhs.

If the name Orāon was conceived in contempt by those who coined it, the Orāons of our generation tell a story more complimentary to themselves by which they seek to account for the name. Long—long—ago, a Mūni or ascetic, so runs the Orāon story, sat absorbed in divine contemplation in the heart of a dense forest. Day after day, month after month, and year after year, the ascetic remained seated in the same posture on the self-same spot, without food, drink, or sleep, till at length his body got rooted to the ground, and was covered over with an ant-hill. Round the ant-hill grew up a thorny creeper, a long thorn from

* This derivation of the name Orāon was given me by more than one Orāon. My informants were all illiterate people and they told me that their Hindu neighbours began by calling them 'Rawna-pūt,' and thence finally the name *Orāon* came to be applied to them. But my informants did not know the reference. Col Dalton (*Ethnology*, 245) explains the name as a nickname 'assigned to them possibly with reference to their many migrations and proneness to roam.'

which actually entered his chest. At length it so happened that a wood-cutter who had been to the jungle to cut wood, mistook the ascetic for the ant-hill-covered stump of a tree. And against this supposed stump he struck the butt-end of his axe to shake off the ant-hill. But to his astonishment, the wood-cutter soon discovered it was a living man. The ascetic, thus rudely disturbed in his meditations, got up on his legs. As he stood up, the thorn sticking into his chest got broken, and blood began to ooze out of his chest. The ascetic, not willing to allow a drop of his own blood to stain Mother-Earth, took all the blood in the folded palms of his hands. As, however, he had now to satisfy a call of nature, he put the blood in a cup improvised for the purpose out of a *Korkota* leaf, and placed the cup in a shady place close by. When the ascetic was about to leave the place, out of the blood there came into life a boy and a girl (called in the story *Bh'yi-bh'yin* or brother-sister). And they called out to the ascetic and said, "Stop, pray, stop. It is you who brought us into the world. And now if you leave us here, what shall we do to get a living?" The ascetic replied, "You shall be cultivators. Clear this jungle, and make agriculture your occupation. Your granary will be full of grains. And when people of different castes will approach you for alms, give a handful of grain to every suppliant." Thus, then, the *Bhāyā-bhāyin*, the first parents of the Orāons, having been born of the blood of the chest (Saṁskrit, *Uras* or *Ur*) of the holy ascetic, their descendants came to be known as *Urāgon Thākurs* or Urāons.* And in those olden days they were quite as respectable as the Brāhmans, and wore the sacred thread. When, later, the Orāons fell from their high state, and began to eat indiscriminately whatever food, clean or unclean, that came to hand, they forfeited their claim to the name of Urāgon Thākūrs, and came to be called simply *Orāons*.* The point

* Compare the supposed origin of the 'four main castes' of the Hindus from the different limbs of Bramhā, the Creator.

* This story has a significant similarity with that given in the Rāmāyana (Uttara kānda, XLII. 7—12) concerning the origin of Sugriva, king and leader of the Vānara (monkey) followers of Rām Chandra, and appears to confirm the suggestion we have made in the following section as to the Orāons having formed part of the monkey host of Rāmachandra. The legend as given in the Rāmāyana is as follows: While Bramhā, the grandfather of the human race, was seated on Mount Merū, rapt in contemplation, a drop of tear fell from one of his eyes. Bramhā held the drop of tear in the palm of his hand and besmeared his body with it. As soon as a particle of tear came in contact with the earth, out of the particle there came into life a monkey with long hair like those of a bear. This bear-

of this story, again, is their renowned ancestry, and their honourable occupation of agriculture.

iii. ORIGIN AND MIGRATIONS.

Affinities.

For the racial and linguistic affinities as well as for the origin of the Orāons, the student has to look to Southern India. The traditions of the people point to the Deccan as their original home. Philologists trace a connection between Kūṛukh and the Tāmūlian languages of Southern India, the Mālto, Kui or Khond and Gondi of Northern India, and the Brahūi of Beluchistan.* All these languages

like monkey seeing his own image in a pool of water, mistook the image for an enemy and jumped into the water to punish him and finally emerged from the water transformed into a female monkey. She was impregnated successively by Indra, the chief of heavenly spirits, and by the Sun (their semen falling on her head), and gave birth respectively to Sugriva and Bāli.

* The Tamulian languages are Tamil, Malayalam, Kanarese, and Telugu together with such minor dialects as Koragu, Tulu, Toda, and Kota. The latest authoritative opinion classifies the Dravidian family of languages into two groups, called respectively the *Dravida* and the *Andhra* with a third group intermediate between them. The *Andhra* group, spoken by 24 millions, comprises Telugu, Kandh or Kui and Kolami. The intermediate group (15 million speakers) occurs sporadically in the Central Provinces, and

were first classed together by Bishop Caldwell* under the generic name of Dravidian, the adjectival form of *Dravida*, *Dramila*, *Tamil*. And the name has since been extended to these and other peoples in an ethnological sense, and have gained currency as such. But, although language in itself is no test of race, yet in the case of the peoples named above, with the exception of the Brāhui, race and language appear to coincide. The Orāons, at any rate, appear to be both linguistically and ethnologically a Dravidian tribe. Although more than one theory † has been propounded by eminent anthropologists

Berar, and the east of the Hyderabad State. The Dravida group, with a total of 37 million speakers, includes Tamil (18·1 millions) Kanarese (10·5 millions), Malayalam (6·8 millions), and Tulu (0.6 millions). It also includes several outlying languages, the chief of which are Kuṛukh (0·8 millions) in the Chōta Nāgpur plateau spoken by the Orāons, who have traditions of emigration from the peninsula, and Brahūi (less than 0·2 millions) in Beluchistan, whose existence in that distant spot is one of the greatest riddles of Indian philology." *Census Rep. of India*. Part I. 335-6.

* *Dravidian Grammar*, p. 4ff.

† For a summary of these theories, see Thurston's *Castes and Tribes of Southern India* (Madras, 1909), Introduction, XIX-XXXVI. See also the Introduction by Mr. E. A. Gait, in S. C. Roy's *Mundas and their Country* (Thacker Spink and Co., Calcutta, 1912).

and philologists to connect the Indian Dravidians linguistically and ethnologically with races outside India, no convincing reasons have so far been adduced to show that they came to India from outside and were not real autochthones of the peninsula. Nor do the traditions of the Dravidians appear to mention any country outside India as having ever been their home.*

The Vanaras of the Ramayana, and the Oraons.

Their own traditionary legend as to the origin of the tribe coupled with the account of the Vānaras contained in the ancient Saṁṣkrit epic, the Rāmāyana, would lead one to suppose that the Orāons formed part of the Vānara army that helped the Aryan hero Rāmchandra in defeating the non-Aryan king Rāwana of Lankā, whose dominions probably included part of Southern India. In the long story‡ of the genesis of man and the spirits recited by the Orāons at their periodical Dāndā-kattā or ceremony, of 'cutting the [evil] teeth'. Rāma is spoken of as their 'grand-father', his wife Sitā as their 'grand-mother', and his monkey-general Hanūmān as their 'uncle'. Hanūmān, as we

* Except that one solitary legend of the Orāons speaks of their having been to 'Mecca-Medina,' in the course of their migrations. *vide* Appendix.

‡ Vide Appendix.

learn from the epic, became a devoted follower of Rāmchandra whom he came to regard as God personified. And in some versions of the Orāon legend we find the name Rāma used interchangeably with Dharmeś (God) Himself, and Sitā also called *Pārvati*, and described as the wife of Dharmes. In the Rāmāyana, the Vānaras are described as a dusky 'cloud-coloured' people (*Kiskindhya kanda*, xxxvii, 5 ; xvii, 1), with large teeth (ib, xxii, 24 ; xxvi, 4), and their men and women are represented as addicted to drink (ib, xxxiii, 38ff; xxxvii,45,)and as taking a great delight in singing to the sound of the *mridanga* or *māndal* (ib, xxvii, 27ff). All these characteristics are to be met with in the Orāons of Chōtā-Nāgpur, in common, indeed, with many other Dravidian jungle-tribes ; and dancing and singing to the sound of the *māndal* is still a favourite amusement with Orāon men and women, as with several other jungle tribes. It does not, however, appear to be without significance that whereas ancient Saṁskrit writers describe other aboriginal peoples in general terms, as 'robbers', 'monsters', and 'goblins' indiscriminately, certain Dravidian hillmen with whom the Aryan hero Rām Chandra lived long on very intimate terms, should be described in particular as 'monkeys', and that different sections of them should be always specifically described as belonging to different species of monkeys, such as the long-haired bear-like monkeys (*Riksa-vanara*), the common monkey (*Vanara*) and a kind of ape with tails like those of cows (*gō-Lāngula*).*

As we have said, these different sections of Vānaras are never confounded, one with the other, in the epic, and each section is represented as having its own leaders and generals who are specifically named. It does not appear at all probable that the Aryan king Rāma Chandra, who is invariably represented as a model of wisdom, discretion, righteousness, human sympathy, and charity, should call his own trusty friends and faithful followers by any epithets of contempt; and the names of monkeys and bears, would ordinarily appear to be contemptuous epithets when applied to men. As a matter of fact, we find that Rāma Chandra while calling them 'Vānaras,' always addresses them in very cordial, complimentary, and grateful terms, as 'friends, brethren, and limbs of my own body' (*Suhridomé bhabantascha sariram bhratarastathi*). The Aryan hero must therefore have had good reasons for calling his trusty friends and helpers 'monkeys' and 'bears;' these names must have really belonged to them in some particular sense. There are passages in the Rāmāyana which go to show that these

* Vide, Ramayana, *Kiskindhya Kanda*, XXXIV, 24ff.

Vānara soldiers actually took pride in their name of 'Vānaras'.* It is again significant that whereas in speaking of other aboriginal tribes ancient Saṁṣkrit writers hurl any number of contemptuous epithets at them, it is different in the case of these Vānaras: We hear them spoken of as 'amiable-looking' (*priya-darsana*) good fellows.† What, then, could have been the reason for calling them 'monkeys'? The reason seems to be that monkey was the tribal totem of the leading section of Dravidian hill-men who formed Rām Chandra's aboriginal army. Even to this day, there are monkey-totems amongst the Orāons of Chōtā Nāgpur. There are Orāons of the *Haluman* (baboon) *gotra* (totemic sept) and the *Gāri* (common monkey) *gotra*, who have each a species of the monkey for their totem, and who abstain from killing or injuring or even domesticating a monkey. The further fact that the flesh of the monkey is tabu to all Orāons, irrespective of their sept-totem, although they eat the flesh of almost every other animal, large or small, would seem to support the suggestion that 'Vānara' or monkey was

* See Ramayana, *Kiskindhya kanda* XXVI, 6; XV, 2ff.

† Ib. XXXIII, 6., Dalton writes, 'The Orāon youths, though with features very far from being in accordance with statutes of beauty, are of a singularly pleasing class, their faces beaming with animation and good humour.—*Ethnology* 249.

once the tribal totem of the Orāons, and the totem was derived from the mother's side, descent being matrilineal in those days and paternity imperfectly understood. Recently we were told by an Orāon of the Palāmau district that in a village there, not long ago, monkeys used to eat up the gram-crop standing on an Orāon cultivator's field. The cultivator, who did not belong to any subdivision of the monkey sept, at length caught a monkey in his net and beat it to death. Within a short time after this, most of the members of the man's family happend to die, one after another. All the Orāons of the locality attributed this misfortune to the sacrilege of having killed a monkey.*

Thus, then, it is not unreasonable to conclude that the forefathers of the Orāons had the monkey for their tribal totem, and formed part of the aboriginal army of the Aryan hero of the Rāmā-

* As may be expected, the present-day Orāons when asked for the origin of this tabu, cannot give any explanation ; and, those who attempt any explanation, only state their own inferences. Thus, I was given by an Orāon the explanation that it was because the monkey always makes *salams* (bowing salutation) and looks entreatingly when a man approaches the animal, that it is not ill-treated or killed. Another explanation I have heard is that as Haluman was the nephew of God, a monkey is not to be killed nor its flesh eaten.

yana. Again, the similarity of the story told by the Orāons as to the origin of the name 'Orāon', * with the story given in the Rāmāyana as to the birth of the Monkey-king Sugrīva would seem to confirm the view here suggested.†

In further support of this suggestion, I may refer to the address of the Vānara chief *Sugriva* to his followers in the forty-first chapter of the *Kiskindhyā kānda* of the Rāmāyana, in which he speaks of a female witch of the Rākṣasa race, by name Angārika, who 'eats people by attracting their shadows' (*chhayamaksipya bhojani*). Here we find not only the Orāon belief in witchcraft and the Orāon's suspicion of the magical powers of all alien peoples, but even something like the Orāon theory of 'chhāin' (O., *ekh*), or the magic power of the shadow of a man

* *Vide* foot-note p. 16.

† In the Chotā Nāgpur plateau, although the tabu against eating the flesh of the monkey is invariably observed by the Orāons, the prohibition against injuring a monkey is now occasionally disregarded. But some septs, such as the 'Iron' (Panna) *gotra*, besides the 'monkey' septs, invariably observe the tabu against eating as also killing or injuring the animal. The Birhoṛ tribe who kill monkeys, are, for this reason, looked down upon by the Orāons, and the latter do not take water at their hands.

Original Habitat.

We gather from the Rāmāyana that although the leading chief of the Vānaras had his seat at Kiṣkindhyā†—a locality which antiquarian scholars locate on the north bank of the Tūngābhadra river, a branch of the Kriṣnā, about twenty miles to the north of the town of Bellary, different sections of the *Vānara*-race occupied different hills and jungles up to and beyond the Vindhya mountains on the north. It may be noted that it was on Mount Malai where the Vānara king Sugrīva was then living, that Rāma Chandra first made the acquaintance of the Vānaras. And the subsequent name of that race as the 'Mālé' may not improbably be connected with that mountain. (*Kiskindhya Kanda*, V.) When after the recovery of Rāma's wife Sitā from the capital of Rāwana, the Aryan hero went back to his own kingdom of Ayōdhyā (Oudh), his Vānara followers, with their families, we are told (*Lanka Kanda*, cxxiv), accompanied Rāma Chandra to witness his installation ; and the Aryan king, we learn, loaded the headmen of the Vānara clans (*Vanara juthapas*) with valuable presents (*ib.* cxxx). But the most valuable of all boons that the Aryan hero appears to have conferred upon them was to put them in the way

* Dey's *Geographical Dictionary of Ancient and Modern India.* See also J. A. S B., XIV. 519.

of attaining a somewhat higher level of primitive culture. When they first came in contact with the Aryâns, the Vānaras were living in cave-dwellings (*Kiskindha Kanda*, xxvii, 1). Even Kiṣkindhyā, the seat of their suzerain king, is said to have been in a mountain-cave, (*ib.* xxvi, 41.) Sticks* and stones are the weapons with which they are represented as having fought with their enemies. (See *Lanka-kanda,* xvii, 8, xxiv, 20, xli, 29 ; xliii, 41 ; to ii. 3, and numerous other passages in the *Lanka-kanda*). They were fond of eating wild herbs (*sags*) and roots (*kanda*) and drinking liquor (Uttarākānda xlix, 26). A few references in the Rāmāyana would seem to show that even the physiological conditions of paternity were not yet understood by this people in those days, as, we are told, they are not understood to this day by such people as the Arunta of Australia. Thus, the Monkey-general Hanūmāna is said to have been born of his mother Anjanā, wife of Keśari, after she was impregnated by the Wind. (Uttarā kānda, lx, 19, 20). Sugrīva, the king of the Vānaras, is said to have been born of the wife of king Rikṣa, on her being impregnated by the Sun (*Aranya Kanda*, lxxii, 11ff.) The monkey-general

* It is worthy of note that the Oraons still use about half a dozen varaities of sticks in their hunting excursions. *vide* chap. IV. *post.*

Dadhi-mukha had the Moon for his progenitor, and the monkey-general Neel had Fire for his progenitor (Lankā-kānda, xxx, 22, 24), and the Vānaras, in general, are said to have been born of Vānara women impregnated by the gods and the spirits. (Kişkindhyā-kānda, xxxviii, 29.) Such was the primitive stage of savagery in which the forefathers of the Orāons once lived in the hills and hill-caves of Southern India, wandering about, ill-clad and ill-armed, winning as best as they could a precarious subsistence from the hill and the forest.

Migrations.

If our identification of the Vānara followers of Rāma Chandra with the ancestors of the Orāons be correct, it was probably during their long association with the Aryan hero and their long travels in his company through the country of the more civilized Dravidians of the plains who had already taken to agriculture and evolved a much higher civilization than their own, and more particularly during their friendly visits to Rāma Chandra's dominions in Northern India, that the Orāons first understood the benefits of cattle-breeding and agriculture, and the use of metal implements and utensils, and thus got a moderate lift in the ladder of civilization. To their nomadic or herdsman state before they settled down as regular agriculturists, their folklore bears some testimony. Thus in one folk-tale we are told that when in the course of their wanderings, an Orāon family did a piece of good service to the king of the land of their sojourn the Rājā wanted to make a gift of five villages to the family, but the latter preferred to have a large herd of cattle instead.* With their newly-acquired knowledge of agriculture, however, they gradually settled down on the fertile valleys of some great river like the Narbadā. Either owing to over-population, or external pressure, or for some other reason, which cannot be ascertained at this distance of time, they appear to have moved forward from Southern to Northern India. Wherever they met with green field, so their tradition goes, they would 'take down their mats and pots, and settle down.' After many wanderings, in Northern India, in the course of which their traditions represent them as having passed through Nandan-garh, Pipri-garh, and Hardi-nagar,† places which

* Hahn, *Kurukh Folklore*, 4. A similar story is also told to account for the burning of lamps on the *Sōhōrai āmāwas* night.

† It is not unlikely that these names might have been picked up from the Mūndas, and, as a matter of fact, the Orāons went up the Narbada from the Deccan, and passed across the Vindhyas to the valley of the Son. These names do not appear in the traditions of the Māles. It is true we read in the Mahābhārata of the Kāruṣas as taking part in

To face p. 29.

The Rohtas Fort (Rohtās-garh).

can only be doubtfully identified, they at length went to what is now the Shāhābād district in Bihār. Here they settled down as agriculturists and land-owners. Here, as we have seen, one of their chiefs known as Kaṛakh is said to have established his suzerainty and to have given his name to the country. When, in the whirl-gig of time, some other tribe,—probably the Kolarian tribe of the Cherōs,—became predominant in the Karuṣ-deś, the ancestors of the Māler and the Orāons appear to have taken shelter on the Rōhtās plateau, which they claim to have fortified. But even this fortress plateau they were at length constrained to leave.

Dislodgement from Rohtas

A people whom their traditions sometimes call "Mlechchhas", appear to have dislodged them from Rōhtāsgarh. It is sometimes supposed that these "Mlechchhas" were the Muhammadan conquerors of

the Great War. But the word Kāruṣ used in the Māhabhārata is the adjectival form of Karuṣ, and simply means people from the Karūṣa country. It may, for aught we know, refer to some other tribe who occupied the country after the Kurukhs had left the country. Moreover, this may not improbably be one of the interpolations with which the epic, as competent authorities tell us, is replete, and which were made by subsequent writers to show off their geographical and ethnological knowledge.

Vide the attempts at identification of these places in

India.* But there appear to be strong reasons against the correctness of this supposition. The traditions of the Chōtā Nāgpūr Rāj family agree with the traditions of the Orāons in asserting that the Mūndas as well as the Orāons were present at the coronation of Phanī Mūkūt Rāi, the first Nāgvanśi Rājā of Chōtā Nāgpur. The chronicles† of the Rāj family fix the date of this coronation at A. C. 64. But the first Muhammadan conquest of Bihār was made by Muhammad Bakhtiār Khiliji so late as in the year 1193 A. C., and it was not until 1539 A. C., that Rōhtāsgarh passed into the hands of the Muhammadans through the trickery of Sher Shāh. Again, Ptolemy (2nd century, A. C.) in his 'Ancient Geography' appears to refer to Chōtā Nāgpūr when he says,—"Further east than these towards the Ganges are the Kokkonagai with this city Dosara."‡ Although Lassen's

Anthropos (vol iv. no. 1), and in S. C. Roy's 'Mundas and Their Country (Calcutta, 1912).

* *Vide* Risley, *Tribes and castes of Bengal*, Vol II, p. 139.

† Published in Hindi verse under the title of the *Nagvansabali*. The tradition referred to has been given in detail at pp. 139-140 of S.C.Roy's *Mundas and their Conntry*(1912), where the probable date of this coronation has also been discussed.

‡ '-gai,' or '-gahi,' it may be noted is the genetive suffix in the Orāon language so that 'Kokkon-a-gai' may be a contraction of *Kurukhar-gahi* and may mean *the land of the Kurukh.*

identification of Dosara with the village Doesa may not be correct inasmuchas Doesa, if it then existed at all, must have been an insignificant village until the seventeenth century, when it became the seat of the Nāgvansi Rājās, his identification of Kokkonagai* with Khokherā or Chōtā Nāgpur is not an unlikely one. And as the name Khōkhera or Khūkhrā which is derived from the name 'Kūrūkh,' came to be applied to the Chōtā Nāgpur plateau after its occupation by the Kūṛukhs or Orāons, this people must have been dislodged from Rōhtāsgarh before Ptolemy's time and consequently long before the Muhammadan invasion of India. Again, there appears to be a tradition amongst the Orāons still living in the Shāhābād District, that it was the Hindus who dislodged them from Rōhtāsgarh. Thus in the *Bihar Census Report* for 1911, we read, "The traditions of the Orāons relate that they held the fort of Rohtasgarh till ousted by the Hindus."† In the District Gazetteer of Shāhābād, we read, "The tradition that Rohtas was once the seat of their rule lingers among the Khārwārs, Orāons, and Cheros. The Orāons

* Mc Crindle's Edition, 167-168. (Trubner and Co., 1885).

† *Bengal, Bihar, and Orissa Census Report*, 1911, Part I., p. 402. By L. S. S. O'Malley (Calcutta, 1906), p. 9, ante. also p. 17.

assert that Rōhtāsgarh originally belonged to their chiefs and was finally wrested from them by the Hindus who surprised them at night during their great national festival, when the men had fallen senseless from intoxication, and only women were left to fight."

We have referred to the tradition which names their enemies as the Mlechchhas. A second tradition which we have heard amongst the Orāons calls the people who expelled them from Rōhtās the 'Hākims'—a word popularly used in the sense of 'authorities' or 'men in power'. The word Mlechchha is used by the Hindus in the sense of ceremonially unclean people,* and may refer equally to some non-Hindu aboriginal tribe or to the Muhammadans. And the Orāons appear to have learnt the name 'Mlechchha' from their former Hindu neighbours in Bihār. The early history of what is now the Shāhābād district shows that it was occupied successively by the Kūṛuk͟hs or Orāons, the Khārwars, the Bhars, three Rajput brothers, the Cheros (twice), and the Savaras. Though the order of succession of the first three tribes cannot be ascertained, it is known that the Cheros were conquered by the Savaras† and that even

* See quotation from Walter Hamilton, at p. 9 *ante*.

† "Dr. Buchanan's *Eastern India*, Vol I. 405-407, and Mr. L.S.S. O' Malley's *District Gazetteer of Shahabad*, 17-18.

as late as in Asoka's time (271-231, B.C.), Shāhābad was only nominally included in the Aryan kingdom of Magadha. It was not until the rise of the Gupta empire in the 4th Century A. C., that the country really came under Hindu rule; but on the downfall of the Gupta dynasty, the country again came under the sway of the Cheros for a second time.

Now, the bulk of the Cheros may well have been called 'Mlechchhas' by their Hindu neighbours, and 'Hindus' by themselves and other aboriginal tribes. As to this, Dr. Buchanan writes, "The Cheros, once lords of the Gangetic provinces, and whose sovereign was probably king paramount of India, are in this district thrust into the lowest dregs of impurity. All of them, that I have seen, say, that they live exactly in the same manner as Rajputs, and those of Palāmau who are rich, wear the thread, although the poor do not. But the Brahmans allege, that the Cheros live as impure as the highland Kherwars."* Thus, then, it seems probable that when the Cheros, once 'hakims' of the land, either during their earlier term of sovereignty in the Karūṣ-deś or during their temporary eclipse, sought to occupy the Rōhtās plateau, they succeeded in dislodging the Orāons

* *Eastern India* Vol. I. 494.

therefrom.* Thereupon the Orāons split up in two branches;—one branch still known as the Mālé proceeded northwards up the valley of the Ganges and established themselves on the Rājmahal Hills; the other branch, the ancestors of the Kūrukhs went down the Sōn and up the North Koel south-eastwards through Palāmau into the Chōtā Nāgpur Plateau. A probable explanation for the mention of the Hindus in one tradition and of the Muhammadans in another tradition as having expelled the Orāons from the Rohtās Plateau, appears to be that two different waves of Orāon immigration into Chōtā Nāgpur took place, one at a long interval after the other. Linguistic and cultural differences between the Orāons of the Western and those of the Eastern parts of the Chōtā Nāgpur Plateāu would seem to support this suggestion.

We shall conclude this section with the account that the Orāons give as to how they were dislodged from Rōhtāsgarh. The Orāons say

* Of two other traditions that we have heard from the Orāons, one names 'the Khāngārs of Patna' as their assailants, and the other the 'Turukhs' a name, which is generally taken to mean the Muhammadans. But when asked as to who the Turukhs were, our Orāon informants told us that the enemy were called Turukhs because they opposed the Kurukhs, a name which rhymes with Turukhs.

that they once dwelt on the Rōhtās plateau under a Rājā or king of their own tribe. The place was well fortified so as to defy the strongest enemy. The Orāons had erected a stone rampart about a mile in height, and the enemy long sought in vain to effect a breach. At length the 'Hākims' caught hold of a milk-woman of the Ahir caste who used to supply milk to the Orāon Rājā, and who had therefore free access to the fort. Inducements were offered to this woman to suggest to the enemy a practicable means of occupying the fort. She accordingly advised them to wait till the ensuing *khaddi* or *sarhul* festival when all the Orāon males were sure to get dead drunk. This turned out to be correct, and the enemy followed her instructions and succeeded in entering the fort. Although the Orāon women who had been at the time pounding rice with their wooden pestles to prepare bread for the *Khaddi* festival, came out with their pestles and valiantly met the foe, these amazons were soon overpowered. The Orāon Rājā and his subjects, it is said, fled the fort through a subterranean passage known only to themselves. The enemy lighted huge torches 'each of which consumed four maunds of oil,' but they failed to discover their exit.

IV. Later History.

In Chota-Nagpur.

From Rōhtās the Orāons went up the valley of the Koel which falls into the Sōn not far from Rōhtāsgarh, and finally entered the Chōtā Nāgpur Plateau. On their way, so runs their tradition, they passed through vast jungles where, with the help of their iron-tipped arrows, they secured plenty of game for their food.

When the Orāons reached Chōtā Nāgpūr they found the Mundās already in occupation of the country. The Orāons have a tradition that as they had first taken shelter, on their arrival here, in the houses of the Mundās and took whatever food the Mundās offered, they came to eat things which they had hitherto considered unclean. The basis of truth in this tradition seems to be that, thus cut off from contact with more civilized peoples, the Orāons in time went down a little in the scale of civilisation.

The claim sometimes advanced as to their having conquered the western parts of the Chōtā Nāgpur Plateau and driven the Mundās further to the east and south appears to be exaggerated. It was, at best, a moral rather than a military conquest which the Orāons may be said to have effected in the end. For some time, the Orāons appear to have lived in tolerable amity with the Mundās. But with their comparatively superior equipment for the struggle for existence, their comparatively better intelligence, better knowledge of agriculture, and their rapid multiplication due perhaps to better food secured through agriculture, they became gradually predominant in the north-western and central parts of the plateau, and made extensive clearances which they brought under the plough. It appears probable that a later wave of Orāon immigration from the Rōhtās side added considerably to the strength and importance of the Orāons in Chōtā Nāgpur The conservative Mundās, so long sole masters of the country, were too proud to brook rivalry, and retreated in hauteur to the southern and eastern parts of the plateau.

The Mundāri names of a number of what are now Orāon villages in the north-west of the Rānchi District, and the existence of the characteristic Mundā graveyards in many places in these parts with little or no Mundāri population, testify to the former occupation of that part of the country by the Mundās.* The fact that the Orāons in some of these places retained one or two Mundā families to propitiate the village-deities, would prove, if any proof were needed, that the Orāons acted in a

* The matter has been more fully discussed in *The Mundas and their Country*, pp. 123-130, 140-143.

conciliatory spirit. Up till now the Orāons have always shown due consideration for the Mundās on the score of their prior occupation of the country. Theirs was a victory not of arms or of physical strength but of improved tools and of qualities like patience, industry and perseverance which have survival-value in the struggle for material existence.

Pre-Hindu Period of Oraon History in Chota Nagpur.

As the Orāons increased in population, they gradually extended their settlements, as we have seen, from the north-western parts of the country up to the very heart of the Plateau. Each village, thus established, had its own sacerdotal and secular headman (originally combined in one and the same person), selected either by supernatural election or by hereditary succession. This headman and his assistants or colleagues managed the executive administration of the village and also took care to maintain agreeable relations between the village and the supernatural powers. The administration of justice amongst villagers *inter se* remained in the hands of the village-community as a whole represented by its elders as 'Panch'. Federations of seven, twelve, twenty-one or twenty-two villages formed what is called a Pārhā. And over this group there was a Rājā who was the headman of one of the villages of the group, the headmen of the other villages acting as the different office-bearers of the Pārhā association.

The Pārhā court or Pārhā-panch decided questions of tribal interest, and disputes between village and village. Although the autocratic name of Rājāh was adopted by the Pārhā-head, the pārhā was an essentially democratic organization. The assembled elders of the tribe took part, as of right, in the deliberations of the Pārhā tribunal. Tribal custom was the recognised law to which the Pārḥā-Rājā and other dignitaries were quite as amenable as the humblest member of the Pārhā. Expulsion from the tribe was the direst punishment in the eyes of the Orāon. Here were the main essentials of government; and under favourable circumstances, the Orāons might have developed their Pārhā organisation into a full-blown state of the modern type*.

Hindu Period.

An unforeseen event, however, destroyed the chances of further development of the Pārhā confederacy. While the Mundās and the Orāons were living together in the central parts of the Plateau, a king arose amongst them in the person of a reputed foster-son of a

* For a detailed account of the village and Parha organization of the Oraons, see *post*.

Mundā patriarch. Tradition as well as the annals of the Rāj-family of Chōtā Nāgpur speak of his election by the assembled Mundās and Orāons as their king and leader. But in course of time this elected chief appears to have succeeded in establishing a hereditary kingdom over the head of the Orāon and Mundā Pārhā confederacies.

Whether this personage known to posterity as Phani Mukut Rāi was of pure aboriginal extraction as some writers suppose*, or was of mixed descent as tradition would seem to imply, his descendants in course of time became completely Hinduised, and through frequent intermarriages with Aryan families became, to some extent, Aryanised. For a long time, however, Phani Mukut Rāi and his successors do not appear to have interfered with the internal administration of Orāon and Mundā villages and Pārhās, or even with their proprietory rights in their respective villages. The suzerainty of the Nāgbansi chief appears to have been acknowledged in the beginning by small periodical presents from the villages or groups of

* Dalton (*Ethnology*, 162,168) is of opinion that he was of Mundari extraction ; Sir Herbert Risley (*Tribes and Castes* II. 121) describes the Nagbansis of Chota Nagpur as 'a sub-tribe of pseudo-Rājputs, probably of Drávidian descent'; Rev F. Grignard (*Anthropos*, Vol. IV) suggests they might have been a branch of the Chero family.

villages, in the shape of grains and jungle-produce, and by feudal services in the nature of honorary attendance in his court on ceremonial occasions and following him in war. In course of time these voluntary presents were converted into fixed tribute. But the villages and the Pārhās remained, to all intents and purposes, perfectly autonomous.

Mahomedan Period (1585-1765, A.C.)

The autonomy of the aboriginal village communities of Chōtā-Nāgpur appears to have remained quite as undisturbed during the greater part of Muhammadan rule in India. It was in 1585 A. D., for the first time, that the Raja of Chōtā Nāgpur (then called Khukrā) was reduced to the position of a *Malguzir* (tributary) of the Moghul Emperor of Delhi. The necessity of raising the tribute which the Muhammadan Emperors or their Subādars or Viceroys demanded from him may have first suggested to the Rājā and his advisers the neccssity of converting the periodical supplies or aids hitherto obtained by him from the Orāon and the Mundā village-communities into regular payments in the nature of revenue. But this innovation was apparently resisted by the Orāons and the Mundās; and the Rājā generally found it difficult to raise the amount required by the Muhammadan Government. And, consequently, in the year 1616 A. C., the then Rājā, Dūrjan Sāl by name, was, under the orders of Emperor Jāhāngir, taken captive, and kept confined in the fort of Gwalior for twelve long years. There the Nāgvansi Rājā had for his fellow-prisoners a number of other Hindu Rājās. On his return to Chōtā Nāgpur after his release, he assumed, under imperial authority, the title of Mahārājā and changed his surname of Rāi into 'Shāh' or 'Shāhi.' Hitherto his own native plateau was practically all the world he knew. His contact with the greater world outside Chōtā Nāgpur, now created a change in the spirit of his regal dreams. The dazzling splendour of the Muhammadan Emperor's court, the pomp and pageantry, the wealth and power, which he had witnessed in the courts of the Hindu Rājās of Northern India whose acquaintance he had made, revolutionised the Nāgbansi Rājā's ideal of royalty. And the 'Rāi Rājā', now a full-fledged 'Shāhi Mahārājā', soon gathered about himself a pompous retinue of Brāhman priests, Rājpūt and pseudo-Rājput courtiers, and *amlahs* and place-hunters belonging to various Hindu and Hinduised castes. It was these alien adventurers who gradually introduced into Chōtā Nāgpur the idea of rents in cash and kind (*rakumats*) and cesses (*abwabs*) of various sorts.

The now-despised Orāons and Mundās naturally refused to submit quietly to such degradation, and stoutly resisted such exactions. And, as a consequence, more foreigners were called in by successive Nāgbansī Chiefs to overawe the aborigines into submission. These military mercenaries had to be remunerated for their services, and accordingly the Mahārājā's feudal dues in a number of villages came to be assigned to these adventurers. And thus the system of service-jāgir grants came into existence in the country.

This was the beginning of the agrarian troubles of the Orāons and the Mundās of Chōtā Nāgpur. Not content with the small tribute which the village-communities hitherto paid to the Mahārājā, these new Jāgirdārs sought to grasp some of the best lands of each village as the Jāgirdār's share (*manjhihas*) and also to levy rents on such lands (now called *Rājhas*) as had been given away by the descendants of the original settlers to outsiders—generally relatives who had come to live in the villages. The village-communities naturally showed fight. And the closing years of Muhammadan rule in India was a period of great turmoil in Chōtā Nāgpur, as it was in the rest of India.

The British Period 1765—1914.

At length, Providence, in His mercy, brought the mighty British Lion to introduce law and order into this distracted country. Unfortunately, the large area of the Plateau;

its inaccessibility and distance from the head-quarters of Government, and the want of correct information about its history and its affairs, for a considerable time prevented the authorities from taking effective steps towards putting a step to the aggressions on the rights and privileges of the Orāons and the Mundās of Chōtā Nāgpur. And although, goaded to desperation, these aboriginals now and again rose in revolt, they were put down with a strong hand by the British Government to whom they were represented as lawless savages and unscrupulous dacoits. And so the Jāgirdārs went on merrily with their campaign of expropriation of the descendants of the aboriginal clearers of the soil and founders of villages. They found a new unconscious instrument for effecting their purpose in the British Courts at distant Sherghāti and Chātrā where the Orāons would rarely go, or, even when they were obliged to go, would out of sheer stupidity or from the novelty of the situation, stare in blank astonishment and confusion at their proceedings which they could not understand ; and thus the landlords would easily secure what were no better than *ex-parte* decrees.

The terrible rising of the Orāons and the Mundās in 1831-32 at length made it clear to the British authorities at head quarters that there was something radically wrong in the affairs of the

Chōtā Nāgpur Plateau. And accordingly in the year 1834, the seat of District administration was removed from distant Sherghāti * and Chātrā to the very heart of the Plateau.

The form of administration was changed by making the new South-Western-Frontier-Agency more direct and patriarchal than its predecessor. The operation of the ordinary 'Regulations' was suspended, and, in their place, the Governor-General's Agent who had his head-quarters at Kiśanpur (Rānchi) made a few simple rules for the administration of justice. The spirit, but not the letter, of the substantive laws of the Regulation-districts were to be followed. An Assistant to the Agent was stationed at Lohardaga, and his seat was removed ten years later to Rānchi. Attempts at further spoliation of ancient rights, whenever discovered by the officials, were promptly checked. But only a couple or so of British officials however much they were filled with an ardent desire to save the tenantry from ruin, could not effectively control the never-ceasing attempts, open as well as covert, of an ever-increasing host of alien land-

* Sherghati is now in the Gaya district and Chatra in the Hazaribagh district. In those early days the Judge-Magistrate-Collector of the Ramgarh district (which included Chota Nagpur *proper*) had his seat alternately at Sherghati and at Chatra for every six months.

lords scattered over an area of more than seven thousand square miles. A new agent to effect the ruin of the aboriginal peasant-proprietors had already appeared on the scene in the early years of the nineteenth century. These were the itenerant merchants, money-lenders, and other creditors of the then Nāgbansi Mahārājā. Unable to pay them in cash, the Mahārājā farmed away villages to them or made assignments of lands or revenue. The greedy foreigners, who had naturally no sympathy whatever for the aborigines, succeeded in reducing a large number of Orāon and Mundā families of peasant-proprietors almost into miserable serfs. A number of improvident and impecunious Jāgirdārs were only too glad to emulate this new class of 'thikādārs,' as they were called.

Unfortunately for the aboriginal population of the Plateau, the more direct and patriarchal form of Government established in 1834 was abolished twenty years later, and a Commissionership such as existed in the more civilized parts of the Province, was established, and most of the legislative enactments obtaining in the rest of the Province were one after another re-introduced into Chōtā Nāgpur. As Messrs Slacke and Lister in speaking of the Chōtā Nāgpur Plateau observe,—"The Evidence Act and the Civil Procedure Code may or may not be suited to the needs of advanced commercial communities, for jungle tribes they are instruments of oppression.'*

The Government sought in 1869 to remedy what it considered the most crying grievance of the aboriginal tenants by getting a register prepared of such of their originally reclaimed (Bhuinhāri) fields as they had still left to them. But this was only a partial measure which temporarily allayed but could not effectively cure the discontent which had its foundation on wider and deeper grounds.

In the years 1889 and 1890, this discontent manifested itself in agrarian disturbances amongst the Orāons of the western parts of the district During the whole of the last quarter of the nineteenth century, the Sardārs, 'a band of unscrupulous aboriginal agitators' have been taking advantage of this chronic discontent to raise large sums of money by holding out false hopes of getting their wrongs redressed and their lands restored through petitioning the King Emperor. Though it is a shameful swindle on the part of some of the 'Sardārs,' the fact that several hundreds of the poorest Orāon and Mundā cultivators thus easily throw away their

* Quoted in the *Ranchi Settlement Report* (1912), p. 105. Similar observations were made in 1832, by Mr. Blunt, a Member of Governor-General's Executive Council. See *The Mundas and their Country*, p. 211.

hard-earned money testifies to the sense of grievous wrongs that rankles in their minds.*

The same sense of wrongs unredressed led a number of Orāons to join the Birsāite movement (1896-1900) at its inception. At length Government ordered the preparation of a record of existing rights in land, and sought to put the relations between landlord and tenant on a better footing by legislative enactments in 1903 and 1908. But for these belated legislative measures and the still more belated Record-of-Rights† completed in 1910 even the miserable fragments of their old rights in

* An exhaustive account of the agrarian history of the district, of the Sardar movement and the Birsaite movement, and also of the efforts of the Christian missions to civilize the aborigines and save them from further aggressions on the part of the landlords, will be found in *The Mundas and their Country*, Chs. IV and V, and Appendix III.

† The preparation of a Record of Rights was suggested as early as 1854 by H. Ricketts, Esq. C.S., Member of the Board of Revenue who had officially visited the country in the year. "If anything is to be done for the protection of the occupants of the soil," wrote he, "it must be by means of a Pergunah-wari investigation and record of rights. The class of indigenous village Zemindars is gradually, or rather quickly, disappearing in that character, though still existing as discontented Ryots brooding over their wrongs."—*Selections from the Records of the Bengal Government* No. XX., PP. 15-16. (1855).

land still left to the aboriginal tenantry would, at no distant time, have been swept clean away. These measures have, to some extent, served to arrest further spoliation and impoverishment of the Orāons and to allay the unrest of a century.

With the establishment in April, 1912, of a new Province composed of Chōtā Nāgpur, Bihār and Orissa, a new era of abiding peace and active progress appears to have at length dawned on the land. With the seat of a most sympathetic Government now at their own doors, the Orāons look forward to a steady improvement of their moral, material and intellectual condition. With gradually increasing facilities for education calculated to enable them in time to compete on equal terms in the race of life with their more civilised neighbours, with the wide diffusion of co-operative banks calculated to save them from ruin at the hands of the Sāhu money-lender and with similar other institutions sure to be devised and started for their uplifting by a paternal Government ever solicitous for their welfare, the Orāons, it is fervently expected, will soon take rapid strides in the path of material, moral and intellectual progress, and find for their capacities improved by education better fields of activity, which will more than make up for their loss of ancestral fields and ancient rights in land,—a loss, to which, as devoted agriculturists, they have not yet been able to reconcile themselves.

Conclusion.

Such is a brief outline of the history of the Orāons. We have traced them from their original home in Southern India where they dwelt in hill-caves, lived on jungle roots and fruits and the precarious gains of the chase,* and fought their enemies with sticks and stones; we have followed them to the valley of the Sōn where they evolved a primitive civilisation based on an agricultural life; and finally we have seen them settle down on the Chōtā Nāgpur Plateau where they opened out extensive lands for cultivation, established well-organised villages, and confederated them into socio-political groups known as Pārhās. These Pārhās, as we have said, possessed most of the essential elements of a state and might under favourable circumstances have developed into something better; but unforeseen circumstances, as we have seen, not only checked their normal evolution but made for their disintegration

* In the Rāmāyānā, the Vānaras are mentioned as living on roots and fruits. The reason for not making any specific mention of hunting was obviously the epic writer's desire to maintain the consistency of their habits with those of actual monkeys. Moreover, their difference with the man-eating Rākshasas was obviously sought to be emphasized (*vide Kiskindhya Kanda* XL. 27).

and degeneration. Thus for the Orāons, the Deccan has been the area of their physical characterization, the valley of the Sōn the area of their economic, social, moral and mental characterization, and the Chōtā Nāgpur Plateau the area originally of their consolidation and subsequently of disintegration and degradation.

CHAPTER II.

—:o:—

Geographic and Social Environment.

1. Geographic Environment.

We considered, in the last chapter, the tribal history of the Orāons, which has exerted a considerable influence on the life and manners of the people. Let us now pass on to consider their present geographic and social environment, whose influence on Orāon life has been no less important.

Nagpur

The central and western parts of the Rānchi district in the Chōtā Nāgpur Division of Bihār and Orissa form the present habitat of the bulk of the Orāon tribe. It is these central and western parts that are locally known as 'Nāgpur' and generally described as the Chōtā Nāgpur plateau.

General Physical Aspect.

We must picture to ourselves this land of the Orāons as an elevated table-land dotted over with numerous hills and pretty scrub jungles and intersected by a number of small and shallow hill-streams that fall into one or other of the two principal river-systems of these parts—the South Koel and the Subarnarekhā. The whole surface of the plateau is thrown up into long undulations, the depressions between the ridges of which have been cut up for purposes of cultivation into innumerable terraces rising one above the other like series of steps. The surface of the plateau is further diversified in appearance by expanses of arid gravelly land, exposures of naked rock, ranges of wooded hills, and here and there gaping ravines and sounding cataracts, and stately remnants of ancient sāl forest. As one travels from the western hills and jungles of the district where the tiger prowls and the semi-savage Hill-Koṛowa hunts, further eastward to the central parts of the plateau, the ruder features of the scenery gradually get softened, bleak ravines give place to cultivable valleys, the forests and hills become less numerous, the surface less broken, the undulations gentler, villages and open fields comparatively more numerous and extensive, and the population denser and comparatively more civilized.

We shall now proceed to give a brief account of each of the principal topographical and climatic features of the land of the Orāons.

Area and Boundaries.

The district of Rānchi lies between 22°20′ and 23°44′ North Latitude, and 84°3′ and 85°57′ East Longitude. It is bounded on the north by the Districts of Hāzāribāgh and Palāmau, on the east by the District of Singbhum and the tributary state of Gāngpur, now in the Central Provinces, and on the west by the Palāmau District of Chōtā Nāgpur, and the tributary states of Jāśpur and Sirgūja now in the Central Provinces. The District has an area of 7, 104 square miles and is by far the largest District in the Province of Bihār and Orissa.

The plateau.

The Chōtā Nāgpur plateau consists, broadly speaking, of two levels of undulating table-land resting at average elevations of 2,000 feet and 1,000 feet respectively above sea-level. The upper plateau is also the larger in extent, as it covers about two-thirds of the entire area of the District, and comprises its northern, central, and western parts. It is here that the bulk of the Orāons have dwelt for centuries.

Ghats.

Connecting these two levels of plateau with each other you meet with rugged and precipitous hill-passes locally known as *ghats*. These Ghāts are generally covered over with abundant forest growth and often present a highly picturesque scenery. Of these the most well-known are the Chūtu-pālū Ghāt on the north and the Chām-ghāti on the east.

Pats. Among the peculiar hill-features of the District are the *pats* on its north-western corner. These are small isolated table-lands perched up on lofty hills which rise abruptly out of the upper plateau, and appear to be the remnants of an ancient third and highest level of plateau. Captain G. C. Depree, who was in charge of the Topographical Survey of the District in 1868, gave the following account of these *pats* :—"They are of a nearly uniform height, 3,600 feet above the sea. Looking at them from a distance, their summit is as level and uniform as that of a masonry wall, and they form as perfect an horizon as the sea itself. On a near inspection, however, they are found to consist of rocky spurs of various heights, with deep valleys and many precipitous ravines radiating from the central mass. The ascent of these *pats* is steep. On the summits there is generally a small depth of soil overlying a rock, consequently very little can be cultivated ; forest trees however grow, and the slopes of the *pats* generally grow heavy timber. It is probable that the *pats* at an early period were one continuous mass, forming a plateau. If this be so, then Chutia Nāgpur was formerly made up of three separate levels of 3600, 2,100, and 800 feet, respectively, above the sea."

Water-falls

What impresses the traveller as the most interesting scenic feature of the Rānchi District is perhaps the few water-falls locally called ghāgs. Any one of these, as the *Imperial Gazetteer of India* observes, would "in a Western country be regarded as worthy of a visit even from a distance." Of these the most notable are the Hūndru-ghāg and the Dasam-ghāg. The former is situated about 30 miles east-north-east of the town of Rānchi. Here the Subarnarekhā river rushes down a rocky chasm from the higher plateau to the lower to a depth of 320 feet, and forms one of the most picturesque water-falls in India. The Dasam-ghāg, about 22 miles south-east of Rānchi, is formed by the river Kānchi falling down from the higher plateau to the lower in a sheer drop of 114 feet amid a rocky and sylvan scenery of great beauty. Besides these, the two Perōā-ghāgs, one in thānā Kōchedegā and the other in thānā Basiā, are worthy of notice: They are so named from the hundreds of wild pigeons (perōā) nesting in the crevices of the surrounding rocks. Even the little frequented Sādni-ghāg, formed by the river Sankh on its way from the Rājderā plateau to the plains of Borway, is well worth a visit.

Rivers

The one thing that the traveller in the District misses very much is a large sheet of flowing water.

Natural lakes there are none. The rivers of the District with the exception of a very few are narrow streams of water which are almost dry except during the rains. The principal rivers are the Subarnarekhā and the South Kōel, both having their source near the village of Nāgri about 12 miles west-south-west of the town of Rānchi.

Springs

Surface-springs, locally known as Dāṛis or Chuās are very common, and supply good drinking water to most villages in the District. Almost every Orāon village has at least one such spring.

Hills

The hills and rocks that strike up on every hand throughout the District add to the beauty of the landscape. These hills are gneissic in formation. In fact, the District is marked by the preponderance of gneisses and transition rocks. The highest hill in the District is Sāru in pargana Kāsmar, and the next highest is the Baṛāgain Hill near Rānchi. The former rises to a height of 3,615 feet, and the latter to 3,445 feet.

Jungles.

The greater portion of the District was at one time covered over with dense forests. It is principally the Mundās and the Orāons, as we have seen, who opened up the country by clearing jungles and establishing villages. And at the present day the central and eastern parts of the District are mostly denuded of their forests. Such jungles as still remain on hills and river-banks in these parts can hardly be called forests, for not many big trees are now left. Pātrās or small scrub jungles of *sal* saplings and other trees, are scattered throughout the District, and greatly contribute to the verdant freshness and wooded beauty of the scenery. By ancient custom, these pātrās have been reserved for the periodical supply of wood for the domestic, agricultural and building requirements of the village-communities, and also of the landlords since the latter class arose. But the conflict of rights between landlords and tenants are at the present day leading to a ruthless destruction, by both parties, of many of these pretty scrub-jungles. The western and south-eastern parts of the District are more fortunate in respect of their jungles. It is in these parts that you still meet with miles upon miles of unbroken forest. And the people of the District very appropriately nickname the whole of the District west of Pālkōt as the Ban-rāj or the forest-kingdom, in contradistinction to the portion of the plateau eastwards from Pālkōt which they style the Tānr-rāj or the land of bare fields.

In this forest-kingdom, the majestic *sal* (*Shorea robusta*)—the characteristic tree of the Chōtā

Nāgpur jungles—reigns supreme. The other dignitaries of the forest are the sacred *pipar* (*ficus religiosa*), the graceful *mahua* (*Bassia latifolia*), the gay *semar* (*Bombax malabaricum*), the stately *pesar* (*Cassia fistula*), the comparatively rare *sisu* (*Dalbergia sisoo*), the light *gamhar* (*Gomelina arborea*), and the sturdy *Dhautha* (*Anogeissus latifoluis*). Among courtiers of humbler rank are the sacred *karam* (*Nauclea Cordifolia*) the magical *bhelwa* (*semicarpus anacardium*) the *asan* (*Terminalia Tomentosa*), the *Khayer* (*Acacia catechu*,) the *palas* (*Butea frondesa*), the *tetar* (*Tamarindus Indica*), the *bael* (*Aegle Marmelos*), the *Karanj* (*pongamia glabra*), the *jamun* (*Eugenia Jambolana*), and the *Kusum* (*Schleichera trijuga*).

Forest trees

The stunted *khajur* palm (*phanix acaulis*) serves as the fan-bearer of the court, and the dwarfish bamboo (*Bambusa stricta*) piping in the breeze acts as the court-musician. Flower-bearing creepers of different kinds wreathe garlands round the king of the forest and his courtiers, and lovely orchids of different varieties add to the decoration of the sylvan court.

Fauna.

Among the denizens of this forest-kingdom the more important are the tiger, the leopard, the hyena, the bear, the wolf, and the antelope. The Nilgai (*Boselaphus tragocamelus*) and the Sambar (*cervus unicoler*) roam in the larger forests.

Birds.

Among the feathered denizens of the jungles of the District may be mentioned the peacock, the partridge, the duck, the teal, the plover, the pigeon, the snipe, and parrots of different species. Orāon boys while out in the jungles to graze their cattle, often take their *iahsa thongi* (bird-lime) with them, and amuse themselves by catching birds therewith.

Reptiles.

Snakes of different sorts and sizes, some poisonous and others harmless, are to be met with in the jungles and hills of the Chōtā Nāgpur Plateau.

Fish.

The streams and rivers of the District are not known to contain any of the larger species of fish. But various small species, such as the *putia*, the *khairā*, the *bans-pata*, the *magur* and the *garai*, are met with in almost every stream and pool.

Minerals.

The district of Rānchi is believed to be rich in minerals. Diamond, gold, lead, copper, tin, graphite, and manganese have been known to exist in some quantities. Limestone, mica, and quartz occur in beds of gneiss. A soft kind of steatite allied to soapstone is found in the south-eastern parts. Iron ores abound in the District.

Climate

The greatest glory of the land of the Orāons is its salubrious and genial climate. It is only in the more jungly portions of the district, especially at the foot of the ghāts, that a kind of malarial poison lurks in water and air and produces jungle-fever in the unacclimatized, although the indigenous population appear to resist the noxious malaria fairly well. Owing to its elevation, the Chōtā Nāgpur Plateau has a much cooler climate than that of the adjoining districts. Except for about a month in summer, when the sun beats fiercely and the heat is somewhat trying, the weather is generally agreeable and the nights delightfully cool. In fact, the variation of temperature between day and night, is much greater than in the plains of Bengal and of Bihār *proper*. The average mean temperature rises from 62·2° in December to 87·8° in May. The mean minimum in the cold season is 51° and the mean maximum in the month of May is 100°. The highest recorded temperature in summer has been over 110° and the lowest recorded temperature in winter has been 38°. The annual rainfall varies from 50 to 65 inches. The undulating nature of the ground gives the country the advantage of a natural drainage. Situated at a distance from the sea and at an altitude of over 2,000 feet above sea-level, the plateau possesses a dry atmo phere, and except during the three rainy months, cloudy weather, when it occurs once in a way, is of a very transient duration ; and the country enjoys a genial sunshiny weather for the greater portion of the year.

The Seasons

In Chōtā Nāgpur, we have three distinct and well-marked seasons,—winter, summer, and the rains. The cold weather begins about the middle of October and lasts up till about the middle of March, when the hot weather may be said to begin. The month of March, however, generally passes for the Spring in Chōtā Nāgpur. The hot weather continues till about the middle of June, about which time the monsoon bursts and ushers in the rainy-season. The rains generally continue off and on till the end of September or the beginning of October.

The Monsoon.

It is these annual monsoon rains that form the chief controlling factor of the climate and the vegetation. With the advent of the later monsoons, the face of the country is transformed. The drooping paddy-plants of the lowlands revive, the parched up-lands are covered over with verdure,—and the Orāon rejoices at the prospect of a bumper harvest for himself and abundance of grass and other fodder for his cattle. Except a few of the lowest fields that retain moisture throughout the year, the rest of the cultivable lands could yield no crops but for these monsoon rains.

Soil

For agricultural purposes, the soil of the Chōtā Nāgpur Plateau is generally poor. It is only in the hollows between continuous ridges of uplands that good clayey (*nagra*) soil is met with. In many of the lower terraces of rice fields there is a good deal of admixture of sand with clay. In many of the upper terraces of low (*don*) lands the proportion of sand is very large, and some of them (*chowra don*) have even gravelly soil. The quality of the soil in the uplands (*danr*) is still poorer. These uplands consequently require to be manured every year they are cultivated, and most of these lands have to be left fallow at intervals of one or two years. Except in the jungly parts, the soil is deficient in humidity. The productiveness of the soil in any particular year depends largely on adequate and seasonable rainfall. This short account of the soil shows with what considerable amount of hard labour, the Orāons and the Mûndas have converted the slopes of the depressions between the ridges into terraces of smiling fields of paddy; and with what difficulty they extract crops of pulses, oil-seeds and other grain out of poor gravelly uplands.

The effects of geographic environment on Oraon life.

The effects, direct or indirect, of his geographic and climatic environment may be traced in almost every aspect of Orāon life—in the Orāon's physical and mental characteristics, his economic condition, and his animistic religion. The coal-black skin which we saw in his forefathers who lived in the Deccan has been modified into brown-black in the comparatively cooler climate of the Chōtā Nāgpur plateau ; the tonic effect of his agreeably cold winter has made him hardy and long-lived. His native jungles provide him with a number of edible roots, leaves, and fruits ; the comparatively fertile valleys of the central plateau provide him with rice and other cereals. And as the country is now denuded of a greater portion of its jungles, and game is not plentiful, the Orāon lives mainly on rice and other cereals that he grows on his fields, and on edible roots, leaves and flowers that his womenfolk gather in the jungles ; and although he is fond of animal food, he can now only indulge in it on particular occasions—either after the periodical hunting expeditions or on occasions of religious or social festivals and ceremonial visits. Owing to the absence of excessive cold in his country, meat diet is not in fact a climatic necessity with this people. Climatic control may also be traced in the material and construction of the Orāon's huts and in the furniture he ordinarily uses. These huts have walls of mud or of split bamboos, and either sloping roofs of burnt clay-tiles or thatches of wild grass supported on posts, beams, and rafters made mostly of *Sal* wood. Bamboos, *sal* trees, and wild grass grow in abunonce in his native jungles and waste lands ; and although stone for building purposes may be had in plenty, he prefers wood, bamboo and wild grass, as these are much easier of transport and collection, and as owing to the absence of dampness in the atmosphere of the plateau these stand no risk of decomposition. To keep out the hot winds of a tropical summer, the Orāon builds his huts without windows, and to drain off the rain-water that pours in torrents in the rainy months, he makes the roofs and thatches of his huts somewhat sloping. Living in a tropical climate, the Orāon does not require an abundance of clothing or furniture ; and thus his huts are not overburdened with furniture, and his dress is of the scantiest. His low culture is indeed principally responsible for the poor type of his dwellings and the poverty of his furniture and dress ; but the effects of climatic conditions are not to be overlooked. Climatic control may also be traced in the colour and material of his dress. As may be expected in a tropical climate, white is the ordinary colour of the Orāon's clothing, whilst Orāon youths are fond of ornamenting their scanty clothing with gay-coloured embroidery and tassels of red thread. Climatic control may be further traced in most articles of household use among the Orāons, in their outdoor sports and games, and in their other habits and customs. The laborious method of terrace-cultivation by which the Orāon cultivator manages to secure the advantages of rain-water for every plot of land in the higher as well as the lower terraces of his fields, further illustrates the effects of geographic and climatic conditions. Owing to the isolated geographical position of the plateau to which access was not easy until recently when a railway line was opened, and owing also to the poverty of the soil and of its natural products, the Orāons are not a commercial nor even a trading people, and the economic condition of the tribe is indeed very miserable. As for manufactures, the only thing worth mentioning is the mat made by Orāon women with leaves of the date-palm (*Fœnix Sylvestris*) which grows in their native jungles. The effects of geographic and climatic conditions may be similarly traced in the Orāon's mental characteristics and his religion. The warmth and sunshine of his climate is reflected in his gay, vivacious temperament; and the ruder and grander features of the scenery of the plateau nurture sentiments of fear and awe of the supernormal and mysterious powers that appear to him to reside in heaven and earth.

Such, then, is the present habitat of the main body of the Orāons,—a land of dry climate and dry soil where the agriculturist must work hard to live, —a land of rugged hills and stubborn valleys which make people hardy, patient, and persevering,—a land of pretty scrub jungles, purling hill-streams, smiling fields (the outcome of the Orāon's industry), shady groves and dancing-grounds (seen at their best in clear moon-lit nights),—a land of clear skies, cheering sunshine and invigorating west winds during the greater part of the year,—which all help to keep up the Dravidian's characteristic vivacity and geniality of temper ;—a land too of a brief spell of powerful Sun in summer, of frequent heavy downpour of rain in July and August, of a few roaring cataracts, and of some heavy forests infested with wild animals—which all combine to inspire and feed a 'superstitious' awe of invisible powers working more often for evil than for good.

II. Social Environment.

Like geographic environment, social environment has an important influence on the life of a people.

The Neighbours of the Oraons.

There are very few villages, in the Orāon country, with an exclusive population of Orāons. The landlords of Orāon villages are for the most part Hindus, and, occasionally Muhammadans resident in the country. Again, as the chief, and practically the sole, occupation of the Orāon is agriculture, and he considers it derogatory to himself to engage in such occupation as weaving, basketry or wicker work, pottery, and working in iron, he necessarily requires the services of people of other tribes and castes to supply his few simple needs. And thus in most Orāon villages we find a sprinkling of families of Lohrās who make or mend the Orāon's ploughshares and other tools and implements,—Āhirs, who tend his cattle,—Kūmhārs who make earthen-ware for his domestic use and tiles to roof his huts with,—Jolāhās and Chik Baṛāiks who weave his clothes,—Tūris, Māhālis or Oṛs, who weave or plait his baskets and *Gōṛāits* and Ghāsis who play music at his social festivities and who serve him in some other ways. There are very few Orāon villages without at least an Ahir family and a Gōṛāit family.

Besides these low-class Hindu or rather Hinduised castes, there are in Chōtā-Nāgpur a few other purely aboriginal tribes living side by side with the Orāons. The more important of

To face p. 69.

Handloom weaving in the Orāon country.

these aboriginal tribes are the Mundās, the Khāṛiās, the Kōṛwās, and the Asurs. The Mundās and the Khāṛiās stand on the same level of culture as the Orāons. If these tribes occupy a low level of culture, the Kōṛwās and the Asurs represent a still more primitive culture. As, however, these aboriginal tribes are not necessary factors of the Orāon village organisation, we shall here briefly notice only those castes and tribes whose services are indispensable to the Orāons,* and who consequently form component parts of a typical village-community in the Orāon country. Such are the Ahirs, the Lōhārs, the Gōrāits, the Ghāsis, the Māhālis, the Kūmhārs, and the Jōlāhās,†

The Ahirs

In every Orāon village, in or near which there are jungles and pasture land, you find at least one family of Ahirs. The duty of the village-Ahir is to graze and look

* It must, however, be noted that the Munda tribe with whom the Orāons lived together when they first entered the Chotā Nāgpur plateau, have exerted a much stronger influence on the customs, manners and beliefs of the Orāons than any of these other castes and tribes.

† As the Jolahas of Chota-Nagpur, who belong to the Sunni sect of Muhammadans, hardly differ in material respects from the same class of Muhammadan weavers in other parts of India, we do not give any account of them. But the accompanying illustration represents a good type of the Chota-Nagpur Jolaha.

after the cattle of the villagers. For his services, the Ahir gets a certain measure of paddy (from 30 seers to a *maund*) every year for each pair of plough-bullocks and buffaloes owned by the Orāon whose cattle he grazes. The plough-cattle are left in his charge only for about six months in the year, that is to say, from after the harvest till the commencement of the next sowing season. In addition to his annual allowance of paddy from each client, the Ahir generally gets one day's milk out of every two days' for each cow left in his charge and one day's milk out of every three days' for each she-buffalo. The cattle of the Chōtā-Nāgpur village are a very poor breed, and the cows and she-buffaloes yield a very small quantity of milk.

The Ahirs of Orāon and Mundā villages appear to have a strong admixture of either Dravidian or Mundā blood, if they are not actually a class of Hinduised aborigines. They eat fowls and sometimes, it is said, even pork, though beef is tabu to them. They are sometimes served by Brāhman priests, but only of a degraded class. Like the Kumhārs and the Kurmis of Chōtā-Nāgpur, the Ahirs are given the title of Māhāto. In some villages, the village Ahir also acts as the *panibhara* or water-carrier of the landlord and has to keep the landlord and his agents during their visits to the village supplied with water.

The Lohras

To the Orāon village community, the Lōhrā or blacksmith is even more indispensable than the Ahir. For, whereas in some villages, the Orāon cultivator manages to have his cattle tended by the boys of his own family or by a servant (dhāngar) when he can afford to engage one, the necessary repairs to his ploughshares and other tools and implements cannot be similarly managed. * The Lōhrā like the Ahir, is remunerated by a certain measure of paddy (generally a *maund*) annually for every yoke of cattle owned by each cultivator who requires his services. In addition to this annual allowance, he is paid separately for his services in making or mending other tools and implements, and for these each client finds his own iron. These village Lōhras of the Orāon country are partially Hinduised Dravidians, and are popularly known as 'Kol Lōhārs', or rather 'Lōhrās', as distinguished from purely Hindu Lōhārs locally known as 'Sād Lōhārs'. These Lōhrās act as their own priests.

The Goraits

Almost every Orāon village has its family of Gōṛāits. The Chōtā-Nāgpūr Gōṛāits are, like the Lōhrās, a

* The Lohrā of one village often, however, serves the Orāons of a number of surrounding villages.

Hinduised aboriginal people. The function of the village Gōṛāit is aptly described as that of the village drudge. He has to carry messages to the Zemindār and to the village headmen, act on ceremonial occasions as the village drummer, and perform several other miscellaneous functions. He makes combs, cards cotton, and the services of his women-folk are requisitioned in tatuing Orāon girls. In some places, again, where there are rivers that are not fordable during the rains, the Gōṛāit acts as the ferryman by poling a canoe which is only the hollowed-out trunk of a sāl tree. In some villages, the Gōṛāit also acts as the village-Kōtwār in which capacity he has to call the tenants to the landlord, carry letters, and collect fuel and provisions for the zemindār or his agents when they visit the village. The village-Gorāit like other village-officers are generally paid a certain measure of grain annually by each cultivator. In a number of villages, he holds a plot of rent-free service land under the village-community, known as '*Goraiti khet.*' Like their neighbours the Orāons, these Gōṛāits eat beef, pork, and fowls, and are great consumers of spirituous liquors. The Goṛāit house-holder performs his own *puja* (worship), but a Brāhmin priest is sometimes secured to perform the worship of *Debi Mai* and *Surja.*

The Ghasis

In many Orāon villages you meet with one or more families of Ghāsis. Although they profess to be Hindus, they appear to be a purely aboriginal tribe who eat beef and pork and indulge freely in spirituous liquor. Fishing is a favourite occupation with this tribe. They also turn their hands to bamboo-work. Their men are good players on flutes and pipes and are hired to play music at weddings and other social festivities, and their women act as midwives and nurses. A Ghāsi will not feel ashamed of begging for alms from door to door. And the tribe has a very bad reputation for thievish habits. They are only nominal Hindus, and are denied the services of Brahman priests.

The (Bans) Mahalis, Turis, Ors, or Oreas

Here and there in the Orāon country you come across families of Māhālis, Tūris, Oṛs or Oṛeās. These are the basket-makers and workers in bamboo in the Orāon country. They appear to be of purely aboriginal extraction. Though more or less Hinduised, beef, pork, fowl, and liquor do not come amiss to them. They have not yet secured the services of Brāhman priests.

The Kumhars

Higher in the social scale than the castes hitherto described is the potter caste of Kūmhārs. They have better features, are served by Brāhman priests though not of the best type, and conform more strictly to orthodox Hindu tenets. They cannot however resist the temptation of partaking of the meat of fowls when the opportunity occurs. The Chōtā-Nāgpur Kūmhār is not exclusively devoted to his wheel, but engages in cultivation and thus ekes out the scanty income he derives from his caste-occupation by the produce of his fields. Kumhars are found only in the comparatively larger villages of the district—generally in villages, which have resident landlords. In many of these villages, the village-Kūmhār holds a plot of land called 'Khāpar khetā' (land given for services in making *Khapra* or roofing tiles) in lieu of which he has to supply pots and pans to the Zemindar and his agents free of cost.

In villages where there are no Kūmhārs, an Orāon desiring to have tiled roofs to his huts or houses, has to get a Kumhār from another village. And the Kumhār, generally with an assistant, comes to his house with his wheel and other appliances, and they have to be fed and lodged by their employer and paid at a certain rate for every thousand roofing tiles made for him. But this is what the poorer Orāons cannot afford to do. It is only in the parganās nearer Rānchi that many Orāons go in for houses with tiled roofing. But in the jungly *parganas* in the west

To face p. 75.

Semi-Hinduised aboriginal women in the Orāon country. The woman on the left is carrying a child in the manner of an Orāon mother.

and south-west of the district, where plenty of thatching grass and bamboos are easily available, houses with grass thatching and plaited bamboo-walls, as in the accompanying illustration, are more numerous. The wild tribes of Chōtā-Nagpur, such as the Kōṛwās, especially that branch of them known as the Pāhāṛiā Kōṛwās or Hill-Kōṛwās (as distinguished from the *Dih-Korwās* or Village-Kōṛwās) live in huts of the rudest style thatched with wild grass.

The habits, beliefs and customs of these tribes and castes and those of the Orāons have necessarily acted and reacted upon each other to some extent. All these tribes and castes now use the same sort of household utensils, agricultural implements, tools and weapons,—live in the same style of huts,—and wear the same kinds of ornaments, as the Orāons do. Women of the comparatively more respectable of these castes—such as the Ahirs, the Kūmhārs and the Bhōgtās,—wear in addition to the 'jwellery' in use among Orāon women, a few ornaments on the nose and ears, of which specimens are given in the accompanying illustration. It is, of course, different with the Hindu and Muhammadan Zemindar and money-lender. With their comparatively higher civilization, they live in a better style of houses (though generally made of the same materials), have better furniture, better food, and better dress, and look down upon the Orāons as untouchable *Chuhars.* And the Orāons, on their part, look upon them with distrust, though long years of submission have made them somewhat docile. There is a saying amongst the Orāons that sooner or later evil befalls the village in which a *Teli* lives. Some of these Telis are notorious usurers and oppressive landlords. As for the other castes and tribes we have spoken of above, friendly relations generally exist between them and their Orāon neighbours, except where the Zemindar, for purposes of his own, creates a spilt amongst them.

All these peoples are more or less completely Animistic in their beliefs. They all believe in an ever-increasing host of indeterminate powers and shapeless spirits in whom there is more of malevolence than of beneficence. These are believed to bring rain, storm, drought and other pests on earth and to afflict men and animals with all sorts of diseases and ailments, great and small, and cause misfortune and death. All these tribes and castes regard the Orāon and Mundā Bhuihārs as occupying a higher social status than themselves, though not as superior in point of 'caste' or race. They share with the Orāons their superstitious beliefs about omens and dreams, and the powers of wizards and witches, observe the same ceremonies as the Orāons do to expel disease from man and cattle and to send it on to the next village, make use of the same charms and amulets for protection from the evil eye and employ the same methods for exorcising evil spirits when they 'possess' people and cause epilepsy and other diseases. Most of their gods and godlings too are common to all these tribes and castes. Among gods, the worship of *Gāon-deōti* (village-deity) and *Devi Māi*, the Būṛhā-Būṛhi or ancestor-gods, Barpāhāri (the Marāngbūrū of the Mūndās and the Sāntāls), and the Sun-God, is known to all these peoples. The manner of worship of, or rather the nature of the offerings to, the different gods sometimes differ in different tribes. Some of these tribes have indeed special gods of their own; but that does not prevent the other tribes and castes from revering or rather fearing such special gods. Thus, the *Gōṛea bhut* is particularly the God of the Ahirs, but other castes and tribes, including the Orāons, offer sacrifices to this *bhut*: Again the Nature-spirits and stray godlings (bhūlās), the souls of men and women who died a violent death (*muis, chuṛins, baghouts, &c.*) are common to the spirit-cult of all the castes and tribes of Chōtā Nāgpur. There is another class of peculiar godlings which may be said to form the place-cult of the Chōtā-Nāgpur plateau. These are places hallowed by some unusual and awe-inspiring occurrence such as the immolation of a Hindu *sati* on the funeral pyre of her deceased husband,* and weird-looking rocks and unusual natural features which inspire fear and awe in the minds of these simple folk. In such cases it is to the soul of the departed or to the spirit of the water-fall or hill, or other place, as the case may be, that homage is really paid by the Orāons and their neighbours.

This sort of Animism may be said to be the local cult of the Chōtā Nāgpur Plateau to which the Hindu and even the Muhammadan residents of an Orāon village readily subscribe. As his Hindu neighbour has given the Orāon the worship of the Debimāi and the Mahādeo, so the necessity felt by the Orāon for the propitiation of the special local powers residing in hill and jungle, land and water, is recognised as a matter of course by his Hindu and even his Muhammadan neighbours. The Chōtā Nāgpuri's idea of his relation to his physical and super-physical environment expresses itself in Animism and Magic, as his idea of his relation to his social environment expresses itself in elabo-

* As, for example, in the Orāon villages of Hendlaso and Jovi in Thana Lohardaga.

rate rules of ceremonial pollution and avoidance* (*chhut*) or tabu.

* People not belonging to their own tribe are generally looked upon by the Orāon with suspicion, for who knows but that they may have the evil eye, or have at their back and call some familiar bhūt or spirit who may be set on to do him harm? To a similar reason, we think, is to be attributed the tabu against food touched by people of other castes and tribes.

CHAPTER III.

Physical Characteristics and Personal Adornment.

I. Physical Appearance.

Although the natural beauty of health, cheerfulness, and simplicity, invests the Orāon youth of both sexes with a certain comeliness, Orāons of either sex, when past middle age, are generally ungainly in appearance. In fact, the Orāons have what are termed "low" features. They are a short-statured, narrow-headed (dolicho-cephalic) and broad-nosed (platyrrhine) people. The colour of their skin is dark-brown often approaching black, their hair is black and coarse with an occasional tendency to curl; and although wooly hair is rare, it is not altogether unknown : we have come across one or two Orāons whose hair is distinctly so. Although the hair is plentiful on the Orāon's scalp, it is usually less plentiful on his cheeks, and lips, and still less so on the chest, back, and legs: Such beard and moustache as he has, generally begin to appear rather late, ordinarily not before a lad is out of his teens. The chest is well-developed and so are the calves of his legs. The eyes

To face p. 81.

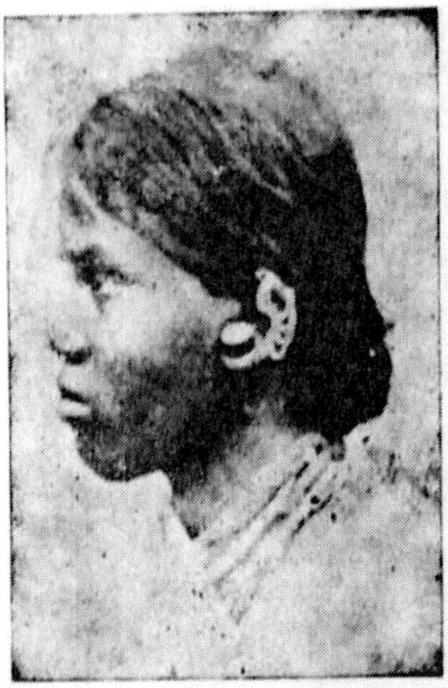

A. Type of Orāon girl (profile).

(Front view of A).

B. Type of Oraon boy.

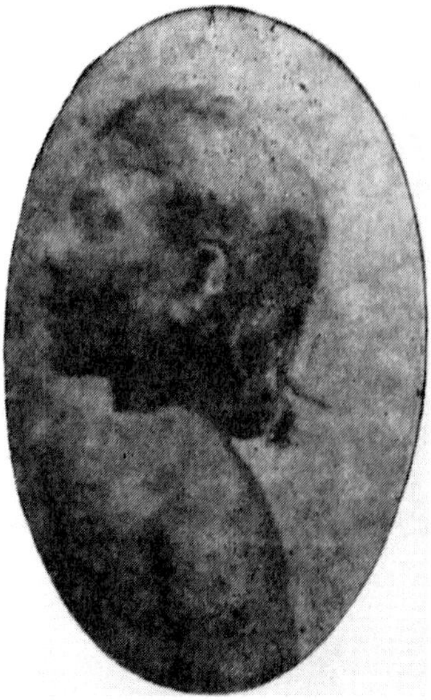

(Profile of B).

are medium-sized and occasionally small, the colour of the iris is dark, and there is no obliquity in the axis of the eye-lids. His jaws are somewhat projecting, lips rather thick, and the nose is depressed at the root.

Anthropometric Indices, and their Value.

The average anthropometric indices for a hundred Orāons measured by Sir Herbert Risely are given as follows :—

(1) Stature :—

Average	...	1·621 m.
Maximum	...	1·744 m.
Minimum	...	1·480 m.

(2) Proportions of the head :—

(Glabelo-occipital) Length

Average	...	184·6
Maximum	...	198
Minimum	...	165

Extreme breadth :—

Average	...	139·3
Maximum	...	158
Minimum	...	131

Cephalic Index :—

Average	...	75·4
Maximum	...	87
Minimum	...	67

(3) Proportions of the Nose.

Height :—

Average	... 46·2
Maximum	... 53
Minimum	... 38

Breadth :—

Average	... 39·8
Maximum	... 47
Minimum	... 34

Orbito-nasal Index :—

Average	... 86·1
Maximum	... 113
Minimum	... 70

From a comparison of these indices with those found by him for a hundred Mundās, Sir Herbert Risley concluded that there was no difference of physical type between the Mundās and the Orāoṇs, and he classed both the tribes as Dravidians. But this conclusion is open to serious doubts. We may note that whatever similarity there may exist between these two tribes in respect of head-form, the proportions of the nose, and other particular physical features, any one who has lived long enough amongst them and observed them with some attention can in most cases distinguish a genuine Orāon from a genuine Mundā. Thus recently in a batch of about fifty aboriginal boys all dressed in the same fashion, we could at once single out the only Mundā boy from the rest of his companions who were all Orāons. And in the Rānchi law-courts where people of both the tribes come daily as litigants or witnesses, we tried for several days together the experiment of distinguishing by sight Orāons from Mundās and in over three-fourths of the cases we were successful. It may be noted that in these experiments most of the men about whose race we were mistaken either hailed from villages where Orāons and Mundās have long lived together and common social and other environment have operated to make their physical appearance converge to a common type,—or were more or less Hinduised and in some cases ceased to speak their own language. We may also note that amongst children of such Mundās and Orāons as have received English education and have been engaged as clerks, teachers and so forth, in or near the town of Rānchi, and live in a comparatively more comfortable style than their fellow-tribesmen in the villages, we often meet with features decidedly more improved than those of the average Orāon living in the interior of the district. The former often possess a comparatively finer nose, less prominent jaws and cheek-bones, and so forth. Thus occupation, food, mode of living, social and climatic environment, and probably language too, would appear to have some hand, direct or indirect, in moulding or modifying the features. And one is inclined to think that even Anthropometry will in time come to endorse to some extent Spenser's lines :

'For of the soul the body form doth take :
For soul is form and doth the body make.'

Moulding The Features

As for head-form, it may not be out of place to notice a practice common among both the Orāons and the Mundās as also among their aboriginal, semi-aboriginal, and Hindu neighbours. In fact, the practice to which we allude—the artificial manipulation of the features of a new-born babe—appears to be fairly common throughout India, and raises grave doubts as to the value of anthropometry as a test of race in India. An Orāon mother, like a Bengali or a Bihāri Hindu mother, seeks to mould the head of her new-born babe into a 'symmetrical' shape. During the first few days after birth, the babe is profusely anointed with mustard oil every morning and evening; and, while thus rubbing the limbs with oil, the Orāon nurse deftly presses the comparatively soft skull of the babe with the palms of her own hands slightly warmed over a fire. She takes particular care to exert a gentle but persistent pressure with her hands on the back and sides of the babe's head, so that the skull may not remain unduly flat at the top, and the sides of the head may not bulge out in an unseemly fashion. The forehead also is sought to be gently pressed down with the hands, if it be 'unduly' prominent. An Orāon mother also seeks, as Hindu mothers do, to 'elevate the nose' of a new-born babe by pressing the nose upwards with her fingers against its sides. But the practice we have known in certain parts of Bengal of the midwife inserting one of her fingers into the mouth of the babe just after its birth and pressing that finger against the hard palate of the babe so that the bony septum may be slightly elevated and thereby rectify any depression in the bridge of the nose, appears to be unknown amongst the Orāons. As for the flatness of the Orāon's nose, we have heard Bengali Hindu ladies visiting the Orāon country attributing this to the usual habit of an Orāon mother carrying her babe slung at her back with the babe's nose often pressed against her shoulders. But this is obviously going too far. The depression at the root of the nose cannot certainly be accounted for in this way.

Blue patches on the skin and the tongue.

We shall conclude this section by noticing two interesting points in connection with the physical Anthropology of the Orāons. These are the blue patches sometimes found on the persons of Orāon infants, and a blue pigmentation found on the tongues of many Orāons, male as well as female, young as well as old. Sometimes you also find certain blue lines which look like a pigmentation on the true skin and which appear at birth on the chest downwards and on the arms of many Orāon children and generally disappear after a month or two. In some cases the lines are long and parallel to one another, in others broken up and irregular, in some more, and in others less in number. These blue lines, however, do not appear to have any anthropological interest, as they seem to be merely veins.

The blue patches which are more interesting are, however, much less frequent. The few that we have observed on Orāon children vary in size from a tiny speck to a large irregular patch. Some of these blue patches are permanent and are known as 'Janam Khōdā' or 'natal tātū-marks' and others are lighter in colour and disappear within a year or two after birth. Those that we have hitherto seen are, as we have said, but few in number, and therefore afford no solid basis for any speculation. But as for the blue or violet pigmentation on the tongues of Oārons, it appears to be much more frequent. And unlike the blue lines and patches on the chest and arms, this pigmentation on the tongue appears to develop with age, and is found more often and more prominently in grown-up persons than in young children. Surgeon-Captain F. P. Maynard, I. M. S., who first drew attention to these pigmented tongues in 'A Note on Melanoglossia',* states that out of 20 Orāon males and 20 Orāon females that he examined, he found pigmented tongues in 9 males and 10 females, that is to say in 47·5 per cent. We ourselves have examined about four hundred Orāons, adults and children, and we found the proportion of pigmented tongues to be about one-third. The following description given by Dr. Maynard of this blue pigmentation accords exactly with what we observed: "In some cases the fungiform papillæ were each surrounded by a blue or brown rim, giving the tongue a curious speckled look; in others there were irregular blue or black blotches, simple or multiple, and varying in size from a two-anna bit to a rupee on the dorsum or along the edges of the tongue."

* Vide *Indian Medical Gazette*, October 1897.

II. Attitudes and Movements, and Physical powers.

Customary postures.

If the Orāon has 'low' features, he has generally a better physique than many of his neighbours who pride themselves on their 'higher caste.' The Orāon is sturdy in his limbs and erect in his bearing. His body is generally well-balanced and the feet firmly planted n walking. His legs are straightened but the toes are slightly turned out in walking and running. In walking, his arms hang habitually with the palms of the hands rather to the front, when not actually dangling backwards and forwards. The joints are generally pliable. The habitual posture when standing at ease is for the hands to hang at the sides, and, one foot to be turned a little outwards. When standing at attention his arms are either joined together at the back, or one arm is placed akimbo. The habitual posture for sleep is to lie on the side. At dinner, the Orāon generally sits down with his feet on the ground and his knees turned upwards. An average adult Orāon male can carry a burden of about two maunds (160 lbs.) on his shoulders without difficulty. In one day he can carry such a load to a distance of about thirty or thirty-five miles ; and this he can do for several days in succession. We have found an Orāon

To face p. 89.

An Orāon carrying his children in a *sikā-bāhingā*.

walking twenty-three miles of more or less undulating road, in less than five hours with a heavy load on his shoulders ; and the man did not look very much fatigued at the end of his journey, and assured us he could have proceeded further on his journey the same day if it were necessary. And this man was neither a man of more than average strength nor a habitual load-carrier. The usual method of carrying loads in vogue amongst the Orāons and other aboriginal tribes of the Ranchi District is to take them on a *Sika bahinga* (Orāon : *ugi epla*) composed of two rope-suspenders hanging one from each end of a wooden pole placed cross-wise over the shoulders. Women in carrying a jar of water or other burden usually carry it poised on the head.

Pushing, pulling &c.

In moving heavy objects they habitually push rather than pull, that is to say, exert power *from* the body rather than *towards* it. The axe or the hoe is used in the way customary with most Indian labourers, namely, by seizing hold of the handle with both hands, raising it to some height from the ground and then bearing it down on the ground or on the object attacked.

Climbing.

The Orāon is a good hill-climber. A favourite pastime with Orāon boys is to go up to the top of a barren hill with a number of leafy twigs and tnere to seat themselves in a row, each on one of the twigs with his legs stretched forward, and, in this posture, to slip down the sloping side of the hill. Men and women are good tree-climbers. And the inability of a wife to climb trees well, is sometimes urged as a valid ground for divorce, for, the leaves of several kinds of trees are eaten as *sags* and it is one of the ordinary duties of a wife to gather them. The Orãons do not use any mechanical aids or special methods in climbing.

Riding.

Riding is not usual with this people: for, the average Orãon cannot afford the luxury of owning a horse. But Orãon boys frequently amuse themselves by riding buffaloes while grazing them or taking them home after ploughing.

Running, jumping and walking.

The average young man is good at running and jumping. An average Orãon can run long distances,—three miles or more at a stretch,—at a moderate speed. He is a good walker too: He can go on walking day after day at an average rate of from thirty to thirty-five miles.

Rowing and paddling, swimming and diving.

As there are no rivers worth speaking of within the Ranchi District, Orãons rarely row or paddle. Dug-out *sal*-wood canoes are sometimes used to cross the larger rivers during the rains. Owing to the paucity of good tanks and rivers in the district, all Orāons cannot swim and dive. Those who can do so, swim at a fairly good speed, and dive head foremost. The Orāons are good shots with the bow and arrow.

Physical Endurance.

In repose an average Orāon adult can abstain from food for about twenty-four hours, and in exercise for about twelve hours without much inconvenience. As for sleep, although an Orāon generally spends about seven hours out of twenty-four in bed, he can abstain from sleep for a whole night without much difficulty. On occasions of their periodical socio-religious ceremonies, Orāon young men and women usually spend two, three, or more consecutive nights in dancing and singing and indulge in very little sleep. The Orāon can bear cold very well, as well as exposure to the direct rays of the sun,—with his head uncovered.

Such are some of the outward characteristics of Orāon life in Chota Nagpur. In the youth of both sexes, exuberance of health and spirits, a delight in all physical activities, and taking life easy; in the aged of both sexes, dullness and listlessness and in many cases an inordinate love of drink, born perhaps of a sense of relief that their life's work has been somehow fumbled through,—and that reckonings have been somehow made even, with the superior powers, visible and invisible, that have so long threatened to harass them at every step of their journey through life;—these are the prominent outward features of Orāon life that impress the observer.

III. Dress and Personal Adornment.

We have seen that the Orāon mother seeks to mould the features of her new-born babe into a comely shape by skilful manipulation. From the same desire of improving their personal appearance by artificial means, Orāon girls have tatu-marks made on their persons, both boys and girls have the lobes of their ears pierced and decorate their persons with ornaments of various sorts, and all Orāons, young as well as old, use some kind of clothing or other. In fact, the ordinary clothing that the Orāons, male as well as female, wear in their villages, may be said to serve more the purposes of decoration, concealment, and advertisement, than that of an adequate covering or protection,—from the civilized man's point of view. The tropical climate of their country, however, partly accounts for their scanty clothing. Their young men and young women are exceedingly fond of finery. Their old men and women are satisfied with the scantiet rags which barely cover the lower sexual regions. Men and women do indeed feel shame at being seen absolutely naked, but even young women in the villages often go about with no covering above the waist, without any sign of shame.

Male Dress.

The ordinary clothing of an adult Orāon male in his village consists of a piece of cotton cloth about a foot in width and three to five or even six yards in length. It is wound round the waist and then passed between the thighs once tightly and again loosely, the ends being allowed to hang down from the waist. This piece of cloth is called the *Kareya.* On festive occasions, the young Orāon wears a Kāreā with the two endornamented with figures interwoven with red thread and also a number of small round tassels of red thread hanging from the ends. The young Orāon is fond of wearing the *Kardhani,* which is a girdle made either of twisted cotton-thread dyed black, or of the fibre of a creeper similarly twisted and dyed, and worn in coils round the waist. From this showy waist-string a bunch of keys, a cotton-purse, a lime-case, and a pair of small pincers with which thorns are extracted from the limbs, are often suspended. Occasionally too a bamboo-flute is stuck into this girdle. Now and then, you see a young man whose waist-cloth is entirely hidden under these girdles which extend from the waist almost down to the knees; and you may not unreasonably suppose that probably at one time these girdles formed the only covering below the waist that the Orāon knew; and the girdle was indeed a convenient thing in which he could carry as in a pocket all the outfit that a hunter and a wood-cutter might require to carry with him to the jungles.

Old men and poorer people ordinarily wear in the village, only a *bhagoa* which is a short and narrow strip of cloth, about a foot wide and a yard long. This is passed between the thighs and attached by the ends to a waist-string. While going on journey, and also on special occasions, the Orāon covers the upper part of his body with a cotton sheet-covering or *chadar* called *pechhouri*. This is from two yards and a half to three yards in length and about a yard and a half in width. In the cold season, a *barkhi* which consists of two *pechouris* sewn together at the borders so as to have two folds, is used as a more suitable covering for the upper part of the body. Well-to-do Orāons also use blankets as wrappers in the winter. The use of a head-dress is not general. The head-men of Orāon villages are ceremonially invested with the head-dress (Pāgri) as an insignia of office. As for other Orāons, only self-important persons put on a piece of *Karea* wound round the head to serve as a head-dress, while going on a visit to other villages or to the market or to the Courts.*

While walking at night and also in travelling, sticks made of wood or of bamboo, are often carried. A small lime-box made of bellmetal (*chunouti*) or tin or of wood, (*pokoe*), cotton-purses (*batu*) or cotton money-bags (*thaili*), are also carried by an Orāon on a journey. Leather *kharpas* or sandals are occasionally worn by some Orāons while going on a long journey. While going into the jungles, Orāons often carry at their waist iron-pincers (*chimta*) to extract thorns that may prick their feet or other parts of their body. In the rains, occasionally an Orāon wears on his feet a pair of *khatnahis* or wooden soles with a string over each foot. While out in the fields during the rains, a kind of rain-hat (*chhupi*) made of the leaves of the *Gungu* creeper, is used by men, and a kind of waterproof called "*Gungu*' covering the head and back and reaching down to the back of the knees is worn chiefly by women. The latter is also made of *Gungu* leaves and rimmed with bamboo splinters. Bamboo umbrellas or *chhattas* are also used.

* Thus the only mark of distinction in the dress of a village-headman from that of the commoners is now lost.

Female Dress.

In the villages, Orāon women ordinarily wear round the waist only a *khanria* or piece of cloth about four cubits long. This is about two feet wide and reaches down to the knees. The upper part of the body is without any covering. For old women as also for the poorer women, this piece of cloth is often made up of patches and shreds. Women of well-to-do families sometimes wear a borderlers *Sari* ten or twelve cubits long, one end of which is used to cover the trunk. On special occasions they wear a *pudhna* or sheet-covering over the body. But while bathing or cleansing their hair with *nagra*-clay—as they do once a week or so—all women wear the *khanria*.

Clothing of Children.

Children go about naked till their third or fourth year. After that age, a young boy wears a small *karea*, and a female child wears a *putli* or strip of cloth round the waist. An unmarried girl wears a waist-cloth about a cubit wide and five to six cubits long. This is called a *gaji*. Small children when beginning to crawl are given iron anklets to wear. Orāons, in general, use clothes made of home-spun cotton. But those living in or about the town of Rānchi are taking to the use of imported clothes.

Ornaments of Women.

Young Orāon women make up for their deficient clothing by loading their persons with a variety of brass-jewellery. Ornaments of other material are also worn. The arms and the ears are the most favoured in this respect; and next to them come the neck and the ears. One of the first things that attract the attention of the traveller in Orāon villages is the seven thick bracelets made of brass or bell-metal that deck each forearm of the young Orāon woman from the wrist up to the elbow. These become all the more noticeable if, as is usual, she has no covering on her body from the waist upwards. These bracelets or *balas* have to be supplied to the girl by her parents at her marriage. In addition to these heavy bracelets in sets of seven or more on each arm, young Orāon women wear a still thicker brass bracelet, known as *rasnia*, one on each arm. These *extra* thick bracelets are later on exchanged for somewhat thinner ones. On the neck, a necklet called *hansuli* made of bell-metal is worn by a well-to-do Orāon woman, and by the side of the *hansuli*, she wears as many necklets made of beads strung on plaited and coloured thread as her circumstances permit. Those who can afford to do so also wear *Chandoa-malās* or necklaces made of silver coins strung together. Imitation coin-necklaces are extensively used by Orāon young men and girls. Ear-ornaments of different sorts and sizes adorn the lobes of the ears which are pierced for the purpose, and the holes thus made are abnormally distended by inserting pith-sticks into them. On the lowest hole in the lobe of each ear there is worn first a *bindio* which is either a palm-leaf rolled up and dyed red with lac (*tar-bindio*) or a *gangai* stick similarly dyed (*gangai bindio*); above this *bindio*, three pith-sticks called *bich-kanis* are inserted into the lobe of the ear one above the other ; and above them again either a brass-pin called *upar-kāni* or a pith-stick called *bitla danda* is worn. From the middle *bich kani* are suspended a number of *jhika chilpis* or slips of metal attached to metal chains. For the legs, anklets called *painra* (Hindi, *painri*) are worn only by an Orāon bride at her wedding. Nose-ornaments are also worn by girls. At the age of five or six years, a girl gets the left septum of her nose bored and a reed inserted into the hole ; two or three years later the reed is replaced by a nose-pin (*nak-mutri*) ; and, finally, four years or so later this nose-pin is, if circumstances permit, replaced by a silver ornament called *besar*. On the fingers, young women wear as many rings as they can get. Of these, some are made of iron or copper by the village blacksmith and are called *Lohra-muddi* ; and others called *Gōuṛia-muddi* are made by Gōuṛias, or Mālārs, of brass which is melted by blowing ; others again called *sonra muddi* are made by Sōnārs or gold-smiths, by beating pieces of brass sheets into thin plates. On the second toe, three rings made of brass and called *jhutia*, and one made of iron and called *katri* are worn by Orāon women. The *katri* is lighter and thinner than the two *jhutias*, and is worn at the upper end. On the head, a wooden comb (*bagirka*) is inserted into the hair which is formed into a chignon and worn at the back of the head. Hair-pins (*khongso*) of three varieties are also inserted into the chignon. These *Khongsos* are either common single hair-pins (*surra khongso*) or double-pronged ones (*chhatna khongso*), or those with small looking-glasses inserted between the prongs (*aina khongso*). On occasions of *jatras* or dancing-festivals, Orāon women adorn their chignons with flowers and with *bakkā-pencho* which consists of a number of plumes of the white stork with three cock-quills in the middle—all threaded together on a string. Such are the various ornaments with which a young Orāon woman decorates her person, at least until her first child is born and often much later.

Ornaments worn by young men.

Young men amongst the Orāons are as fond of decorating their persons as young women are. Brass bracelets (*bera*) one on each wrist, and *bainkal* or *bijait* also made of brass and worn just above the elbow, a variety of neck-ornaments made of *kasi*-grass (*pondra poon*), *phutchira* grass (*phutchira poon*), *kiskodai* grass (*kiskodai poon*), glass-beads (*kach poon*), china-beads (*mochar poon*); and a kind of crescent-shaped or circular head-ornament called *patoa* made either of kāsi grass or of a thin narrow brass-plate which serves to keep the long hair in position; and a girdle or *kardhani* made of plaited thread or silk dyed black and looking like leather, and worn round the waist in coils;—these are the principal ornaments worn by Orāon young men. They gather up their long hair in a chignon at the back of the head; and into this are inserted one or more iron-prongs (*chhahkar*), wooden combs (*bagirka*), and a small looking-glass or two. At marriage-festivities and dancing-festivals or *jatras*, the young Orāon inserts a few porcupine quills (*surahi chaour*) into his waist girdle—a few at the back of the waist and one on each side. *Patoas* of different sizes and patterns, some of them looking like crowns and made either of *kasi*-grass or of the leaves of the wild *khijur*-palm, are also worn at these *jatras*. The grass-necklaces with his physical structure, a proud delight in showing off to the best advantage his vigorous physique, a self-satisfying expression of personality—these appear to prompt the Orāon's love of finery.

CHAPTER IV.

——:o:——

Village Organization and Economic Life.

The economic activities of the Orāons,—their exertions to obtain food, clothing, shelter and other requirements for the maintenance and improvement of the conditions of life,—centre round agriculture. And consequently it is with agriculture that not only their economic life but much of their social regulations and religious ritual are vitally concerned. For it is on the particular mode of subsistence adopted by a people that their social system and religious observances are to a great extent based.

The Orāon's choice of his present habitat in the more open central parts of the Chōtā Nāgpur Plateau was obviously determined to a great extent by his agricultural mode of life. And so too his village-organization has agriculture for its groundwork. We shall therefore begin with a short account of his village-organization and his mode of land-holding, then see what food and other necessaries of life his lands supply, and inquire into the ways and means by which he extracts you while you are out in the fields or elsewhere'. Cowrie-shells are sometimes worn on the neck of children to ward off the evil eye. A few Orāons, generally Nāg-mātias or snake-doctors, wear necklaces made of the bones of a snake with black and yellow stripes called the 'dhōra' snake. The snake is killed and then buried underground to rot there for a year. After this period, the bones are taken out, chopped into small pieces, and threaded on a string.

Tatuing. Whatever may have been the original object of tatuing, it is now regarded by the Orāon as a mode of decoration. Ordinarily only girls are tatued. When an Orāon girl is seven or eight years of age, three parallel lines of punctures are made on her forehead and three on each of her temples by a woman of the Gouṛiā or Mālār caste. A peculiar iron instrument with three teeth in it is used for the purpose; and a pigment made of powdered charcoal mixed with oil is rubbed into the punctures. Four or five years later, similar punctures are made on the upper part of her arms, on her back and chest, and on her legs. The patterns are preferably of flowers, and are either selected by the girl herself, or, when the girl has no fancy for any particular pattern, other female members of her family may select a pattern

To face p. 102.

These lines are tatued on the forehead and temples.

This is a pattern of tatumarks on the arms and feet of an Oraon woman.

These are the tatumarks on the back.

Patterns of Tattoo-marks of the Oraon.

To face p. 103.

Young Orāon pair.

for her, or the operator may select what pattern suits her client best.

Although ordinarily only women are tatued, a man may have tatu marks made on his person to let out 'dead blood' (*kechchka kheso*), as the Orāons express it, when a long-standing pain in any of his limbs has baffled all other treatment. This process of letting out 'dead blood' is believed to be a sure method of relieving the pain. This is the only case in which tatuing is believed to cure a disease. But tatuing is not believed by the Orāon to protect the wearer against future sickness or evil of any sort. There is a saying amongst the Orāons that whereas all other ornaments of Orāon women are taken off at death, tatu-marks are the only decoration that they carry with them to the next world.*

Such then is a brief account of the dress and personal adornment of the Orāons. The decorative principle appears to be more in evidence than the protective principle, particularly in the case of their young men. A self-complacence in his own individuality which he ordinarily identifies

* But we have not heard them say in so many words that they are after death recognised by the spirits of their deceased ancestors by these marks impressed on the shadow though that may have been the original belief.

To face p. 101.

An Orâon type. The brass band on the fore-head is worn as an ornament

of the young Orāon are generally presents received from the young girl to whom he is attached. Formerly both women and young men allowed their hair to grow. But now-a-days youngmen sometimes crop their hair short in imitation of Orāon Christian converts. But in any case, a non-Christian Orāon male must at least leave a tuft of hair on the crown of his head uncut. Elderly Orāons who generally get their hair cropped always have such a pig-tail or *chundi.*

Ornaments worn as amulets.

As a charm against harm by lightning an Orāon sometimes wears an iron-bracelet (pānnā-berā), plain or twisted, and an iron-ring on one of his fingers. These bracelets and rings are made only of such iron as has been exposed to the open sky during an eclipse of the sun or of the moon. People who are born with the feet foward are believed to be particularly liable to lightning-strokes and so it is such persons who generally put on such bracelets. After an eclipse, the iron—generally some worn-out iron utensil or implement thus exposed—is taken to the village blacksmith to be made into the desired charm. The blacksmith while putting the amulet on the finger or arm, as the case may be, of his client pronounces a blessing on the wearer to the following effect, 'May not lightning strike deities. For these spirits and demons, the Chōtā Nāgpur landlords—at least the majority of them—still entertain a superstitious awe. To this day these public *debottar* lands are not resumable by the landlord so long as a single member of the particular Orāon village-community is alive. The process by which a portion of the Bhūinhāri lands of the original Orāon settlers were taken possession of by the new landlords and converted into their private demesne (*majhihas*), and such of the village-lands as had been given by the Bhūinhār-proprietors to new settlers were converted by the alien landlords into Rājhas, have been briefly described in a previous chapter.* These new settlers, were either relatives by marriage of the Bhūinhārs who were settled on portions of the lands of the different khūnts to which their Bhūinhār relatives respectively belonged, or men of such castes as the Ahir, the Gōrāit, the Ghāsi, or the Lohrā, whose services the agricultural, Orāon village-communities could not dispense with.

Village Organization,

A typical Orāon village thus consists of the Bhūinhārs, subsequent Orāon settlers (called Jeth-rāiyats or ordinary rāiyats, according as they are earlier or later settlers) and a Gorāit family, one or two Ahir families, a Lōhrā family, and

* See Chapter I, p. 43.

sometimes also a family of Kumhārs. In many villages, a few families of Ghāsis, Jōlāhās or in some cases Chik Baṛāiks (weavers), and Māhālis (basket-makers) and a few other castes and tribes are also met with.

Of these, the Gōṛāits, the Ahir, and the Lohrā are practically village-servants. Of village-officials who are Orāons, there are generally three,—namely, the village Baigā or Pāhān, and his assistant known as the Pujār or Pānbhara, and the village Māhāto. The function of the village Baigā (*Oraon*, Nāegās) is to propitiate the village-deities, and of the Pujār to help him at the public religious festivals. The Māhātō is the secular village-headman whose duty originally was to maintain the relations of the village with the outside world on a satisfactory basis, as the duty of the Pāhān or Baigā is to maintain agreeable relations of the village with the world of spirits. 'Pāhān gāon bānāta hai, Māhāto gāon chālātā hāi'—is a common saying amongst the Orāons, and this means that it is the Pāhān who keeps the village quiet (free from disturbances from the world of spirits), and the Māhātō who manages the (secular) affairs of the village. * There is evidence to show that formerly

Village-officials.

* The word 'gaon banata hai' has been taken by Col. Dalton to mean 'makes the village.' But, as a matter of

To face p. 39.

An Orãon Panchāyat.

hārs* of the village, and the lands cleared by them were called the Bhūinhāri lands of their respective khūnts,—stocks or families.†

Khunt-bhuts.

As the process of clearing the jungles involved a disturbance of the spirits residing in the jungles, the duty of making periodical sacrifices to the *nads* or spirits haunting their respective khūnt lands necessarily devolved on the Bhūinhār stocks or khūnts. These spirits as also certain ancestor-spirits were called the khūnt-bhuts or sept-spirits.

Village-deities.

As for the remaining spirits,—for, according to a common Orāon saying, 'the Earth is full of spirits as a tree is

* This term corresponds to the word 'khūntkāttidār' used by the Mundās. It would seem this name was brought by the Orāons from Bihār and adopted in preference to the name 'Khūntkāttidār' applied in the same sense by the Múndās. The name Bhūinhār appears to have been in the beginning applied in the same sense as the term Bhowmik or or Bhūinyā (as in the name 'Bārō-Bhūinyās' applied to the twelve famous chiefs who divided Bengal between themselves in the latter part of the 17th Century).

† This is the reason why almost every Orāon of Chōtā Nāgpur always remembers and names some village or other as his Bhūinhāri village, although his family may have long since removed to another village through the oppression of alien landlords or for other reasons.

full of leaves,'—the spirits that haunted and still haunt the forests and waste lands within the ambit of the village,—they too were not overlooked by the original founders of the village. A portion of the primitive forest was consecrated to the more important amongst them and named the Jāher or Sarnā * Here, to this day does the village-priest, who was originally the village-patriarch and village-chief, offer sacrifices not only to the principal village-deities but to the whole host of general (as distinguished from family) spirits that are of any account. The propitiation of the *khunt-bhuts* and the village-deities are meant to keep the village in general—its inhabitants, cattle, fields and crops,—from harm's way. And these deities and spirits—the chief of whom are *Chalo Pachcho* (Sarnā Burhiā), Dārhā and Deswāli,—can only be propitiated by a Bhūinhār, that is to say a descendant of the original clearers of the jungle. @

* Jaher would appear to be the Orāon name for Sarnā which is the Mundāri name. In many villages, the Sarnā is now represented only by a few trees standing on a *tanr* land which, however, may never be cultivated.

@ That is the reason why in a number of villages originally founded by the Mundās who were subsequently crowded out by the Orāons, one or two Mundā families (descendants of the original settlers) are still retained as Pāhāns or village-priests and are the recognised Bhuinhārs

Necessarily, therefore, the Bhūinhārs of a village have social precedence over later Orāon settlers, however rich such subsequent settlers may be. And thus the Orāon's tenure of land and his social organization may in one sense be said to rest on a basis of religion.

Bhutaha Lands.

As the Orāons in those days had no landlords over their heads, these peasant-proprietors had no rents or taxes to pay. But the only condition of cultivating their lands which the circumstances of the clearance imposed on them was the propitiation of the village-deities and the *khunt-bhuts*. In later times, when land-lordism was established, and rents or services and other impositions came to be attached to some of these Bhūinhāri lands—and in the beginning all cultivated lands were Bhūinhāri,—portions of these lands had to be set apart as khūnt-(family-) bhūtkhetā, Gairahi-(village-) bhutkhetā, Pāhānāi or Dālikātāri (the village-priest's service land) and the Pūjār or Pānbharā khet (service-land of the Pahan's assistant); and these had to be excluded from assessment even by the alien landlord, in consideration of their holders performing the periodical propitiation of village-

of such Orāon villages (e.g., in villages Masiatu, Bhaisadone, Chapadi, &c.)

his food and other necessaries from his lands, and finally examine the material condition that agriculture has secured for him. And as the religious idea is inseparably connected in the Orāon's mind with his 'economics' and his 'social philosophy', we shall, in passing, briefly refer to some of the religious and magico-religious practices connected with his economic pursuits.

1. The Village, Village-lands and Land-holding.

When the Orāons settled in the Chōtā Nāgpūr Plateau, each family, or each group of brothers or cousins with their families, appears to have selected a particular jungle area suitable for clearance and cultivation. The highest level space by its side was selected as the site for dwelling houses. Here a few huts were erected for the families and their cattle. In the beginning it appears these were temporary leaf-shelters such as we still see Orāon labourers putting up for themselves in the jungles or elsewhere when employed as wood-cutters, sawyers, earth-diggers and the like. Gradually these temporary leaf-dwellings came to be replaced by huts with walls of mud or plaited bamboo and thatches of wild grass.

Bhuinhars.

These pioneer families who cleared the jungles and brought suitable lands under the plough, were called the Bhūin-

To face p. 106.

Temporary leaf-huts of Oraon labourers.

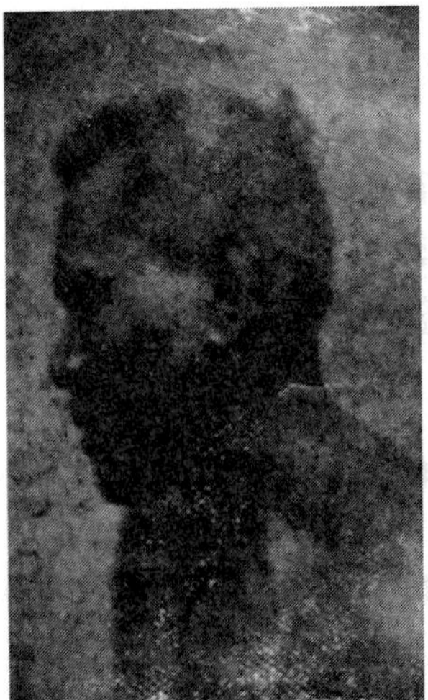

Front view). (Profile)

Type of Oraon adult male.

the Baigā or Pāhān was the secular as also the religious head of the village. To this day there are Orāon villages in which there is no separate Māhātō, but the Pāhān acts in both capacities.

The Pahan, Thus, the Pāhān or Baigā is an essential and indispensable factor of the Orāon village organization. In fact, he is the central figure of the Orāon village. In most Orāon villages a Pāhān is selected triennially (but in a few aberrant instances at longer or even indefinite intervals) by the magic *sup* or winnowing basket. In a few villages, owing to their large Orāon population and large area, there are two or even three* Pāhāns. The reason for this would seem to be that what were formerly more than one village have gradually been amalgamated into one. In a few villages, again, there is a separate Pāhān for the worship of the Mahādaniā *bhut*. He is called the Mahādāniā Pāhān.

Ordinarily the Pāhān always belongs to the Pāhān khūnt, but in a few villages owing to the Pāhān khūnt being very small, Bhūinhārs of other khūnts, too, have been known to be elected Pāhān

fact, the verb 'banana' or 'banao' when used in reference to a village is always used by the Orāons in the sense of 'appeasing' (the deities and demons).

* As in village, Silāgain *thana* Mandar).

(but always by the supernatural method of 'sup-chālānā'). In a few other villages, owing probably to the Pāhān Khūnt having been very small the office of Pāhān has become hereditary. In an Orāon village where a family of the original Mundā settlers has been retained for the propitiation of the village deities, the post of Pāhān has become hereditary in such Mundā family. Any alienation of the Pāhānai-lands *proper* made by a village-Pāhān is not considered binding on his successors; and any alienation of public (*gairahi*) Bhūtāhā lands made by the Pāhān is not valid even during his tenure of office.*

The Mahato. The Māhāto, in an Orāon village holds somewhat the same position that a village-Mundā does in a Mundāri village of the Bhūinhāri type. The office of a Māhāto appears to have been evolved after alien landlords came to the country. Before that, the Baigā or Pāhān appears to have been the sacerdotal as well as the secular head of the village. And, as we have said, even to this day there are villages in which the Pāhān acts also as the village-Māhāto. In most villages, the Māhāto is elected

* Owing to this disqualification of the Pahan, we have found all the leading Bhuinhars of a village joining in executing a mortgage of the Bhutaha lands of the village to meet the expenses of a litigation in which the village-community, as a whole, was interested.

once in three years by the villagers assembled at the ākhrā or dancing-ground. And subsequently the village-landlord or his agent ties a *pagri* or turban round his head as an insignia of the Māhāto's office and as a token of the landlord's approval,—and generally receives from the Māhāto, thus honoured, a *nazār* or present of a goat or a couple of rupees or so. The Māhāto's position as the representative of the village in its dealings with the landlord, with the government authorities, and generally with all outsiders, has in a few villages been degraded to almost that of a Zemindār's agent; and in such villages, the Zemindār claims the right to appoint and dismiss him at pleasure. In one or two villages where the relations between landlord and tenant are exceedingly strained, we have seen two Māhātos,—one elected, as usual, by the villagers, and the other appointed by the Zemindār, but not recognized as 'Māhāto' by the villagers. But, even in such cases, the Zemindār generally takes care to see that the Māhāto appointed by himself, like the Māhāto appointed by the villagers, is a member of the Māhāto khūnt, if there is one in the village. If there is no Māhāto khūnt in existence, the village Māhāto must at any rate be a Bhūinhār.* In Orāon villages where

* Exceptions to this rule are occasionally met with now-a-days. But those are instances of innovation.

there has been no Bhũinhāri measurement, the Māhāto should belong to one of the families of the oldest Orāon settlers. In some villages again the post of the Māhāto is hereditary. The Māhāto, in all cases, enjoys rent-free Māhātoi service-land during the tenure of his office. The Zemindār has no right to resume the old Māhātoi land of the village so long at least as there is a Bhũinhār in the village willing to act as Māhāto. Even in the few villages in which the Zemindār has usurped the right of appointing a Māhāto, when the Māhāto neglects his duties, and the Zemindar wants to dismiss him, he cannot resume the Māhātoi land, but must appoint another man of the Māhāto khũnt (or where there is no Māhāto khũnt another Bhũinhār) to the office, and the service lands will go to the new nominee.* So far as the Zemindār is concerned, the duties of the village Māhāto are to settle disputes as to amounts of rent due, to know the holding of each raiyat, and to assist the landlord or his agent in the collection of rents. Up till recent times the Māhāto and the Pāhān in consultation with each other used to

* But occasionally a Bhuinhar of another Khunt is appointed Mahato, even though there are members of the Mahato Khunt living. This too would seem to be an innovation.

settle vacant rāiyati lands. This they obviously did as representatives of the village-community which was not very long ago the joint owner of all vacant and uncultivated lands. But even this remnant of the old proprietary right of the Orāon village-community over unoccupied village lands, is now mostly lost. For, in most villages, the Zemindār or his paid agents now make such settlements themselves.

Almost the only vestiges of the proprietary rights of the Orāon village-community over the village-lands, that survive to this day, are the rights to jungle-trees and jungle-produce, rights of pasturage, and rights of reclaiming waste lands. But even these miserable remnants of their old rights may now be exercised only under certain restrictions.

Other village servants.

Besides the two headmen or chief officials of an Orāon village, the Māhāto and the Pāhān,* there are generally a few village-servants. Such are the Goṛāit (called the Bhāndāri of the Orāon village-community as distinguished from the landlord's Bhāndāri), the Ahir, the Lohrā, and the Kūmhār,

* The village-Mundā, as a village-official, is unknown to most Orāon villages except those that adjoin the Mundā country. There is, however, a Mundā khūnt in most Orāon villages.

whose remuneration and functions have been described in a previous Chapter.* The Pūjār or Pānibharā or Tahalū who assists the village Pāhān, enjoys as his service-tenure one or more plots of land known as 'Pūjār-khet' or 'Pānbharā-khet.' In villages where the post of Pāhān is not hereditary but elective, the Pūjār is elected generally by the loṛhā process to be described later on, either from the Pūjār Khunt, where there is one, or else from amongst the Bhūinhārs generally. The 'Pūjārkhet', 'Pāhānāi', 'Māhātoi', 'Gōṛāiti', and 'Gairahi-Bhutkheta' lands are the remnants of 'public' lands belonging to the Orāon village-community which the 'landlords', as we have said, cannot resume, so long at least as the Orāon village-community exists, however reduced in numerical strength.

The Oraon village community.

We have spoken above of the Orāon 'village-community'. But whereas amongst the Mundās, at least in an intact Mundāri-Khūntkātti village, the Mundāri village-community as a whole owns all the lands within the village area, and although separate fields are cultivated by individual Mundās for their own profit, the proprietary right to each field belongs to the corporate body of the Mundāri inhabitants, and the consent of all those joint-

* See Chapter II, Pp. 69-72.

owners, must be obtained for the transfer of any land,—amongst the Orāons, on the other hand, the joint ownership of the corporate body of Orāon villagers or rather Orāon Bhūinhārs is not now fully recognised except in respect of these public lands; but not very long ago such ownership extended over all. waste lands and jungles, *etc.*, within the ambit of the village.

Form of land holding.

The idea of individual ownership of land, or rather of separate ownership by each family, appears to have developed amongst the Orāons from before they entered the Chōtā Nāgpur Plateau. And the Orāon's customary laws of inheritance and succession are the outcome of this idéal of ownership of cultivated lands by the family. This is another reason why a married daughter who passes out of the family is not entitled to inherit the lands of her father or brothers; but when her husband, herself, and her children have been living as members of her sonless father's family, and working in his fields, her rights so far as the *rajhas* lands are concerned, revive in her husband (only so long as she is alive) or in her sons.* The *Bhuinhari* lands invariably go to the nearest male agnates of her deceased

* For the rules of Succession, Inheritance, and Partition, see Chapter VI, *post*.

husband; for with regard to these, as we have seen, over and above the merely social and economic considerations, religious considerations supervene.

II. Agriculture.

Village-Fields.

We have spoken of three classes of lands,—the Bhūinhāri and the Rājhās lands of the tenants, and the *Manjihas* lands of the alien landlord. These include both cultivated low-lands and uplands.

Bari-lands.

Attached to each comparatively well-to-do Orāon's house there is generally a plot of what is called *bari* land in which a few kitchen vegetables such as kōhnṛā (squash-gourd), *laua* (bottle-gourd), *jhingi* (*Luffa acutangula*); *dheras* (lady's finger or *hibiscus esculentus*), *simbi* (beans) and *makai* (maize) are grown. Just outside the cluster of houses that forms the village-*basti*, you come to some plots of uplands generally of the same level as the *basti*. These are called *chiras* or *chira-baris*, of which almost every Orāon tenant (at least a Bhūinhār) has one or more. On these a few varieties of pulses are grown, and those tenants who can afford to dig wells on such lands (kūā-bāris), also grow on them such vegetables as mustard, chillies, turmeric, onions, radishes brinjals, *etc.* These are generally the best kind of uplands in an Orāon village (technically known as 'first class tānr') and are cultivated every year. A few of these are used as nurseries for paddy seedlings to be transplanted later on in the low-lands (dōn). Such plots of *bari* lands are known as *bira-baris.*

Tanr and Don-lands

Beyond these lands and further away from the village, come stretches of uplands with their sides sloping down into a depression. In this depression are the best paddy fields (called *don* in local Hindi, and *khal* in Orāon) of the village. And on the other side of the depression, again, you go up either abruptly or over a slope to a ridge. Beyond this ridge, too, are other uplands or *tanrs.* The sides of the slopes are cut into terraces. The lowest cultivated lands in the depressions between the ridges are called *garha don* lands. Of these, such lands as receive moisture throughout the year are called *kudar don* lands. The terraces next above the *garha don* lands are called *sokra* lands, and the terraces further up are the *choura don* lands. Above the *choura don* lands come the *taria don* lands. The uplands just beyond the ridges are generally what are called 'second class' and 'third class' *danr* or *gora* lands. These *danr* lands have generally to be left fallow either every other year or for two out of every three years; and to be manured each year they are cultivated. The low paddy-fields (*don* lands), with the exception of such as retain moisture throughout the year, also require to be manured every second or third year. The manures ordinarily used are old cowdung, ashes, and decayed vegetables. The soil of the country is poor : of 'first class' *don* lands, the area being only 1·18 sq. miles out of a total area of 1,207 sq. miles of *don* lands in the district.

The Rānchi Settlement Report shows that out of a total area of 7,104 square miles in the district, only 2,198 sq. miles (or 31 *per cent*) of lands are under cultivation, and the margin still available for cultivation is 1,293 sq. miles representing only 18 *per cent* of the entire cultivable area.*

Food crops.

The principal food-crop is rice, which is grown on 1,530 sq. miles of land, representing 61·61 *per cent* of the total cultivated lands of the district. Next in importance is a kind of millet called *gondli* (*Panicum miliare*) which is grown on 300 sq. miles of *danr* land, representing 12·08 *per cent* of the total cultivated area. Another millet called *marua* (*Eleusine coracana*) is grown on 110 sq. miles of *danr* land or 4·43 *per cent* of the total cultivated area. *Gondli* and *Marua* form the chief food of the poorer Orāon for about two months in the

* *Ranchi Settlement Report* (1902-1910), p. 118.

year. Of oil-seeds, sūrgūja or the niger oil-seed (*Guizota Abyssinica*) is the principal crop and is grown on 157 sq. miles of *danr* lands or 6·32 *per cent* of the total net cultivated area of the district. Miscellaneous crops including mustard, and a few varieties of pulses,* are grown on 255 sq. miles or 10·27 *per cent* and fruit trees over 43 sq. miles or 1·73 *per cent* of the total cultivated area.

Besides the food-crops mentioned above, some jungle-produce such as the corolla of the *mohua* (*Bassia latifolia*) flower, yams of different sorts and vegetable-leaves (*sag*) are gathered by the Orāons for purposes of food. Among fruits, the jackfruit is the most esteemed, as it supplies a nutritive food and grows abundantly in the district.

Thus the cultivated lands of an Orāon village are broadly divided into lowlands (*don*) in which winter-rice † is grown, and up-lands in which varieties of coarse autumn-rice (*gora*), millets, pulses, oil-seeds, and a few varieties of fibre-crops ‡ and some vegetables are grown.

* Of pulses, the more common are *urid (Phaseolus roxburghii)*, *barai (Phaseolus mungo)*, *Kurthi* (*Dolichos biflorus*), *rahar* (*cajanus Indicus)* and *bodi (vigna catiang)*.

† Winter-rice is broadly divided by the Oraons into two classes (each with numerous sub-classes)—the *Garuhan* or *Barka dhan* which is grown on the lowest *don* lands, and the *Lauhan* or light paddy grown on the upper terraces.

‡ These are cotton (*Gossypium herbaceum*) and *Kudrum*

Processes of cultivation.

The two processes of growing low-land rice are known respectively as the *buna* process or broad-cast sowing, and the *ropa* process or transplantation. The sowing may be either made in dust (*dhuri-buna*) or in mud (*lewa*). The successive operations in these simple methods of cultivation of low-land rice are detailed below.

Manuring.

As we have said above, an upland generally requires manuring every year it is cultivated, and most low-lands generally at an interval of two or three years. The rice-fields are generally manured in March or April. Lumps of decomposed or burnt cow-dung are first distributed over a field and then spread out by the spade or lightly covered over with earth by ploughing the land.

Ploughing.

Before either sowing or transplantation, the rice-fields are generally ploughed at least three or four times ; once immediately after the first heavy showers of rain in January or February ; and two or three times again within a month or two of the first ploughing.

(*Hibiscus Cannabinus*), and, to a very small extent, *sunn* (*Crotolarea juncea*). A few rope-fibres, such as the *chop* (*Bauhinia vahlu*) are obtained from jungle creepers or barks of jungle-trees.

The soil is thus exposed to the heat of the sun. The land is again ploughed up just before sowing. Some time after sowing the weeds that have grown up in the meanwhile are destroyed by a further ploughing.

Repairing Ridges.

Between the first ploughing and the sowing, the Orāon cultivator has to repair breaches, if any, in the ridges that separate one terrace from another. The ridges are also strengthened by adding earth to their sides and top. The object of this is to prevent rain-water from the adjoining terraces suddenly running over the low ridges, or flowing through any breaches into the field.

Regulating water.

From after the sowing down to the close of the rains, the Orāon cultivator has to be on the alert to prevent the accumulation, in any plot, of more water than is needed, or the flowing out of water when water should be retained. When excessive rain-water has accumulated on any field, he cuts a narrow opening in the ridge to let off surplus water in the direction of the lower terraces, and closes the opening again when just sufficient water has been left. The Orāon calls the two operations respectively 'cutting out water,' and 'confining (enclosing) water.' Towards the close of the rainy season by about the middle of September, the ridges are further strengthened by the addition of earth, so that no water may flow out any more.

Sowing broad-cast.

Between April and June, as soon as a few heavy showers of rain have fallen, the land is prepared for sowing (*buna*) by ploughing it up again, breaking clods of earth by means of the mallet, and by pulverizing the soil with the harrow. Then one man takes up the bamboo-basket in which seeds have been brought to the field, and sows the seeds broadcast. The soil is then lightly turned up with one or more ploughs. Finally, the earth is again pressed down with the harrow and the seeds are thus buried in.

Weeding.

Rice-fields are usually weeded of grass and other noxious vegetation three times,—once before the sowing, a second time about a month after the sowing, and finally after yet another month or more. The plough and the harrow are used on the first two occasions. And at the last weeding, such of the grass or other vegetation as escaped the previous weeding are carefully picked up with the hand.

Sowing in mud.

The field in which *lewa* or sowing in mud has to be made, is ploughed at least twice in January-February; and after a heavy shower of rain in July it is thoroughly ploughed up again and harrowed so as to reduce the soil to a state of liquid mud. A day or two after this, when the mud has quite settled down, the water which has come to the surface is drained off, and paddy-seeds are scattered on the mud. Before they are sown, the seeds are made to germinate by being soaked in water for about twenty-four hours and placed in a covered basket.

Transplanting.

In August, paddy seedlings grown on nurseries (*bira-baris*) are taken in bundles to fields reserved for transplantation. A field which has been ploughed up already twice in Aṣār (June-July) is once more ploughed, and harrowed with the *karha*, a couple of days or so before transplantation in Sāwan (July-August), and, if necessary, levelled with the *chowk*. On the day of transplantation the field is again ploughed up, and soil and water are mixed up into an uniform consistence. Orāon women now transplant the seedlings, each woman making small holes in the mud with her fingers at intervals of 6 to 9 inches and planting a few seedlings at each hole.

Watching.

When the paddy crops begin to be ripe, and particularly when they are being reaped or threshed, they require to be carefully watched against thieves (generally non-Orāons) and thievish birds and cattle. In the day-time, women and children generally do the watching, but at night the men keep watch by

To face p. 127.

An Orāon threshing paddy. On the left is the ***Kumba*** or Straw-shed in which the Orāon stays while keeping guard over the ripe paddy in field or threshing-floor.

An Orāon boy setting his bird-lime to catch birds.

stopping in small triangular straw-sheds called *Kumbas* erected for the purpose.

Harvesting.

A threshing-floor (*khalihan*) is prepared beforehand as close to the fields as possible. Rocky places or *chatans* are the most suitable for the purpose. If a *chatan* is not available, a plot of fallow up-land is selected. The same place serves as the threshing-floor of a particular cultivator year after year. This threshing-floor is made clean and tidy (with a cowdung coating unless it is a *chatan*) beforehand, and the paddy-stalks as they are reaped, are made into bundles and carried to the threshing-floor. There the paddy-stalks are left to dry in the sun for two or three days, and then arranged in circular heaps (*chakars*), with their ears to the centre.

Threshing and winnowing.

The threshing is managed with a few bullocks tied in a line. The paddy-stalks are spread out on the ground, and one or two men drive the bullocks round and round over them. As the paddy is being threshed in this way, two other men go on sifting the straw with a pitchfork. Then the straw is thoroughly sifted again with the hand so as to let the grains fall on the ground. Finally, the chaff is removed from the grains by a man taking the paddy-grains in a winnowing-fan (*sup*) and holding it as high up as his own head, and shaking it backwards and forwards so as to let the grains gradually fall on the ground. The chaff, being much lighter than the paddy-grains, is blown away by this process to some distance, while the grains fall near the man's feet. The paddy-grains, thus cleaned, are now weighed and carried home.

Storing rice.

When the Orāon has taken his paddy home, his first business is to repay with interest (generally at 50 *per cent*) to the *Sahu Mahajan*—the rural Shylock,—the grains he may have borrowed from him during the months of stress.* He then doles out to the different village-servants, such as the blacksmith, the Gorāit, &c., the customary measure of paddy payable to each of them for his services during

* Besides paddy-loans thus repaid, an Orāon may have an old interminable account to settle with the *Mahajan*, or money-lender. Once a debt is incurred, although the Orāon goes on paying every year whatever money he can secure by the sale of a portion of his paddy, the debt in many cases seems never to be capable of being altogether cleared off: for the crafty Shylock always manages to make it appear to the illiterate Orāon that most of the money he has been paying from year to year has gone towards the payment of interest and but a small portion of the principal has been yet paid off. The debtor though not convinced has to submit. There may be a few honourable exceptions even amongst the Chotā Nāgpur Sahus.

the year. A quantity of paddy is then kept apart in bamboo-baskets for the consumption of the family for a couple of months or so. The balance left, is stored away in *moras* or circular bags made of plaited straw-ropes.

Husking.

The paddy is husked either with the *dhenki* or with the *samat*. The *dhenki* consists of a very large mortar in the form of a vessel scooped out of a log of wood and sunk on the ground, and a pestle which is the wooden hammer-head of a horizontal lever bar working on a low wooden support. An Orāon woman alternately applies and takes off weight by standing on the level bar and making the hammer-head pound the paddy in the mortar. The *samat* is a wooden hammer with which Orāon women husk paddy which is placed either in a large wooden mortar (*okli*) or in a hole in a rock. When the paddy is boiled before being husked, the husked rice is called *usna* rice. When the paddy is not boiled, but only dried in the sun and husked it is called *arua* rice.

Arua rice.

As we shall see later on, it is '*arua*' rice which is required for offerings to the gods and otherwise used in most of the Orāon religious, socio-religious and magico-religious ceremonies.

Cultivation of other crops.

Of other food crops, upland paddy (*goradhan*) is grown by sowing paddy-seeds broad-cast on an up-land (*gora*) ploughed up several times beforehand. About three days after the sowing, the land is lightly ploughed, and then harrowed to bury the seeds in. Weeding of grass and other vegetation is done with the hands. Upland paddy is sown in June and harvested in September. *Marua* (*Eleusine Corcana*) is either sown broad-cast after the first showers of rain in June or transplanted in July. It is harvested in September or October. *Gondli* (*Panicum miliare*) is also sown broadcast in June and harvested in about a month and a half after it is sown. Maize, pulses, and oil-seeds are all sown broad-cast.

Irrigation.

Orāons do not practise artificial irrigation. But comparatively well-to-do Orāons who grow potatoes, onions, &c., on their *bari* or *chira* lands dig wells to irrigate them. The water is drawn from the well with the help of the *latha khuntha* which is worked by a sort of lever-arrangement, as in the accompanying illustration. The water thus drawn is either poured into shallow drains made on the ground, or on a wooden canoe from which it passes into the drains. In only a very few villages, you meet with reservoirs in which rain-water has been stored by some well-to-do Orāon cultivators by raising embankments or *bunds* at some cost and labour. With this water some fields are irrigated. But most of such *bunds* (and of these there are not many in the district) are constructed by the Zemindārs to irrigate their *manjhihas* lands or private demesne.

Division of agricultural labour.

The part taken by Orāon women in actual agricultural operations, consists in transplanting paddy seedlings after the men have made the land ready for the purpose. Women also weed the fields of grass and other noxious vegetation by hand-picking them, break clods of earth on *danr* lands into powder, and clear the ploughed up *danr* lands of grass with spades. The crops are reaped by men as well as women. Women carry the harvested corn to the threshing-floor on their head, and men on *banghis* or wooden-poles carried on the shoulder. All other operations of agriculture such as hoeing, ploughing, sowing, and levelling, are performed by the men.

Such are the various operations of agriculture amongst the Orāons. It is thus that they extract from the poor soil of the plateau what food they can get. Nor is the fruit of their labour always assured to them. Either deficient or excessive rainfall in any particular year may cause a more or less partial failure of crops. Insects or fungoid pests occasionally do a lot of damage to the crops. And cattle-disease is another evil which from time to time puts the Orāon cultivator in very great difficulties. At times the 'evil eye' not only of a sorcerer or a witch but also of a stranger such as a foreign trader carrying grains on his pack-bullocks and saying to himself 'what a fine crop has grown on this field!'—may cause serious damage to the standing crop. To save his cattle and his crops from all these pests, the Orāon not only offers sacrifices to his village-deities, but invokes the aid of the countless indeterminate invisible powers of the country around him.

Agricultural and other Implements.

Let us now proceed to a description of the principal agricultural implements used by the Orāons. The first and foremost is of course the plough. It consists of five parts or components. The plough-proper (hār) is a thick piece of Sāl (*shorea robusta*) wood about two feet and a half long. (P. L. in illustration). It is generally fashioned into shape by the Orāon cultivator himself out of wood brought by himself from the village-jungle or from some meighbouring jungle. The ploughshare or phār (S. R. in illustration) is made by the village black-smith and consists of a straight piece of iron from three-o face p. 132.

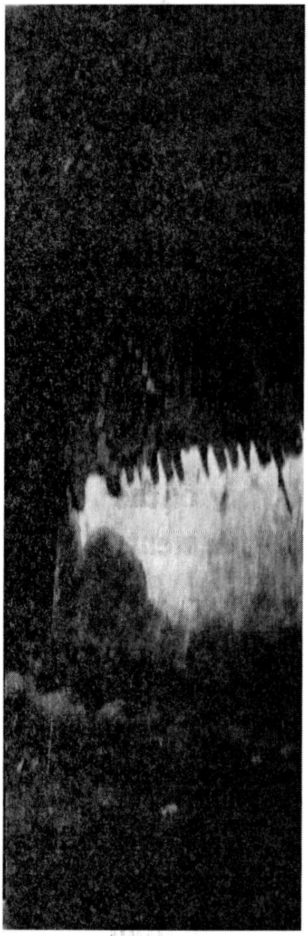

Drawings on the walls of an Orāon's hut

B--M P--L

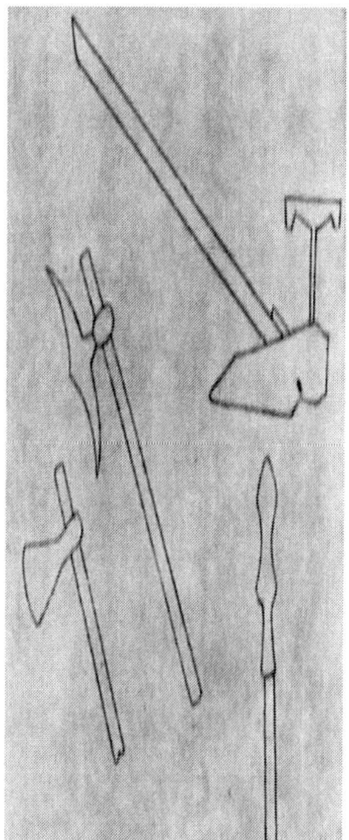

C
A
H
S-R

The plough, axes, and javelin of the Oraons.

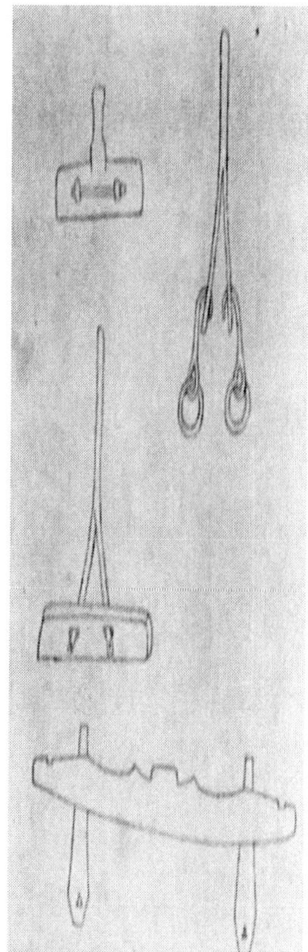

Yoke, Harrow and other agricultural implements of the Orāons.

quarters of a foot to one foot long and about an inch broad. It is fixed on to a groove in the upper part of the plough proper (hār) and fastened in its place by an iron hoop ('H' in illustration). The plough-share when in use requires constant mending by the village blacksmith. The third part is the beam (B M) which is of wood. The fourth part which is the Yoke (not shown in the illustration) is fitted on to the beam with leather-straps (nādhā) bought of a Chāmār or worker in leather. The fifth part is the handle (chāndli) which is a piece of wood with a crook at the end ('C' in illustration). The ploughman seizes the curved end with his hands when driving the plough.

Harrow.

The harrow (pāttā) is a narrow piece of wood about 2 yards long with two apertures in it. Two thin bamboos or split pieces of *dhautha* (*Anogeissus latifolius*) wood are fitted into the two apertures and joined to the yoke at one point so as to form a a triangle. It is worked by a man standing on the pāttā and driving the bullocks attached to the yoke. The *patta* serves to press down and pulverize the soil and to burry the seeds in after they have been sown.

Leveller.

The leveller or *hanga* is required to level fields and press the soil. It is thus described by Mr. (afterwards Sir,)

F. A. Slacke.* "It is like a large oblong wooden shovel which is used to break the larger clods of earth with a short handle. In the blade are two holes not on the same plane, so that when the handle is let go the blade (which is being pulled by bullocks or buffaloes, by yokes passing through the holes in the blade) falls over, leaving behind it the earth it was bringing up."

Earth-remover. The earth-remover, *Karha* or *krur*, used by the Orāons has been thus described:—"It consists of a short plank about 18 inches broad and 4 ft. long. It is drawn by a pair of oxen, in the same way as the *patta*. The plank is held slightly inclined to the ground by means of a short handle at the middle of its upper edge. The Karha is used for levelling down the unevenness of a newly-made rice-field. For this purpose the field is first ploughed, and the Karha is drawn over it to carry the soil from the high parts of the field to the lower. It is held tightly at an angle to the ground and drawn forward, carrying with it a certain amount of loose soil. On reaching a depression which wants to be filled up, the handle is let go, and the soil which was being carried forward is left in the depression."†

* *Report on the Settlement of the Estate of the Maharaja of Chota Nagpur* (1888). page 15.

† Basu, *Report on the Agriculture of the District of Lohardaga*, (1897, Bengal Secretariat Press, Calcutta).

Clod-breaker. The mallet or *dhelphora* is a wooden hammer with a short handle. It is made by the men and used to break the larger clods of earth in the fields.

Pitch-fork. The pitch-fork or *akain* is a wooden rod about five feet long with a bent iron hook at one end. At the time of threshing, it is used to sift the straw.

Mortar and pestle. The mortar (*chunjkga*) and pestle (*man* or *samat*) are both made of wood, and used to husk rice. The men make them and the women use them to husk grains with.

Rice-pounder. The rice-pounder or *dhenki* with which the Orāon woman husks and pounds her rice has been described above. It consists of a long log of wood made into shape by Orāon men, and a *Samba* or cup of iron made by the village blacksmith and fitted on to one end.

Sickle. The sickle or *hansua* is a hooked iron instrument with a toothed edge. It is made by the Lohrā and used by the Orāon to reap his crops with.

Crow-bar. The crow-bar or *Sabar* is a bar of iron sharpened at one end. With it the Orāon cultivator occasionally digs holes in the earth or removes large stones. It is manufactured by the village black-smith.

Chisel and adge-mallet.

The mortising chisel or *rukna* and the adge-mallet or *basila* are used by the Orāons in working wood with, as, for instance, in making their ploughs, &c. The village-blacksmith makes the chisel and the adge-mallet for the Orāon.

Spade.

The spade or *kori* consists of three partrs,—namely, a bamboo or wooden handle about a yard long, an iron socket (pāsā) which fits into the handle, and a flat steel blade which is welded on to the socket. The Orāon uses it for earth-work, such as digging fields, and repairing and constructing ridges and embankments.

Axe.

The axe or *tanga*, like the spade, consists of a bamboo or wooden handle, an iron socket which fits into the handle, and a steel blade. The Orāon uses it for hewing timber, or chopping wood with and for similar other purposes.

Load-carrier.

The ordinary load-carrying contrivance of the Orāon consists of a bamboo or wooden pole about a yard and a half long, called *bahinga* (Orāon : *ugi*) with two rope-nets or *Sikas* (O., *epta*) suspended one at each end of the rod. Things to be carried, such as paddy-seedlings to be carried to the fields or reaped crops to be carried to the threshing-floor, are put into these nets, and the *bahinga* pole is placed crosswise on the shoulder of the carrier.

Country-cart.

The country-cart or *Sagar* of the Orāon is a wooden frame with two block wheels in three pieces, as shown in the illustration.

Grain-measures.

The Orāon measures his grains in cup-shaped *pailas* (O., *acka*) either made of wood by the Orāons themselves or made of brass by braziers.*

Live-stock.

The ordinary live-stock of the average Orāon cultivator consists of oxen, cows, buffaloes, goats, fowls and pigs. Very few Orāons rear sheep. Except in the jungly parts of the district, where extensive pasturage is available, the Orāons do not now-a-days keep large herds of cattle as a form of wealth. Milch-cows or milch-buffaloes are not very common. Even his cows, the Orāon cultivator generally yokes to his ploughs. Such cows are called *gunris.* Those who can afford to do so, keep one or two cows for getting calves out of them. These, when milked, yield a very small quantity of milk.

* For a further account of these, see *post*, under the heading 'Weights and Measures'.

The cattle of the Chōtā Nāgpur Plateau are a very poor breed, and are generally under-fed. The scarcity of pasture-grass in the hot weather and the clearing away of most jungles and the consequent disappearance of herbs and trees whose leaves used to supplement the insufficient grass-fodder, would appear to have contributed to the degeneracy of the small-sized cattle of the Orāon. It is only from July to November that there is plenty of grass-fodder for the cattle. For the rest of the year, the only fodder available is the stubble of rice, millets, etc., and the scanty grass growing on fallow lands. In villages where there are jungles, the cattle are comparatively better off for fodder. Working animals get a stinted ration of straw in the hot weather. In some years, cattle epidemics break out in the villages and carry off a large number of the livestock of the Orāon peasant. Many Orāons have to borrow money at usurious interest in order to replace their dead plough-cattle. The more well-to-do Orāon keeps a few goats and pigs. His poultry consists of a cock or two, a few hens, and their brood of chickens.

Cattle-tending.

The Orāon's cows and oxen are generally made over to the charge of the village-Ahir. At about sun-rise, the Ahir takes out the cattle to the village jungle, if there is any, or to fallow lands for purposes of grazing. Before going out, he milks such cows as have recently calved. At about 10 A.M., the Ahir returns with the cattle to the *bathan* or resting place for the cattle. This *bathan* is situated outside the village *basti*, under the shade of some trees, and has some tank, pool of water or hill-stream close by. Here the remaining milch-cows are milked, and the Ahir goes home to take his meal, leaving some boy of his family to look after the cattle. On his return to the *bathan* after his mid-day meal, the Ahir takes a little rest. He then goes out again with the cattle to graze them and returns home at about sun-set. During the cultivating season, the plough-bullocks are generally looked after by the owner himself. Buffaloes are generally not made over to the village Ahir, at any rate by the more well-to-do Orāons or those with large families. Either a young man of such a family or a servant grazes the buffaloes. The buffaloes are taken out for grazing shortly after cock-crow (about 4 A.M.). At about 9 A.M., the *charwa* or herdsman takes the cattle to the resting place or *bathan* of the village. There such she-buffaloes as yield milk are milked, and the *cahrwa* goes home with this milk, leaving the buffaloes in charge of some other boy who comes there from the house to relieve him. The *charwa*, after taking his mid-day meal returns to the *bathan*, and after resting for a while, goes out again to graze the buffaloes. He returns home with the buffaloes shortly after sun-set.

Besides cattle, you see in some Orāon houses one or two dogs to guard the house, or to attend the men while they watch their paddy-fields at night and one or two cats domesticated so that they may kill the mice that eat up the Orāon's grains. In a very few Orāon houses, pigeons, ducks, and geese may be seen. The Orāon does not keep wild animals in captivity.

The cattle are milked by men, and, when not made over to the village Ahir, the cows and oxen, like sheep and goats are tended by unmarried girls. No ceremonies are performed before or after milking. The dung of cows and buffaloes, but not their urine, is employed to clean and purify houses or grounds but not men (as among the Hindus) from pollution. No classes of persons, such as menstruous women, are forbidden to drink milk nor have the Orāons any objection to selling their milk or other daily produce (such as *ghee*) to strangers.

III. Religious and magico-religious Observances connected with Agricultural Operations.

As we shall see in a subsequent volume, the principal religious festivals of the Orāons are all connected with agriculture. Here we shall only mention a few observances of a religious and magico-religious character connected with particular agricultural operations amongst this people.

(1) In the month of *Baisakh* (April-May) before any cultivator in the village has commenced sowing his low paddy fields (dōn), the village-priest (Pāhān or Baigā) has, on behalf of all the villagers to sacrifice five fowls,*viz.*, a black hen, a white hen, a copper-coloured hen, a spotted hen, and a red cock,—to the village-gods.

(2) In the month of *Asarh* (July-August), sometime after the sowing is over, similar sacrifices are again offered by the village-priest to the village-deities in the hope of ensuring sufficient rain and a bumper harvest.

(3) A little after mid-night preceding the day selected by each Orāon family for commencing the sowing of their paddy-fields (dōn), an adult male member of the family goes to one of his fields with a small quantity of paddy-seeds. He takes particular care that on his way

to the field or while engaged in scattering paddy-seeds on it, nobody may see him. If he happens to meet some person on the way, he does not speak to him. And even when he does not go alone but takes a companion with him, the two men do not generally talk to each other; and, if they must talk, they talk only in low whispers. It is believed that if any one notices him and says to himself,—"There! That man is going to sow his fields!"—such a remark or thought must be prompted by malice, conscious or unconscious, and therefore prove a hindrance to a plentiful crop or a vigorous growth of the paddy-plants. Arrived at the selected field, he scatters paddy-seeds on a portion of it, and goes home, as silently and stealthily as when he came.

During the night on which the cultivator goes to his field for this preliminary sowing, he remains sexually continent and does not lie on the same bed with his wife.

Next morning, before the cultivator goes out to sow his fields, he feeds a chicken on some *arua* rice placed on the ground, and thus consecrates it and sets it apart to be sacrificed to the family-*bhut* (spirit) on the occasion of the harvest-festival (Khālihān puja) in the following Aghān (November-December). After this dedication of the chicken, the cultivator goes first to the field on which paddy-seeds were ceremonially scattered as described above, ploughs it up and sows it again in the regular manner then proceeds to sow his other fields.

(4) The Orāon cultivator who wants to begin the transplantation of paddy seedlings on his fields before any other villager has commenced transplanting his has to invite the village-priest (Baigā or Pāhān) to perform the ceremony known as 'ban-gāri.' The ceremony is briefly this : The cultivator takes a pot of rice-beer* to the field selected where bundles of paddy-seedlings have already been taken. The Pāhān accompanies the cultivator to the field. Arrived there, the Pāhān pours a little of the rice-beer on the ground as 'tapāon' (libation) to Mother-Earth (Dhartimāi) who is thus invoked: "O Mother-Earth! May we have plenty of rain, and a bumper crop. Here is ṭapāon for thee." The Pāhān now plants with his own hands five paddy-seedlings on the spot where the rice-beer has been poured. This done, women commence transplanting the rest of the paddy-seedlings on the fields. The Pāhān is then taken to the house of the cultivator and treated to

* The rice-beer left in the pot becomes the Pahan's perquisite. But now-a-days four *annas* (six pence) or so in cash is generally paid to the Pahan as a substitute for the rice-beer.

a dinner with plenty of rice-beer. He also gets a small sum of one *anna* (one penny) or so as his fee. In some villages, that evening or on the next day the cultivator gives a jar of rice-beer or its value (estimated at four *annas*) to the village head-men (the Pāhān and the Māhāto) for the benefit of all the village-elders. It is said that formerly this used to be given in every Orāon village, but now this present is falling into disuse. In some villages, again, instead of the Pāhān, some female member of every cultivator's family makes *ban-gari* in the family fields in the following manner. She takes a handful of *urid* (*Phaseolus roxburghii*) and paddy to the field, deposits the *urid* and paddy on one of the ridges of the field, and with her own hands plants a few seedlings close to the spot where the *urid* pulse and paddy have been deposited. She then joins the other female labourers and they all transplant paddy-seedlings on the rest of the fields.

(5) To ward off from the paddy-plants on his low (*don*) lands, the 'evil eye' of malicious persons and the mischievous attentions of evil spirits and to ensure a bumper crop, the Orāon cultivator plants on the morning of the *Karam* festival in the month of Bhādo (August-September) one or more twigs of the Kend (*Diospyros melanoxylon*) tree or, failing that, of either a Sinduār (*Vitex Negundo*)

plant or of a Sākhuā (*shorea robusta*) tree, or of the Piāl (*Buchanania latifolia*) shrub on each of his *don* lands (low paddy-fields), magic potency having been imparted to these twigs by the *mati* or ghost-doctor during the Bheloā-Pujā ceremony on the previous day. To one of the twigs thus planted on each field is tied up with a straw-string a *bheloa*-leaf containing a few grains of the rice offered at the *Bheloa-puja*.

(6) Similarly, to ward off from the crops on their uplands (dānrs) the 'evil eye' of malicious persons and the mischievous attentions of evil spirits, and to ensure a bumper harvest, Orāons fix on each cultivated up-land a wooden pole about a cubit higher than the height of the plants. Over this pole is placed upside down an earthen vessel, with its upturned bottom painted black and white. Sometimes instead of placing such an earthen vessel over the wooden pole, the upper half of the pole itself is split into three prongs. Whether these contrivances serve to keep off the evil eye or not, they do indeed serve to some extent to keep off birds and virmin from the crops.

(7) No Orāon cultivator may thresh his paddy or celebrate his *Khalihāni Pujā* (threshing-floor or harvest festival) before the village-priest has performed his own *Khalihani* pujā. The Pāhān, when celebrating his own *Khalihani* pujā, brings out a

few jars of rice-beer and entertains with food and drink such of his fellow-villagers as assemble at his house on the occasion.

(8) The first fruits of the crops are offered to the deity called Sarnā Būṛhiā or Chāālō Pāchchō. The eating of the new rice (Nawā Khāni) is a solemn occasion with the Orāon. And as with the harvest-festival (Khalihāni pūjā), so also with regard to this ceremony, it is the village-priest who has to celebrate it before any other villager is allowed to do so. This has to be celebrated in the month of Bhādo, when the up-land rice (goṛā dhān) is ripe. On a day appointed beforehand, the village priest (the Pāhān or Baigā) with his assistant (the Pūjār or Pānbharā) goes out before day-break to a goṛā (up-land rice) field of a neighbouring village. There they gather about two *seers* (four pounds) of upland rice, and, with this, return to their own village. The man whose rice is thus taken is generally informed beforehand, so that he may not use expressions of annoyance, for such expressions are considered as of bad augury. The paddy thus obtained is made over to the wife either of the Pāhān or of the Pūjār to make it into *chiura*. This is done by steeping the paddy in water, then drying it and heating it over a fire, and finally husking and winnowing it. The elders of the village then assemble at the Pāhān's house.

When the *Chiura* is ready, the Pāhān, after purifying himself with cold-water ablutions, takes the *chiurā* to the room in his house where the winnowing-basket sacred to the village-goddess known as Sarnā-buṛhiā or Chāālō Pāchchō is hung up. There the *chiura* is offered to the goddess. Then the Pāhān distributes the *chiurā* thus sanctified to all the villagers who may be present at the Pāhān's house. In case any important Orāon villager is absent, his share of the *chiurā* is sent to his house. The Pāhān also entertains with food and drink the elders of the village assembled at his house. After the Pāhān's Nawā-khāni celebration is over, other Orāon villagers celebrate their own *nāwa-khani*, each family on such a day as suits their convenience. At these other *nawakhani* celebrations, no particular ceremony is observed, only plenty of rice-beer is drunk, *chiura* made of new upland rice is prepared and eaten, and those who can afford to do so entertain their friends and relatives with plenty of food and drink.

(9) Every Orāon family carefully preserves until sowing-time a handful of rice 'blessed' by the village-Pāhān during the annual *Sarhul* festival. Magic virtue is imparted to this rice by placing it on the sacred *Saṛna-sup* or winnowing-basket on which the 'Lady of the grove' or *Sarna Burhia* is believed to have her seat, and

which is ceremonially hung up at the Pāhān's house. With this sanctified rice is sometimes mixed a little cowdung ; and a piece of copper (generally copper-coin) is put into this rice. When, at the sowing season, the Orāon cultivator takes out his paddy-seeds and proceeds to sow his fields, he mixes this sanctified (aśirbādi) rice with his paddy-seeds in the hope of securing a good crop through the magic virtue of the sanctified rice.

(10) Before an Orāon cultivator begins to reclaim for cultivation some waste land which is believed to be the seat of some malignant spirit or *nad*, some fowl or animal (generally indicated by a dream) is offered to appease the spirit so that no misfortune may befall the family. The same procedure is followed when a house has to be built on such a land, or a tree believed to be the seat of a spirit has to be cut down. If within a short time of the reclamation of a plot of waste land, or the building of a house on a particular land, or the felling of a tree, any case of sickness or death to man or cattle occurs in the family, it is the hitherto unknown spirit of the land reclaimed or built upon, as the case may be, or of the tree cut down, that is believed to have been offended. In such a case, a vow is made by the master of the family that a particular animal or fowl will be offered to the offended

spirit in the event of the recovery of the sick person or animal, or in the event of no other case of death happening in the family within a certain period. And by way of a pledge, the animal or fowl promised to be sacrificed is ceremonially fed on *arua* rice and set apart. After such a ceremonial vow, recovery from illness is believed to be certain. Even non-Orāons in Orāon villages believe in the efficacy of such vows, and, when their desire is attained, make the Orāon village-Pāhān offer on their behalf the sacrifices they had promised. These sacrifices are generally offered either on a Tuesday or on a Friday—the two days in the week that the Orāon regards as particularly auspicious.

(11) The few days in the month of Baiśākh (April-May) during which the Orāons celebrate the *Sarhul* festival, and which just precede the commencement of sowing operations, appear to form a period of general license. Men and women get drunk to their heart's content, and the young men and women sing and dance and make merry at the village ākhrā, without practically any restraint whatever except their own sense of decency. It appears probable that this period of almost unrestrained license originated in a belief in a sympathetic connection of such license with the fertility of their fields.

(12) In the month of Kārtik (October-November), on the morning of the *Amawas* day (Sohorāi day), when the Orāons have commenced harvesting their low-land rice, the annual flea-driving festival is celebrated by the bachelors of each village. A few young bachelors strip off all their clothes from their persons, bathe themselves in cold water, and wrap themselves up from head to foot with paddy-straw. Various flowers, prominent among them being the yellow *surguja* (*Guizotia Abyssinica*) flowers, are inserted into this straw-covering. The young men thus arrayed are called 'Dundu'. Thus decked, they go about at cock-crow from house to house shouting in a sing-song tone "Give us pumkin-gourds : give us rice. Gnats and fleas leave the houses."—"*Kohrade, chaul de. Dasa masa ja-ja*". In this way they collect some rice from the maidens of every house and also get vegetables from some houses. These are taken to some open space outside the village-*basti* and cooked together as 'Khichri', and all the young bachelors (old bachelors are unknown in Orāon villages) have a jolly feast. This ceremony is supposed to compel the gnats and fleas to leave the houses and cattle-sheds. The bachelors take charge of the cattle of the village for that day, and depute a few persons from amongst themselves to graze the cattle. Next day the bachelors have another feast at the same place. That day

they boil rice in milk, and eat this delicious dish.

Such are some of the Orāon observances connected with agriculture. The Orāons of our days do not appear to have any other superstitions about the first or last sheaf of corn cut, or about threshing, winnowing, etc. Persons engaged in agricultural operations, such as sowing, reaping threshing, gathering fruits, making oil, and the like, do not appear to be regarded as sacred or tabued in any way. They have a special ceremony at breaking up the land by ploughing for the first time during the spring Hunt in the month of Phāgun. This will be described in the next chapter. The pestle for pounding rice is not used for superstitious purposes, but the winnowing-basket (*sup*) is an indispensable element in most magical operations and religious ceremonies. Although the plough is not used for such superstitious purposes as procuring rain, averting epidemics, and the like, worn-away ploughs are generally used by the Orāons as pegs which are planted on the ground to serve as the seats (āsthāns) of spirits. At Orāon marriages, three bundles of straw are placed over a yoke, for the bride and bridegroom to sit upon. These are calculated, by sympathetic magic, to bring prosperity in agriculture to the wedded pair. The different crops are not supposed to be each animated by a spirit or deity. Human sacrifices in connection with the crops have now fallen into disuse; but in years of drought and impending famine, rumours of human sacrifices having been offered somewheré or other are not unknown in the Orāon country. In the hot months, many Orāons are to this day afraid of going alone outside the limits of their villages for fear of *Otongas* or men who are believed to spirit away persons to be offered as sacrifices.

Customs and ceremonies connected with Pastoral Life.

The Orāon pays no attention, as the Toda of the Nilgiris does, to the pedigree of his cattle, nor does he ascribe any sanctity to the grass or to the fodder of the cattle. The only occasion on which grass appears to be regarded as an auspicious thing is at marriages, when a few young blades of grass together with a little *arua* rice, three bits turmeric, a few sheaves of paddy, and a few mustard-oilseeds are put into a small earthen vessel over which a lamp is kept burning. Again, in contracts of sale of cattle between Orāons, the seller hands over one or two young blades of grass (*dub*) to the purchaser by way of sealing the contract. After this symbolic transfer (the grass representing the cattle), the vendor may not sell the cattle to any one else even if a higher price is offered, nor may the former purchaser decline to take the cattle and pay for it. Should either the seller or the buyer seek to resile from the contract of sale and purchase thus made, the Panch will compel him to fulfil his obligations under the contract. The Orāon attaches something like sanctity to his cows and oxen, which, in imitation of his Hindu neighbours, he sometimes calls *Lachmi* or the deity of wealth. The *Gorea puja* ceremony is performed annually with a view to increasing the fertility of the cows.

IV. Hunting.

Hunting Excursions.

Hunting is no longer practised as an occupation by the Orāons. But, as that was one of the earliest methods adopted by them in their quest for food, and the social and religious life of the people in that stage of culture centred round it, they still celebrate the memory of those days by periodical hunting excursions of a socio-religious nature. These periodical festivals are three in number, namely,—the great tribal hunt called *Bisu Sendra* held annually in the month of Baiśākh (April-May), the less important *Phagu Sendra* held in the month of Phāgun (March) every year, and the Jeth-Sikār held in the beginning of the rainy season. These will be described in the next chapter. Besides these they have what are called Dourāhā Sikārs or informal hunts held at option according to the pleasure convenience of each village or group of villages.

Weapons of hunting.

The principal weapons used by the Orāon for purposes of hunting are the bow and the arrow, the axe, the sword, the spear, and clubs and sticks of different varieties. His bow (*dhanu*) consists of a thin bamboo and a bow-string (eṛet) made either of a slender strip of split bamboo, or of *chop* or *sunn* string; and the arrow consists of a reed-shaft (chār) generally with a pointed iron-arrow (kānnā). Iron arrows without a pointed end are called *thuthis*. Often, a pair of feathers of the white stork or some other white-plumed bird, are attached to the lower end of the shaft. These feathers not only serve as ornamentation, but, what is more important, make it easy for the hunter to recover his arrow after it has been shot. Spears used by the Orāon are of two varieties; the larger variety called *ballam* having a bamboo shaft four to five cubits long and an iron or steel point, the shorter variety called *barchi* having a bamboo handle about a cubit long and a smaller iron or steel point. The *barchi* is shot at game with the help of the bow, whereas the *ballam* is not shot but thrust at game. Axes used

To face p. 155.

Oraons out for a hunt.

in hunting are also of different varieties, such as the *ballu* or *balua*, the *pharsa*, and the *surhi*. With these axes the animals are hacked to pieces. The *Khanra* or sword is also used to cut down the prey. Among clubs and sticks, the one worthy of notice is the *dabsa lebda* which is a wooden stick, a yard or less in length, the upper end of the stick being very much thicker than the rest. This stick is hurled at small game. Some of these sticks are slightly curved, and look like non-return hunting boomerangs. They are held in the hand at the lower end, and hurled at deer and other game with the concave side forward. When the game is at some distance, it is hurled with a swing of the hand ; at close quarters it is simply flung at the game. These sticks, as also the bow, and the wooden handles of the other weapons are made by the Orāons themselves, whereas the portion made of iron is manufactured by the village blacksmith.

Mode of Hunting.

For every regular hunting expedition the Orāons must have a leader of the hunt. On the appointed day, this chosen leader summons the intending hunters, who thereupon assemble and start under his leadership for the hill or jungle selected for the expedition. The hunters, as we have said, are armed with axes, swords, sticks, bows, and arrows. One or more men take nets with them, and those who own dog lead their dogs by string leashes. The person or persons carrying nets and the men with dogs go ahead. One or more nets are spread on the way leading to that part of the jungle to which the animals pursued are likely to go for refuge. The other hunters arrange themselves in long rows three or four lines deep. When any one of the party catches sight of a game he whispers to the man next to him to keep silent, and the latter similarly whispers to the man next to him, and so on till the whole party are informed, and all maintain silence. The man nearest to the game either shoots his arrows or hurls his spear or stick or boomerang* at it. Should he fail to bear it down to the ground, word is quickly passed on to the men in his front or behind him, according as the game flies forward or backward. If the game eludes the arrows shot at it, the baffled huntsmen generally shout out warnings to the men with the nets and the men leading their dogs, and these men manage to entangle the game in the net, and then the hunters come up and kill it. When no game is in sight, the huntsmen pelt stones all directions and make a loud noise so as to frighten

* Mr. E. A. Gait, to whom I showed one of these *dabsa lebdas*, first pointed out its similarity to boomerang.

the game and make them run about. When a game is bagged, its mouth is tied round with *sal* leaves and sometimes its ears are torn out. When the party arrive at some open space on the outskirts of their village, the slain animals are dressed, and the meat divided amongst the members of the party. Generally each hunter gets an equal share and even the dogs that assisted at the hunt are given each a share equal to that of a man. In some villages, young boys who join a hunting expedition get each half the share of what an adult member of the party gets. The man who actually bagged the game gets two shares, one for having killed the animal and another as a villager and a member of the party. The entrails (*potta*) of the animal are, however, not divided in this way, but are boiled with any vegetables that may be procured, and all partake of this delicious dish.

Other modes of capturing and killing wild animals.

When an Orāon cultivator finds his crops being eaten up night after night by animals, such as a wild hog, a porcupine or a deer, he either spreads one or more nets on the track or tracks which the animals are likely to follow, or encloses the field by planting small branches of trees all around it leaving one or more passages for egress and ingress, and over each of these passages spreads a net set on poles lightly resting on the ground so that the net may fall down at the slightest touch of the animal and entrap it in its meshes. After evening meal, the owner of the field and one or more companions proceed towards the field with clubs and axes, and lie in wait. When the animal is caught in the net, they come out of their ambush and hasten to the spot and either beat the mischievous animal to death with their clubs or hack it to pieces with their axes or swords. Should the animal succeed in entering the field without getting entangled in the net, the men run to the field shouting so as to drive it towards the net.

Capturing animals by magic.

Besides these ordinary methods of capturing mischievous animals, there is a particular method by which tigers and wolves are sometimes said to be caught and killed. This method, in which the magic art of the sorcerer or *mati* is employed, is known as 'Pāti-dharna'. Ordinarily, it is said, a tiger never approaches a dead body whether of a human being or of a beast or a bird. But the *mati* or sorcerer is believed to be able by his magic spell to attract a tiger irresistibly to such a dead body or part of dead body. So, when a tiger or wolf is found repeatedly visiting a village and carrying off cattle or men, a *mati* is called in to make *pati*. A human corpse or the carcase of an animal (or, failing that, a portion of such a dead body) is placed in some suitable spot, and the *mati* electrifies it with his *mantrams* or spells and goes away. A man with a loaded gun lies in ambush within shooting distance, and when the animal, attracted by the charmed bait, appears at the spot, as it is sure to do, he fires at it.

V. Fishing.

Fish-traps and Fishing nets

Although fish is not abundant in the Orāon country, and consequently does not form a principal article of food, the Orāons use more than half a dozen varieties of fish-traps and fishing-nets. Among these are the common 'kūm' which is a bamboo-trap with one 'tooth', the 'jhimri' also a bamboo trap but possessing two 'teeth', the kūrūa which is another bamboo-trap with two doors so constructed that when a fish once enters the trap, it cannot get out. These bamboo-traps are made generally by men of the Tūri, Goṛāit, or Ghāsi castes, but sometimes also by the Orāons themselves. *The Pondra Kum* is a trap made by Orāon boys by plaiting *Kasi* grass. It is used in catching small fish. The *Phutchira Kum* is a similar trap made of *phutchira* grass, also by Orāon boys. This latter trap is now falling into disuse, as owing to the extension of cultivation, the supply of *phutchira* grass is no longer sufficient. The *girgo* or *gira* is a small triangular or circular proddling net made of cotton-thread and put up on a triangular or circular bamboo-frame. The water of the stream or tank where it is used is disturbed by the fishers so as to make fish enter the trap. The *pilni* is a small pull-net woven by Jōlahā weavers with thread and attached by its two sides to two bamboo-rods. It is dragged through a stream or tank. The *churguria* is also a drag-net. The *Jalli* is a casting-net made of thread by the Orāons themselves and also by men of other castes and tribes. Fishing with the *dang-bansi* or the common fishing rod and line is known to the Orāons, though not extensively practised. The fish caught by the Orāon is kept in a *Koncho* which is a bamboo basket made by men of the Turi caste. Fish is eaten either by frying it in oil, or roasting it, or making a curry (āmkhi) of it by spicing it with a little pounded turmeric and salt and boiling it in water.

Ceremonial Fishing.

When the Orāon is comparatively free from his agricultural labours, he sometimes catches fish in water-logged *don* fields, and in tanks, streams and pools. The only occasion on which fishing is now regarded as something of a ceremony is two or three days before the Sarhūl festival in the month of Baiśākh (April-May), all the young bachelors (dhāngars) of the village with a sprinkling of elderly men go in a body to a tank or stream to catch fish. All the fish caught on that occasion are kept in one or more common baskets and finally distributed amongst all the Orāon families in the village. Some representative of every family which has male members residing in the village is generally present at the fishing, and takes home the share of his family. Even those families in which there are only women and small children and so cannot send representatives to join the fishing party, get their respective shares sent to them. On the day of the Sarhūl festival, some female member from each of these last-mentioned families takes a pot of rice-beer to the headman (Māhtó) of the bachelors as a present to the young Orāon bachelors (*dhangars*) of the village.

VI. Bird-catching.

Bird-catching is with the Orāons more an amusement than an occupation. The Orāon catches birds with the help of the *Laḥsa thongi* which consists of bamboo splinters smeared over with gum obtained from the *pipar* (*Ficus religiosa*) or the *bar* (*Ficus Bengalensis*) trees. A number of such gummed splinters are carried by boys in a bamboo tube (*thongi*) and are planted all round on a bit of ground, and, in the middle, as a live-bait, a small mouse is tied by its tail to a small piece of bamboo. As birds come down to catch the bait, they are themselves caught by the gummed splinters sticking fast to their wings. Bird-catching with the help of traps too is practised. And bows and arrows are also used to kill birds with. A few Orāons practise bird-catching with the help of a raptorial or *Sikra* bird which is trained to the pursuit of other birds. It is held in the hand with a small string tied to one of its legs. When the prey is in sight, the bird-catcher lets it go, and when the bird has seized its prey, it is called back and returns with the prey.

VII. Material condition.

Having now examined their methods of food-quest, we shall proceed to examine the material condition of the Orāons,—the food they eat, the drinks they use, the houses they live in, the furniture with which their houses are furnished, the manufactures and trade they engage in, the outside labour they employ, and their own daily routine of work.

Food.

The staple food of the Orāon is rice, which is boiled as 'bhāt' fcr food.* But the average Orāon cannot pro-

* Rice is also occasionally used as 'ālkhārā' or Chiurā which is prepared by steeping paddy in hot water and leaving the paddy in the water one night, then parching this

vide for himself and his family a full diet of rice all the year round. When, in August, the poorer Orāon gathers in his *gondli* (*Panicum miliare*) crop, he and his family live on it for two or three weeks. Even the Orāon of ordinary means gets rice and *gondli* mixed together and boiled for his meals at this season, thus eking out his moderate store of paddy with his crop of *gondli*. After this, when, in August, his *gora* or upland rice is harvested, and not until after his *marua* (*Eleusine Coracana*) is gathered in, the coarse goṛā rice forms the principal article of food till November when his lowland (*don*) paddy is harvested. From November to April or May, the Orāon has plenty of food and drink ; and consequently that is the period when he celebrates his principal religious and social festivals and marries his children.

The months of May, June and July are generally bad months for the average Orāon cultivator. Soon after the winter paddy is harvested, some member or members of many Orāon families annually go to Calcutta or its suburbs or to the 'labour districts' to work there for a few months.

paddy in an earthen vessel put over a fire and then husking and flattening it in a rice-pedal. This preparation of rice is not made by the Orāons but women of the Bhogatā caste.

In the jungly parts of the Rānchi district, a number of wild roots or yams are collected by the Orāons in January and February and stored for use in the months of want. The corolla of the flowers of the mohuā tree (*Bassia latifolia*), collected in March and April, is also similarly used by the poorer people.

For a side-dish, the more well-to-do Orāon uses dāl or pulses of various sorts. His dāl is boiled in water with a little turmeric and salt. To the Orāon of ordinary means, dāl is a luxury which can be indulged in only on special occasions. But the poorest Orāon manages to have some sāg or edible leaves every day, and for a side-dish takes such sāg boiled in māṛ (the starchy liquid drained off his boiled rice) with a little salt added. The ordinary Orāon living amongst Hindu neighbours sometimes uses oil, though very sparingly, for culinary purposes. The oil thus used is obtained either from mustard or from Niger oil-seed or surgujā (Guizotia Abyssinica). As for vegetables,—pumpkins, some sorts of arum, sweet potato, brinjals, jhingi (*Luffa actangula*), lady's finger, beans, radishes, onions, and chillies, are used by the Orāon, when he can get them. Vegetable-curry is called by the Orāon 'ahra āmkhi'. In some villages only, potatoes are grown in limited quantites by well-to-do Oraons. This is generally grown for sale and not for consumption. Eggs are eaten. As for milk, it is drunk with relish when available. The same is the case with *dahi* or curdled milk.

Religious and other restrictions on food.

Although the Orāon relishes animal-food, such food does not often come in his way, and he lives ordinarily on a rice-and-vegetable diet. But when he has the opportunity of doing so, the Orāon eats any and every fish and the flesh of almost all birds and animals with the exception of monkeys which abound in the jungly parts of his couutry and of asses, horses, elephants, and a few other animals of which many are not seen in his country. The average Orāon eats even the mouse and the crow with relish. Flesh and fish are either boiled in water, or fried in oil, or roasted. The beast, or bird, or fish, or plant that forms the totem of a particular sept is tabu to members of that sept. The flesh of the monkey, as we have seen, is tabu to the whole tribe. Cannibalism is unknown. No particular food is forbidden to a woman during pregnancy, or to people at such periods of life as childhood, puberty, adult years, etc., or to men engaged in agricultural operations or in fishing. When the men of a village go out on a hunting excursion, no Orāon of the village or at any rate of the families of which any member has joined the hunting party, is allowed to kill any animal or fowl or other living being until the party return home. When this restriction to animal food is removed and before animal food is partaken of for the first time again, a red cock which was kept apart for the purpose on the morning of the Phāguā festival, is sacrificed to the *Darha* spirit after the usual *tapoan* or (liquid-) offering of a little rice-beer on the spot where the *Phagu*-tree was burnt. This sacrificed fowl is cooked at the village-Pāhān's house, and every villager who goes to the Pāhān's house that day partakes of a little of this sacrificial meat. After this, every Orāon family of the village have a hearty meal of their portion of the game brought home by the huntsmen.

The Orāon has certain superstitious practices or beliefs with regard to the refuse of his food. Although ordinarily no pains are taken to hide or destroy such refuse, it is believed that a person walking across such refuse may get a pain in the gullet. The refuse of sacrificial food is carefully hidden away.

As we shall see later on, the belief that by eating the flesh of certain animals, the qualities of that animal is acquired, is not altogether absent. As for occasions of fasting, every Orāon bride and bridegroom has to remain fasting on their wedding-day until the actual marriage-ceremony is over,

What may appear to be a fanciful extension of this practice is the fast observed on the day of the *Sarhul* festival by every master and mistress of an Orāon family from sun-rise until after the Pujā is over. The *Sarhul-puja* is supposed to be the marriage of Mother-Earth with the Sun and this union is symbolised by the mock-marriage of the Pāhān and his wife. Until the *Sarhul* ceremony, the Earth, it is said, has remained a virgin since the preceding harvest, and no Orāon may manure his fields until the *sarhul* ceremony has been celebrated in his village. Even breaking clods of earth on his fields after midday is not permitted to an Orāon before the *Sarhul*. No fruit or edible leaves of the season may be eaten by the Orāons of a village before the *Sarhul* ceremony has been celebrated in the village.

Drink.

Rice-beer (*hanria*) is the favourite drink of the Orāons, as of other aboriginals of Chōta Nāgpur. The method of preparing this drink is as follows : An earthen jar (gāgri) with water in it, is placed over a burning hearth. When the water has been sufficiently heated, about four *seers* or eight pounds of māṛūā (*Elensine corocana*) is put into it and, a little later, about half a *seer* or a little more of rice is added. When this *marua* and rice are both sufficiently boiled (*dar-sijha*), and the water in the jar has dried up, the jar is taken down from over the hearth and left to cool down to some extent. Then the contents of the vessel are spread out either on the floor which has been previously cleaned with a coating of cowdung diluted with water or on a mat spread out on the floor. When the contents have quite cooled down, the medicinal *ranu* (Orāon,—*bichchi*) is mixed with the contents. This *bichchi* or *ranu* is made of a few vegetable roots which are powdered and mixed with rice-flour and then formed into the shape of small tabloids. These *ranu* tabloids are now-a-days sold at the bāzārs at about a dozen per *pice* (farthing). The inside of the jar is now thoroughly rinsed and dried over the hearth. Then the contents spread out on the mat and mixed with the medicinal *ranu*, are put into the jar, and stowed away. In summer it takes about three or four days, and in winter about a week or more for the *ranu* to work and produce fermentation. Now, when it is desired to use it, water is poured into the jar and mixed well with the contents by pouring the contents, water and all, into a capacious brass-plate and back again into the jar, and repeating this process several times. The rice-beer thus prepared is now put into another earthen vessel and is ready for use. Country-beer or *arkhi* made of the corolla of mohuā (*bassia latifolia*) flowers, and sold at grog-shops, is now-a-days very much in demand. In fact, their excessive love of drink and characteristic improvidence have spelled the ruin of many an Orāon family. The use of imported liquor is practically unknown.

Religious Ceremonies connected with drink.

No religious or superstitious ceremonies are now observed in the preparation of this rice-beer or *hanria*. As for the religious aspect of drink, *hanria* or rice-beer is a necessary offering to the gods or spirits at almost every religious festival except at the worship of a few deities borrowed from the Hindus. As an expiatory drink, mention may be made of the blood of a sacrificed fowl or animal. Thus when an Orāon on his release from prison (where he had to mix with, and take food prepared or touched by, men of other tribes and castes), or owing to pollution from the touch of a non-Orāon during his meals, or after being excommunicated for sexual intercourse with a non-Orāon woman, seeks re-admission into his community, the candidate for re-admission has to drunk, a little blood of a white fowl or white goat sacrificed on his behalf to *Dharmes* (the Supreme God). Into this blood, before it is drunk, a few leaves *of the basil plant* (*tulsi*) and sometimes also a bit of gold are dipped to add sanctity.

Fire.

Fire.

And here it will not be out place to say a few words about his method of making and using fire. Before lucifer-matches were introduced amongst the Orāons some years ago, in almost every Orāon house fire used to be always kept burning in a moderate-sized earthen vessel (*bursi taoa*) containing sun-dried cowdung-cakes and grain-husks. An Orāon family by whom fire was not thus kept, would, when necessary, borrow a little fire from some other family by whom fire was so kept. A solitary house away from the main *basti* would always have its own *bursi-taoa* of fire for domestic use.

Religious awe of Fire.

Although fire is not ordinarily considered sacred, 'lightening-fire' (*bajar khatarka chich*) is regarded as 'sent by Heaven.' Thus, not long ago, at village Hāril (in thānā Māndār), a tree on whose branches an Orāon cultivator had stacked his straw, was struck with lightening and the straw caught fire. Thereupon all the Orāons of the village assembled in a meeting and decided that as God had sent this 'lightening-fire,' all existing fire in the village should be extinguished, and a portion of this 'Heaven-sent fire' should be taken and carefully preserved in every house, and should be used for all purposes. And this was accordingly done. Fire is not now made by the friction of stones, nor is there any custom amongst the Orāons of extinguishing old fire and kindling a new fire on such occasions as after a death, during a drought, at harvest, etc. In such Orāon villages as have got a Mahādeo-āsthān (seat of the God Mahādeo), Orāon Bhagats, as an act of religious merit, ceremonially walk over burning charcoal on certain occasions. It is believed that on such occasions, by the grace of the god Mahādeo, his devotees (Bhagats) pass unscathed over this burning charcoal although they actually stamp their feet on it.

Village-basti

An Orāon village-*basti* consists of a cluster of mud-huts huddled together without any definite arrangement. Bits of winding alleys or pathways form the only thoroughfare inside the village. There are no roads or paths used for special purposes or ordinarily forbidden to any particular class or sex. The interior of the village with its stinking manure-pits, filthy sink-holes, and, in the rains, stagnant pools of foul water made all the fouler by pigs and cattle wallowing in it, is as dirty and disagreeable as its outer surroundings—its bits of pretty scrub-jungle, the open fields, and here and there a hill, a hill-stream, or a mango-grove,—are pretty and delightful. Among the public places of an Orāon village are the ākhṛā or dancing-ground and the dhumkuṛiā or dormitory for the bachelors of the village. Except in the central parts of the Plateau, the *dhumkuria* is fast disappearing. The villages are not fortified or walled in. Outside the *basti* is the grove called *Sarna* or Jhākrā, sacred to the principal village-duty called *Chalo Pachcho* or *Sarna Burhia.* In some villages, the sacred grove now consists of only one or two ancient trees standing on a bit of fallow land. But ancient custom forbids any one to cut trees or branches of trees standing on the *sarna* grove. When a tree or a branch dries up or falls down of itself, any one may take it on payment of a price to the Pāhān and Māhto who represent the village community. But no Bhuinhār of the village may take or use the wood of *Sarna* trees.

Houses.

The average Orāon tenant has two huts, each with four low side-walls made of mud, one opening or door-way, and a roofing of tiles or grass-thatch. The grass-thatch has now been mostly displaced by tiled roofs in the central plateau, but, in

To face p. 173.

Orāon's hut in the western parts of the Ranchi District. The human figures are those of Orāon Christian converts.

the more jungly parts in the west and south-west of the Ranchi district, thatched houses are still common, and the walls are sometimes made of twigs plastered over with mud and cowdung. The floor of the hut is also of mud, and is slightly raised above the level of the ground. The bigger hut is ordinarily divided into two main compartments, the larger compartment serving the purposes of a sleeping-room, dining room, and kitchen,—and the smaller compartment serving as the lumber-room and granary where paddy and other grain as well as all sorts of pots and pans are stored. A small veranda is often attached to the hut, and serves as the sitting-place, and old men generally sleep in this veranda. At one corner of the large compartment, a small space is usually partitioned off with a bamboo-fencing to serve as a fowl-pen. The smaller hut is ordinarily used as cattle-shed, and a small lean-to or verandah attached to the cow-shed serves as the pig-sty. In larger families, the central portion of the smaller hut is also used as a sleeping-room, the cattle-pen and the fowl-pen being separated each on one side of the central portion by a bamboo partition. The poorest Orāon who owns only one hut uses the larger room as his sleeping-, eating-, and cooking-room, and the side-room as his granary and store-room, whereas a portion of the sleeping-room is partitioned off with a bamboo fencing to serve as his cattle-pen, and another corner as a fowl-pen. Very well-to-do Orāons with large families have more than two huts or rather houses with a quadrangular courtyard or open space called *angan* in the interior, and at the back a bāri or plot of land for growing kitchen-vegetables, maize and the like. The houses of these well-to-do Orāons are more commodious and respectable-looking than those of poorer people. The posts, rafters, and beams used in Orāon houses are generally made of *sal* wood procured from the jungles of the village, and, where there are no jungles in the village, from the jungles of some neighbouring village. There are no windows and rarely more than one door to a hut. A very few Orāons living amongst Hindu neighbours have taken to imitating them in the matter of adorning their house-walls with drawings of animals, flowers, and human beings.

Social and magico-religious customs in connection with building and repairing houses.

When an Orāon first occupies a hut newly built, he generally gives a feast to his fellow-tribesmen of the village. His Orāon fellow-villagers who have assisted him in relaying the tiles or grass-thatch of his old huts are also given a feast when the work is completed.

When an Orāon wishes to build a new house, he puts, of an evening, unobserved by anybody else, a few grains of rice on the intended house-site. If, in the course of the night, the grains of rice disappear—having been eaten up or removed by birds, beasts, ants or other insects or in any other way,—he gives up the idea of building a house on that site, as the omen clearly indicates that there will be want and poverty in such a house, or, to use the Orāon's own phrase, 'rice when boiled will decrease in quantity instead of increasing.' If only a portion of the rice thus exposed at night disappears before morning, the intended house-site is, though not absolutely bad, an undesirable one, and should, if possible, be avoided. If, on the other hand, the rice remains intact, the intended house site is a very desirable one, where prosperity will attend the family, or, in the Orāon's own phrase, 'a little rice when boiled will turn into an unusually large quantity of *bhat* (boiled rice).' When, in the morning, the Orāon examines the rice left in the evening, for purposes of prognostication, and finds the rice intact, he makes a mark on the ground around the rice. And on the site thus selected, the Orāon builds his house.

Household Furniture.

The furniture of the average Orāon house is neither numerous nor costly. A few mats (*pitri*) which

Orāon women weave with date-leaves gathered in the jungles, form the only bed that the poorer Orāons can afford to have. These mats are spread out for guests and visitors to sit upon. The comparatively well-to-do Orāon may afford to have the luxury of owning one or more *khattis* (chārpoys) or beds each with a coarse web of string supported on a rude four-legged wooden frame. It is only in a very few Orāon families that you meet with one or two low string-bottomed stools (*manchia*) to sit upon. Many Orāons squat on small planks of wood called *kandos*, or on similar seats made of straw (*busuhi kando*), while taking their meals. All these articles of furniture are ordinarily made by the Orāons themselves.

Household utensils, Earthenware and Basketry.

Among the utensils used by the Orāons, the more important are brassplates of two varieties, namely, the *thari* which is a large circular dish in which boiled rice is served to adult men and women, and the *chhipni* which is a smaller brass-dish with a high rim, and in which rice is served to children. Brass-cups called *dubhas* are used for holding vegetable-curries and similar other things and brass *lotas* or spherical water-jugs (without handles) for holding water, used in washing the mouth or the hands and feet. These brass utensils

1, 2. Kendera (guitars). 3. Sahnai (a kind of clarionet). 4. Murli (Bamboo flute). 5. Mandar or Mandal (clay-drum). 6. Tangi (Small axe). 7. Gulel (bow for shooting stones with). 8. Dhanu (bow for shooting arrows with). 9 and 10. Girgo (fish-traps). 11. Lasa thongi (bird lime). 12. Supli (diminutive winnowing-fan). 13. Bira (pad of ricestraw for squatting). 14. Toki (bamboo receptacle for various things).15. Lota (brass-jug). 16. Tumba (pumpkingourd for carrying water on journeys). 17. Malwa with Chamka (Oil lamp with stand). 18. chhipni (curry-plate) made of brass. 19. Tharia (rice-plate) made of brass. 20. Peti (basket made of rice-straw with lid, in the shape of a box). 21. Khijur or binda (pad of palm leaves for head.) 22. Chatai (mat of palm-leaves). 23 Dhurua. 24. Banghi 25. Wooden cow-bells. 26. Topor (cap worn at war dances). 27. Tarkis (ear-plugs, ¾ inches thick worn on the lobes of the ears.) 28. Tarkala Parpat (Earplugs of rolled up painted palm leaves). 29. Rita Mala (Necklace). 30. Kangi (wooden-comb). 31. Mala (necklace with long woolen string). 32. Hansli (solid brass crescent-shaped necklace). 33. Tainri (solid brass rings for ankles). 34. Dori (woolen string with tassels to tie women's hair into a knot). 35. Thotiya (4 thick brass-rings for toes with 2 copper wires for fastening them on to the toes). 26. Tarka Parpat (same as 28 but without ornamented top). 37. chilpi tayna (brass ring worn on the forehead of young men to keep their hair in place). 38. Kardhani (belt of leatherstrings worn by men). 39. Amulets. 40. Tatta parpat (Earplugs of rolled up leaves, 1 inch in diameter). 41. Hansuas (saw edged sickles for mowing grass). 42 and 43 yam (edible roots, taste like potatoes). 44. Sup (winnowing basket). 46. Bamboo umbrella 47. Thota (arrow with wooden head to shoot birds with). 48. Thota (arrow with iron head to shoot birds with). 49. chiari (arrow for shooting small game). 50. Patra (Sewing apparatus for joining two pieces of cloth into one). 51. Bainthi (kitchen knife). 52. Keya (Snuff-box.)

To face p. 177.

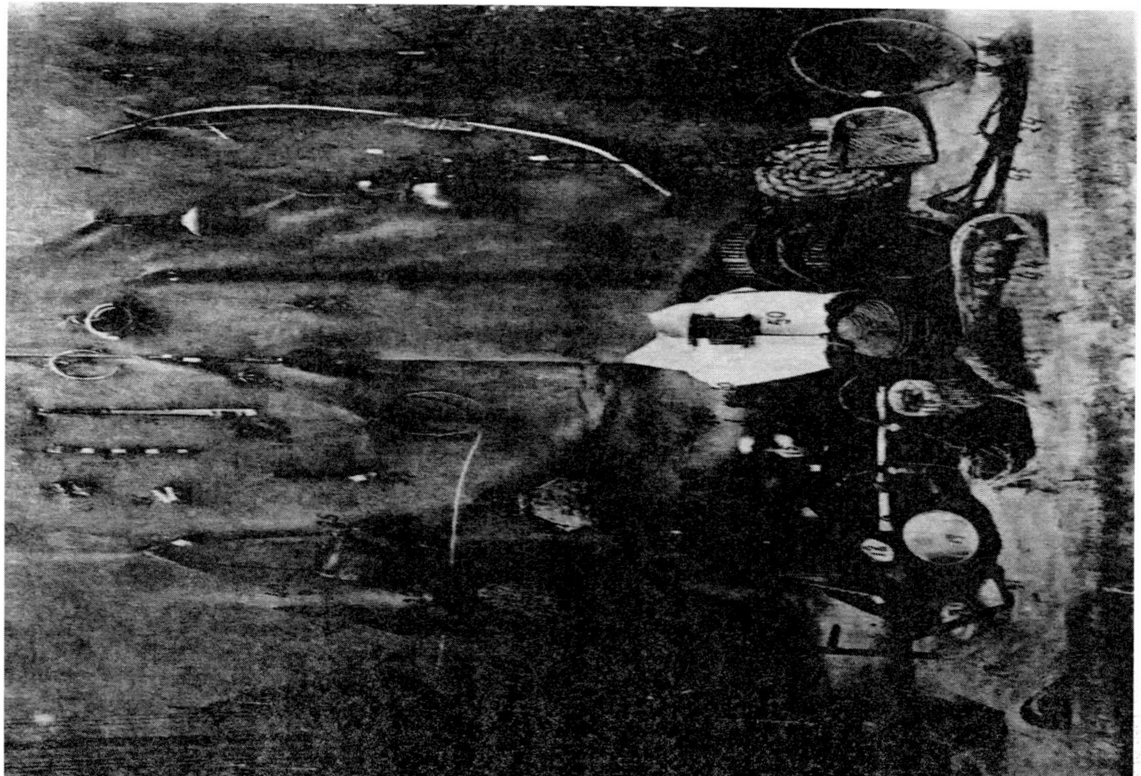

are manufactured by Hindus of the Kaserā caste from whom the Orāons buy them at the *bazars*.

In the kitchen, an iron spoon called *Karchhul* manufactured by the village blacksmith is occasionally used for stirring rice in the cooking pot; an wooden spoon, called *dui*, made by carpenters, is used by the Orāon for stirring pulse, vegetables, and meat in the cooking-pot. The *Koha kanto* or large knife made by the blacksmith is used for cutting meat, vegetables, *etc.* The dried-up hollow outer rind of the bottle-gourd is used for carrying water, particularly on a journey. Plates and cups of different sizes, are made by Orāon women by stitching together leaves of the sāl tree with thin bamboo splinters or bits of reed. These are used to eat rice and pulse and curries from. Poor Orāon women living near towns, sell these leaf-cups and leaf-plates at the bāzārs.

The Orāon's earthen ware are made by Hindu potters of the Kumhār caste. The pottery usually used are the *Kathi* in which rice is boiled, the *taoa* in which vegetable-curry and pulse are cooked, the *chukka* used by the poorer Orāons for drinking water from and holding water to wash the mouth and hands and feet with; the *ari* or *ghara* for drawing or carrying water, the *bisali* which is a bigger *ghara* in which paddy is boiled before being husked, or grains for domestic consumption is sometimes stored; the *dabna* or plate-like vessel with which cooking pots, *gharas* (water-vessels), *etc.*, are covered at their mouth; the *dhudiwa* which is a small pot in which oil is kept, the *tatthi* which is a diminutive cup used to hold a little oil and a lighted wick and thus to serve the purposes of a lamp, and the *chumkha* or earthen lamp-stand on the top of which the *tatthi* is placed.

The basketry of the Orāon consists of bamboo baskets of various shapes and sizes made by men of the Turi, Māhli or, and Dōm castes. Among these baskets may be mentioned the *chhatka* which is a very large basket in which rice is stored, the *dilingi* which is a smaller variety of the *chhatka*; the *uddu* which is a smaller basket holding about a maund (80 lbs) of grain; the *khachila*, a still smaller basket, in which paddy, rice, charcoal, and manure are carried, and in which various things are kept, the *daura** in which grains and other things are carried or kept; the *bowgi* or *nachua* which is a small basket, one important use to which it is put being to carry paddy-seeds to the fields for sowing; the *tunki*, another small basket carried

* An important variety of the daura is the *Karam-daura* a small basket in which flowers are gathered by Orāon girls for the *Karam* festival.

about by Orāon women and children for gathering edible leaves (sāgs), *makua* flowers, and the like ; the *koncho* which is a small bamboo-receptacle for carrying fish ; and the *sup* (*keter*) or winnower used by the Orāon for cleaning grain with, and for religious and magical purposes.

Useful Instruments.

In every Orāon house, you will find one or more axes (tāngi or tablā). These are used for cutting wood with and for various domestic purposes. The implements, tools, and weapons employed by the Orāon in agriculture, hunting and fishing have been already described. Knives of different shapes and sizes, made of soft iron by the village blacksmiths, are used by the Orāon. Such are the *ep kantos*, the small knives which are worn by young men at their waists, *the talma kanto* used for peeling mangoes and stuck by young men into their long hair in the mango season for cutting mangoes with ; the *khola kanto* used for shaving and hair-cutting, the *kanto kuba* used in making necklaces of kāsi grass ; and the *khurpi kanto* used for making reed necklaces with. To sweep the floors and courtyards of their houses, Orāon women use the *chalki* which is a broom made by themselves with the *birni* grass. Orāon women also make a circular straw pad for the head. On these pads placed on the head water-jars, *etc.*, are carried. Similar straw-pads, larger in size, are used as stands for *moras* and *tibsis*. To trace out cattle which may have strayed into the jungles an wooden bell called *tharki* is tied with a string to the neck of cattle. To catch rats and mice, a trap in the form of block and trough is used. This trap is made of clay, and called a *charpa*. Traps made of wood and called *osga-bajhro* are also used.

Musical Instruments.

The musical instruments used by the Orāons comprise drums and gongs, horns and trumpets, cymbals and clappers, pipes and banjos, besides bamboo flutes, metal ankle-bells, a kind of tambourine, and even the conch-shell. Of these, the bamboo flutes and the wooden clappers appear to have been independently evolved by the Orāons themselves, whereas all or most of the other instruments appear to have been borrowed by them from other peoples. Most of these musical instruments are used at their socio-religious dances and jātras; a few are used only at social festivals such as weddings; and a few others—the bamboo flutes and gourd banjos—are played upon by young men and shepherd boys at their leisure by way of amusement. We shall here briefly describe the principal musical instruments now in use amongst the

To face p. 181.

Orāons fishing.

Orāons of Chōtā Nāgpur. Of drums, the Māndal or Māndar (O., *khel*) is the most popular, and one or two may be found in almost every well-to-do Orāon family. It is made by men of the Gōṛāit caste, and played upon by Orāon males at some of their dances. It is a cylinder-shaped drum with earthen sides and with tops of baboon skin. It is slung from the shoulders of the drummer, and is sounded with the hands and not with sticks. Another cylindrical drum is the *dhol* which is similarly slung with a strap over the shoulders and rests crosswise on the chest of the drummer. It is a hollowed-out block of wood with a cow-hide cover on its left top which is sounded with a small stick, and a goat-hide cover on its right top which is sounded with the hand. It is played upon both at weddings and at some of the dancing festivals. At Orāon weddings, you also see the Dhāk, a very big drum slung over the shoulders of the village Goṛāit. It has a goat-hide on its right top and a cow hide on its left top. The goat-hide alone is sounded by the Goṛāit-drummer, with a stick in his right hand and a bamboo-reed in his left hand.

The most important drum is, however, the Nāgerā (O., dāmuā) which has iron sides and bottom and a buffalo-hide cover. It is by sounding the Nāgerā at the different village markets that notice of any great social or socio-political gathering or of an intended inter-pārhā hunting excursion or of an important decision of a Pārhā-panch, is circulated to the persons whom it may concern. It is, again, the sound of the Nāgerā that summons the village youth to the nocturnal dances at the village-ākhrā, and also notifices to the villagers the approach of a religious festival. And, last, but not least, the Nāgerā is an essential accompaniment to certain dances of the Orāons.

If the Nāgerā is the most important drum in use amongst the Orāons, the most interesting drum is the *Runj*, as it appears to be more ancient than the drums described above, and is now fast falling into disuse. The Rūnj has an earthen body of a peculiar shape with a depression at the middle, and its tops are made of goat-skin. A number of leather-strings are strung across the earthen-body to protect it. It is sounded at the tops with two curved wooden sticks, and is played upon at the Karam dances and jātrās. The earthen sides of the instruments are made by men of the Kūmhār or potter caste and the goat-skin tops and the leather-straps are made by the Goṛāits.

At Orāon weddings one or more pairs of bhēnrs (O., Bhōmbé) or long trumpets made of

To face p. 183

Orâon Musical instruments viz :—1. The Sainkho ; 2. The *Tuhila ;* 3. The Nagera 4. The Thechka ; and 5. The Murli ; (from left to right).

brass or copper are blown by Orāon young men, and one or more pipes called the Sānhāi made either of brass or of bell-metal are played upon by men of the Ghāsi or of the Gōrāit caste. And both at weddings and jātrās, and during hunting excursions you hear the Orāons blowing the horn called Narsinghā (O., bānk) which is made either of brass or of copper. A kind of tambourine known as the Dhāmplā may occasionally be seen at the jātrās. It is made by the Goṛāits and has wooden sides and a goat-skin top. The most noticeable musical instruments of the Orāons are, the Theskā clappers and the Soenkhō rings. These, like the *Runj* drums described above, are gradually falling into disuse. The Soenkhō which is played upon at the Karaṁ dances consists of a pair of large iron rings about nine inches in diameter placed one above the other and soldered together at one end. Into each of these rings are fitted a number of very small iron rings about an inch in diameter. The player holds a Soenkho in each hand, and waves his hands rhythmically backwards and forwards so as to produce a tinkling sound by the small rings striking against one another. Although it is doubtful whether the Rūnj and Soenkho, now used almost exclusively by the Orāons, were actually invented by them, there can hardly be any doubt that the wooden clappers called Theskā, which look like a rude original of the modern brass cymbals, are an Orāon invention. These are manufactured by the Orāons themselves and used during the Karam dances. Brass cymbals called Jhānj which the Orāons now buy of men of the Thaṭherā or brazier caste are fast supplanting the wooden Theskā. The Conch-shell (*gaegunghi*) is sometimes used, like the Nāgerā drum and the Narsinghā horn, on occasions of the tribal hunting excursions. A peculiar musical instrument which Orāon boys make for themselves is the small pyramid-shaped hollow earthen instrument, from six to nine inches in height, known as the Gūgūchū, or Tōrō-rōrō. 'It has its narrower end covered over with a spider's net, and is blown with the mouth of the player at the other end. It is played upon by young boys and girls at the *chhali bechna* or *angan* dances. Orāon young men play on two kinds of banjos—the more common Tūhilā and the less common Kendrā—which are both made of pumpkin-gourds and strings of either cotton thread or cocoon silk. Bamboo flutes similarly used are the small Mūrli and the larger Tiriō, generally containing seven holes each. When an Orāon boy goes out to graze his cattle in the jungles or fields, he sometimes inserts his Mūrli into his waist-girdle, and now and then amuses himself by playing on it.

Religious and Magico-religious usages and beliefs regarding Weapons and Musical Instruments.

Before starting on a hunting excursion, an orthodox Orāon hunter has the floor or court-yard of his house cleaned with cow-dung diluted in water. On a spot thus cleaned, all his weapons of hunting, are reverentially placed, and offerings of āruā rice, molasses and sometimes *ghee* or clarified butter are thrown on them, and incense burnt before them. Here and there an Orāon hunter even brings out a chicken before these weapons, ceremonially feeds the chicken on āruā rice, sets it apart with a vow, and on return home from a successful hunt offers it in sacrifice. A sword or other weapon with which a human being has been killed, is regarded with a curious superstitious awe. Such a sword is carefully hung up in the house, and on festival days offerings of a few drops of liquor are made to it. If the Orāon can help it, he will not use it any more, for it is believed that having once had a taste of human blood, it will not, when taken down from its place against the wall, rest until it has had its fill of human blood again. Although no sacrifices are actually made to musical instruments, the power-worshipping Orāon regards them with something like religious awe. Offerings of *aṛua* rice are made by a woman to the drums played on such occasions as weddings, and three parallel lines of vermilion-marks are also made on the drums by the woman sprinkling the rice-offering on the drums.

VIII. Manufactures and Industries.

The Orãons are not a manufacturing people.

Work in cotton.

Only a few raw materials grown on their fields or gathered in their native jungles are worked into suitable forms either with the hand or with some rude mechanical contrivances. Thus, the cotton grown on their fields are spun by Orãon women with a spindle called *charkhi* made of wood and iron. The seeds are previously taken out of the cotton with an instrument called *rahta*, and the cotton is teased out with a cotton-cleaner called *chirkhi*. The thread is gathered on a bamboo *Ghurni*, and twisted with the help of a stone-instrument called *dhera*. Orãon young men are skilful at hemming garments with a bamboo-needle called *thathra*. Decorative borders are made by them on their clothes with red thread, floral patterns being generally used. Fishing-nets are made by the Orãons themselves with the help of a bamboo shuttle.

Ropes are made by the men, with fibres of

Fibre-work.

kudrum (*Hibiscus cannabinus*), of the *sabai* grass, and of *sunn* or hemp. *Kudrum* is grown on the ridges of uplands ; and *kudrum* stems are gathered in October-November, made into bundles, and put out in the sun to dry. Later, these stems are made to rot in water by being immersed in a tank or pool for about a week, and then taken up and dried. The fibre is then extracted from the pith by breaking the latter into small pieces and separating them with the fingers. The fibres thus extracted are twisted into ropes with the *dhera* or rope-twister. Ropes are similarly made of sabāi (*Pllinia eripoda*) grass and of *chop* fibre (*Bauhinia Valu*). These ropes are used by the Orāon in house-building and other domestic and agricultural purposes. The Orāon also weaves ropes into carrying-nets or *sikas*. Less frequently, hemp and aloe fibres are worked up into ropes by the same process.

Work in leaves, grass, and straw.

Orāon women weave mats (*pitri*) of various sizes with the leaves of the wild date-palm *khijur* (*Faenix sylvestris*). Leaves of the *gungu* creeper are made into *chhupi* or a rain-hat with a wide brim occasionally worn by Orāon males while at work in the fields during the rains. A longer water-proof-covering for the head and back is the *gungu*. This is generally used by women, and reaches down to the back of the knees. It is also made of *gungu*-leaves and rimmed with bamboo-splinters. A few kinds of head-ornaments and neck-ornaments of different ornamental patterns are made by Orāon young men and women, with a few varieties of wild grass which grows on high sandy soil, and the *phutchira* grass which grows on damp soil by the side of tanks and pools. Fish-traps (*Kumni*) are also made of these two varieties of wild grass. A few varieties of grass are used by the Orāons in making into brooms for sweeping the floors and court-yards of their houses with. Plates and cups made of leaves of the Sāl tree are made by Orāon women by stitching together the leaves with small thin bamboo splinters or reeds. Pads (*bindi*) for water-vessels, *etc.*, either when carried on the head or placed on the ground, are made by Orāon women with straw and leaves, or only with date-palm leaves. Straw is plaited into long ropes by Orāon men ; and of these are made oval-shaped grain receptacles (*moras and tibsis*) of different sizes. Stands for these grain-receptacles are also made of straw.

Work in Wood.

The Orāon is mostly his own carpenter. With the help of the chisel (*rukhna*) and the adge (*basila*) he makes the mortar (*chunjkga*) and pestle (*man*) with which his women husk rice, the oil-mill (*kulhu*) with which Orāon women extract oil at home, and the oil-press (*tusung chapua*) with which they extract oil in the jungles, the ploughs with which the Orāon tills the soil, the *dhenki* or rice-pounder with which his women husk their grains, the *kando* or wooden seat on which the Orāon squats while taking his meals, and the *balli* or door-plank of his house, the *makri* or bolt with which he keeps the doors of his hut closed, the *paila* or wooden cup with which he measures his grain, and a few other articles of domestic use.

Iron-smelting. In a few Orāon villages, there are iron ores from which the Orāons extract iron in a rude way.

IX. Trade and the Village Market.

There is no special class of traders or merchants amongst the Orāons. The produce of agriculture is, in times of necessity, or when there is a quantity to spare, taken by their women to the nearest market and sold for cash. Of such produce, rice, millets, pulse, and oilseeds are the most important. Coin of Government mintage is the only money now used. But grain is occasionally used as a medium of exchange. Hindu and Muhammadan petty traders attend many of these village-markets with tobacco, salt, cloth, spices, gūr (treacle), thread and needles, china-beads and a few trinkets, and many of them buy up the major portion of the superfluous grain which the Orāon women take to the markets for sale. Agents of big Mārwāri merchants from the towns now-a-days visit the villages and also buy up such superfluous grain, to sell it at a profit in the towns or export it to places outside the district. Besides Orāon women selling their agricultural produce, and the petty Hindu *benias* and other traders exposing for sale their miscellaneous wares, you see at these village-markets—basket-makers with their baskets, Kumhār potters with their pottery, the Teli oil-men or their wives with their oil, and vendors of a few other necessary articles. The custom of silent trade is unknown. In the more important markets, cattle are sold, braziers come with their brass-ware, even the sweet-meat seller is there with his delicacies, and the Ahir with his pot of clarified butter (*ghee*). Dealers of different articles have their seats assigned at the market place. But these more important markets are held only in villages in and about which there is a comparatively large population of Hindu castes. Very few Orāons can go in for more than the bare necessaries of life. The genuine Orāon village-market is in fact the best place you can go to, for guaging the material condition of the people.

Ceremonies in starting a village market.

The Orāon method of establishing a market is briefly as follows :—People of a number of neighbouring villages hold consultation amongst themselves and fix upon a site for holding a weekly market. Information is sent round that a market will be started in a particular village on a particular date. On the day preceding the inauguration day, the headmen of the village in which the market is to be held, sacrifice a goat to the goddess 'Devi' at the 'Devi-āsthān' (seat of the Devi) in the village. In villages where there is a *Mahadeo-asthan*, a goat is sacrificed also to the god Mahādeo. In some villages, a buffalo is sacrificed to the village-spirits. At these sacrifices, a number of Orāons from the neighbouring villages attend. The sacrificial flesh is roasted, and eaten by the assembled Orāons at the selected market-site along with country-liquour which is purchased with a subscription of a rupee or so realised from each of the villages interested in the market.

By ancient custom, these markets are regarded as belonging to the Orāon village communities, and the Hindu or other landlord of the village in which the market is held is not allowed to collect any tax or toll from people who expose their merchandise for sale at such markets.*

* Such markets we understand have been established

Weights and Measures.

The unit of all grain and liquid measure is the *Paila.* Two kinds of *pailas* are in use in the Oraõn country. The *Chhapnahi paila* which is equivalent to one standard *seer* of 80 tolás is in use in parganā Khukrā and a few other places and in the rest of the district, the *bara-gandi paila* which is equivalent to about 14 chittaks of pākkā weight or $\frac{7}{8}$ths of the *chhapnahi paila* is used. The *sawai paila* which is one and one-fourth times as much as the chhapnāhi *paila* is in use in a very few places. The standard weight is the *seer* of 80 *tolas* (a little over 2 lbs.), and its subdivisions,—the kānowā (quarter-*seer*), and Chittak ($\frac{1}{16}$th of a *seer*). A *kat* of grain measured with the chhapnāhi *paila* is equivalent to a standard *maund* of forty seers. At the markets, different sets of pailās (O., *aurka*) called *bikri pailas* are used. These are of three classes called respectively the *anna-paila*, the *dhibua paila*, and the *paisa-paila*,—a pailā-ful of rice selling respectively at one anna (penny), half-anna, or quarter-anna according as the *paila* used is an *anna paila*, *dhibua-paila*, or *paisa-paila*. Grain-dealers have a large number of these *pailas* of different capacities,

even in recent years at many villages, such as at Idri (*thana* Bero), Pipar-danr (*thana*, Bero), Uchri (*thana*, Mandar), and Mahuajari (*thana*, Mandar).

and according to the rise or fall of the prices of grains, bring out larger or smaller *anna*, *dhebua* and *paisa pailas*.

Land measures.

The area of land is roughly indicated by the approximate quantity of paddy-seed required to sow a particular field with. But the area of the *kat* or *powa* varies considerably from village to village, and also in different fields of the same village. The following reasons for this difference are given in the Government Report on the Agriculture of the District (1897), "First, the general, though not universal, custom is for the rate (of rent) *per pawa* to be the same for all quantities of land, and the poor pawas are therefore, by way of compensation, larger than the richer ones. Secondly, *pawas* which abut on *tanr* lands or uplands, though originally of the same size, now differ in consequence of the holder of one *pawa* having enlarged his rice-land by terracing and taking in portions of the adjoining up-land, while another cultivator has been content to keep his *pawa* as he got it. Thirdly, new cultivators come into the village, the customary rate remains the same, but the rent is increased by reducing the *pawa*". For uplands, the kāt is the standard land-measure all over the district; and its sub-divisions are,—the *khandi* which is half of a *kat*, and the *paila* which is one-twentieth of a *khandi.* As for low-lands (*don*), the denominations vary in the different parganās (divisions) of the Orāon country. Thus, in *parganas* Khukrā, Korāmbé, Kuṛū, Lodhmā, Jāspur, and Omedāndā, 2 *kanis* make 1 kānwā, 2 *kanwas* make one *pawa.* and 4 *pawas* make 1 *khari* ; in *pargana* Belkāddi, 2 *kanis* make 1 *kanwā*, 4 *kanwas* make 1 *pawa*, and 4 *pawas* make 1 *khari*, in parganās Biru, Basiā, Doesā, and Pālkōt, 2 *kanis* make 1 *kanasi*, 2 *kanasis* make 1 *kanwa*, and 4 *kanwas* make 1 annā. But in the Mānki patti of Pargana Sōnepur and also in parganā Tāmāṛ (where the Mundā population predominates) and in some other parts of the country (as in Perganā Siri), the *Kat* (sālā) is the standard of land-measure for uplands as well as for low lands. A *Kat* is supposed to be the area which can be sown with one *kat* (twenty seers to forty seers) of paddy-seed. On an average one kāt of lowland approximates to an acre.

X. Different classes of Servants and Labourers.

Even the Orāon cultivator cannot always manage without some extraneous labour to assist him in cultivation. But as may be expected, the Orāon has not much superfluous cash to remunerate such labourers as he employs on his fields. And payment of wages entirely in cash is the exception rather than the rule with the Orāon master. His modes of employing agricultural labour are principally the following :—

(I) **Dhangrai.**

An Orāon who wants to engage a dhāngar or servant by the year goes to the house of some young Orāon in the month of Māgh (January-February) and asks his parents if he may have the services of their son as a dhāngar for the ensuing year. If they agree, terms are arranged, the remuneration (*pogri*) being usually fixed at from six kāts to twelve kāts of paddy for the year and in some places, a small annual sum varying from Rs. 12, according to the age of the servant and the work on which he is employed. The dhāngar gets also his board and lodging free. When terms are settled, a day is fixed for the ceremonial engagement of the dhāngār. On that day, the dhāngar-elect and generally his parents are invited to his house by the intending employer. On their arrival at the house, a mat is spread out for them to sit upon. The mistress of this house comes out with a small cup of mustard oil and a wooden comb, anoints the young man with this oil on his head, shoulders, arms and legs, and combs his hair with the wooden comb, The young man then gets up from his seat and makes obeisance (*johar*) to all present. The young man and his parents are next treated to a drink of rice-beer especially prepared for the occasion, and finally to boiled rice, pulse-soup and other delicacies. Now the engagement of the young man as dhāngar is complete, and from that day he becomes the dhānger of the family. Orāon dhāngars in the villages make very obedient and willing servants, and their Orāon master and his family treat them as members of the family. When the year is out, the parents of the dhāngar are again invited to the house on the day of the fullmoon in Māgh (February), and again entertained with rice-beer and a sumptuous meal of rice, pulse, rice-flour cakes, etc. and the dhāngar's hair is again ceremonially oiled and combed, and one or two combs are presented to him. When the *dhangar* is drinking rice-beer, some member of his master's family asks him—"Does it taste sweet or sour?" If, in reply, the dhāngar says that it tastes sour, it is understood that he will not return to service again. * If, however, he says—'It tastes sweet,' it is understood that he will renew his engagement as *dhangar* for the ensuing year. The *dhangar* now goes home with his parents and comes back after a few days. The fresh contract of

* In some parts of the Orāon country, the dissolution of the contract of service is signified by the dhāngar tying up a yoke with two yoke-ropes.

service is entered into with just the same ceremonies as on the first occasion.

(2) Pasri.

The *Pasri* system of labour is of two kinds. To one class of *Pasri* labourers (called *pasri-dars*) belongs a man who has no plough-cattle of his own, and consequently enters with another man who has ploughs and plough-cattle, into an oral contract under the terms of which the latter will, according to his own convenience, once a week or so, take his ploughs and plough-cattle to the other's (*pasridar's*) fields and plough and sow them ; and the former (the *pasridar*) will, in exchange for this assistance, work in the latter's fields every morning (from about 7 A. M. to about 11 A. M.) during the cultivating season. The second form of *pasri* is the simple exchange of labour. If you help me with your ploughs and plough-cattle and with your labour in my fields, I repay you with the same amount of labour with my ploughs and plough-cattle.

(3) Soukhia

An Orāon who has no ploughs or plough-cattle of his own sometimes engages in the service of another Orāon as a *soukhia*. He is to get no wages but only board and lodging. And, in addition to this his master undertakes to get all his *soukhia's* fields cultivated with his own ploughs and plough-cattle.

As with the *dhangars*, so with the *soukhias*, the engagement is by the year, and continues from Phāgun (February) to the next *Magh* (January).

(4) **Sajha.** By the *Sajha* system, a man who has lands but no plough-cattle, gets his lands cultivated by one who has ploughs and plough-cattle. The latter is called the *Sajhadar* and supplies the required labour, takes his own implements of tillage, and supplies manure to the fields when required, and half (and sometimes the whole) of the seed to be sown on the field. The sājhādār and the owner of the land divide the produce between themselves in equal halves.

(5) **Pacha** When an Orāon requires a number of men to do some particular piece of work, such as roofing his house or doing some work on his fields or embankments, he applies to the headman (Dhāngar-Māhāto) of the young bechelors of the village. A price, generally now-a-days in cash, is settled for the job, and the *Dhangar-mahato* directs the youngmen under his charge to do the work, and they obey with alacrity. Sometimes we have found the services of these young men secured in this way for some unlawful purpose such as looting the standing crops of a field to which the employer of the

dhangars thinks he is entitled but which is in the possession of another person.

(6) **Ghardijoa.**

In the western parts of the Rānchi district, particularly in pergana Borway, you sometimes see a son of poor Orāon parents serving as a dhāngar in the house of an Orāon cultivator on the understanding that he will be in time married to a daughter of his employer, without having to pay any bride-price. Besides board and lodging, such a dhāṅgar (called *ghardija*) gets also a certain *pogri* (an annual allowance of paddy) so long as he works and even after he is married and becomes an actual son-in-law of the master of the house.

XI. The Daily Life of the Oraon.

The daily life of the Orāon male is mainly devoted to the production of food by agricultural work, and that of the Orāon female to the collection of food from field and jungle and the preparation of such food for use.

Men.

Adult Orāons, male as female, will get up from bed in the morning at about 4 o'clock in the cold weather, and about 3 o' clock in summer and in the rainy season. When any upland crops (such as *gora marua*, *urid*, *&c.*) or lowland paddy crops have been reaped, men take their plough-cattle to the threshing-floor and begin threshing the grain from before day-break. Then, after sunrise, they go to plough their fields or bāris or home-stead lands or to do some other work in their fields. They return home from the fields at about 11 A. M. rinse their teeth, wash their mouth, hands and feet, and, at intervals of a few days, bathe themselves in cold water at the village-spring or some tank or stream. Then, they take their breakfast (kālōā). After breakfast, they go out to reap paddy or some other crops, when there is any to be reaped. When there are no crops to be cut, they rest awhile after break-fast and then go out to their fields or make fishing-nets, fish-traps, or some necessary implement or other thing for their own use. Men, and not women as among most peoples, generally mend the garments of the family, or embroider their clothes.

Women.

Orāon women get up from bed at the same hour as the men. Before day-break, they husk paddy for the day's consumption, and, if necessary, for sale. Then at about sun-rise, a female member of the family carries the night's cattle-dung in baskets and deposits it in a manurepit, one or more women go to draw water from some spring, well, tank, or stream, and one proceeds to cook rice, vegetables, *etc.* Once in two or three days the floors of the huts are cleaned by some female member of the family with cow-duug diluted in water. The *angan* or court-yard of the house is similarly cleaned once in four or five days. Women usually take their meals after the men have taken theirs. But during harvesting operations when the male members of the family and sometimes also a few women or girls go out to work in the morning, the women who are left behind do the cooking, take their breakfast, and go to the fields with the meals of the workers in the field, and there join them in reaping the crops. They return home at about sun-set, cook the evening-meal, and after the men have eaten, take their meals. They cleanse the plates and utensils by rubbing them with earth and washing them in cold water. In January and February, women tease cotton with the *ratha* and then after the cotton is carded by *Dhunets*, the Orāon women make *piuris* of them, and then make thread out of them.

Old people.

Old men and women who are incapable of working in the fields, watch their houses when the other members are out, make ropes, or employ themselves in similar other easy sedentary work. Old men also sometimes take care of young children of the house while their mothers are at work. After the harvest, the ordinary routine of work is broken by various feasts and ceremonial visits of relatives. Ordinarily it is the women who cook the meals. But at big feasts, it is the young bachelors of the village who cook the meals.

XII. Economic condition.

Insufficiency of agricultural produce

We have now finished our brief survey of the economic life of the Orāon. Agriculture, which is the principal occupation of the bulk of the people, does not, as we have seen, provide the average Orāon cultivator with the means of supporting himself and his family throughout the year, and to pay his dues to his landlord. Jungle fruit and edible roots, as we have seen, supplement his store of agricultural food. In years of stress he has to borrow money or paddy at usurious interest. The poorer Orāon has to find employment for a son or a nephew as dhāngar to a more well-to-do fellow-tribesman or even to a non-Orāon. And from many an Orāon family, one or more members go every year to work in Calcutta or in the labour-districts, soon after they have harvested their low-land paddy in September, October, or November, and return home in April, May, or June, just in time for sowing or transplanting low-land paddy in their fields. With the savings of their earnings during such temporary migrations, their landlords' dues are paid, and often but a portion of their money-lenders' demand of interest on loans advanced is satisfied.

Indebtedness. Their more open oppression by their landlords has, thanks to the Record-of-Rights recently prepared by the Government, been effectively checked, but they still groan under a more subtle and insidious oppression at the hands of the usurious Chōtā-Nāgpur money-lender.* Once an Orāon gets into the clutches of this Indian Shylock, it becomes extremely difficult to extricate himself from his grip. The paltry initial debt goes on swelling enormously by a process which the simple Orāon can never understand. Interest at the rate of seventy-five per *centum* per *annum* is the normal but not the maximum rate of interest charged on petty loans advanced to the Orāon cultivator. The Co-operative Credit Societies which the Government are doing their best to multiply in the district, are expected in time to rid the Orāons of this crying evil. But, in the meanwhile, the usurious interest he has to pay to

* There may be a few honourable exceptions even amongst the Chota Nagpur money-lenders. Our remarks do not of course apply to them.

his Sāhu money-lender, remains a source of the most grievous oppression. The oppressive demands of their usurious creditors sometimes compel whole families of Orāons to emigrate as labourers to the tea-gardens of Assam, as, not long ago, the persecution of their landlords more often used to drive them thither.* True, in several instances, their own improvident habits and their lamen-

* A typical instance known to many is thus related by Mr. J. Reid, I. C. S., in his *Settlement Report of the Ranchi District* (1912):—"In Tikratoli, thana Bero, the aboriginal raiyats having refused to pay enhanced rents, the landlord began a campaign against them, and has succeeded, mainly through the medium of suits, in ousting the whole aborigiginal population of the village, and replaced them by Hindus." The *Report* (*p.* 101) adds,—"At Turuguru and Sakra in the same thana, the landlord endeavoured to do the same thing, but has hitherto failed"— The aboriginal tenants in these cases are all Oraons; and the present writer has some personal knowledge of the great difficulties and heavy expenses the tenants of one of these villages had to undergo to save themselves from spoliation of their lands. The *Settlement Report* (p. 99) says,— "Illegal enhancements of rent and rakumats were usually effected by the landlords by three methods—I., by sub-letting their villages to thiccadars, with the sole object of effecting enhancements through their agency, II. by bringing a fictitious suit for arears of rent in the Revenue Courts and suing at enhanced rates; III, by private arrangement with the raiyats.

table love of liquor, are, to a great extent responsible for their chronic indebtedness. But even the sober and thrifty Hindu tenant of Chōtā Nāgpur is, in a year of scarcity or cattle-epidemic, obliged to borrow money at high interest. No wonder, therefore, that the slightest stress should drive the unthrifty Orāon into the clutches of the Sāhū money-lender.

Rent.

Again, the incidence of rent on his lands, although it may seem light when compared with that in Bengal and Bihār *proper*, bears heavily on the poor Orāon tenant of Chōtā-Nāgpur. When we consider how the Orāons who were formerly owners of the soil they cultivated and had to pay only a nominal tribute, misnamed 'rent', and how from time to time this 'rent' was in many instances, by force or fraud, enhanced, and how as their rent went on increasing, their tenancies went on contracting in area and the new 'landlord's private demesne—his *majhas* and *bakast* lands—went on expanding in proportion, it becomes clear that any comparison of the incidence of rent in Chōtā Nāgpur with that in Bengal or Bihār, where the history of land-tenures is different, must needs be fallacious. As the Ranchi Settlement Report puts it,—"As their ancestors agreed to pay only a fixed tribute to their feudal Chiefs, they cannot conceive any inherent right of the *Jagirdars* to increase or enhance the rents of their holdings, nor do they in their innermost minds admit that the latter have any *prescriptive rights.*"* As a result of this enhancement of rent and the gradual contraction of the area of the Orāon tenants' holdings, at the present day "enormous numbers of raiyati holdings in the district barely exceed the subsistence limit and the rents are paid not from the profits of the holdings but from the wages derived from extraneous employments."† The Report goes on to say,— "It is in fact the existence of such large numbers of uneconomic holdings, combined with the impossibility of obtaining continuous employment in the villages at fair rents, which mainly accounts for the enormous emigration from the district to Assam, the Duars, and other parts of the province."‡ We may add that the obstacles now thrown by the landlords in the way of their increasing the area of their holdings with the increase of their family lead many an Orāon family to emigrate to Assam, the Duars or the Sundarbans, or sometimes to migrate from one part of the Plateau to another where lands may be had on easier terms. Not long ago, with the increase of his family, an Orāon cultivator would go on

* P 104.
† ‡ p. 119

extending his cultivation by reclaiming portions of the waste lands of his village. And the landlord dared not prevent him, for he knew very well that by ancient custom he had no right to prevent such reclamation, but could only demand half-rents for such lands, when reclaimed. But gradually through a mistaken analogy with the *status* and rights of a landlord in Bengal and Bihār *proper*, the advisers of the Chōtā-Nāgpur landlords thought they should claim, and the landlords came to claim, such a right, and some of the Civil and Revenue Courts in the past, in ignorance of the origin and history of land tenures in Chōtā-Nāgpur *proper*, in most cases, allowed the landlords' new claim. When at length, the mistake was found out,—alas! too late—the right of reclamation could get legislative recognition only in a modified form.

Present condition.

Such, in brief, is the present economic condition of the Orāon. Ill-housed, ill-clad, and underfed, generally over-taxed by the landlord, frequently oppressed by the money-lender, and occasionally duped by the labour-recruiter or fleeced by the law-tout, the Orāon of Chōtā Nāgpur has indeed had an exceptionally hard lot in life.

The outlook.

But, happily, the prospects before him are brightening. Faint streaks of light are shining forth through the encir clinggloom. The school-master is abroad in the land with his torch of enlightenment. The Government and the Christian Missions are doing all they can to spread the light of education amongst the aborigines of Chōtā Nāgpur and otherwise to improve their moral and material condition. Even the non-Christian Orāons are awakening to the necessity of educating their children, and of qualifying them for some additional employment besides their hereditary occupation of agriculture. They have themselves * started an Association to raise funds to assist their boys in prosecuting their studies in schools and colleges ; and many a non-Christian Orāon family contributes its humble mite of one *sup* (winnowing-basket holding about ten *seers*) of paddy at harvest-time towards this most laudable object of the Association known as the 'Orāon-Mundā-Sikshā-Sabhā'. A similar Association has also been formed by a number of energetic young Orāon and Mundā Christian converts.

The Bihār Government are not only earnestly seeking to spread education amongst the aborigines of Chōtā Nāgpur but are taking effective steps, through the establishment or active encouragement of Co-operative Societies, to save them from the clutches of the usurer, and devising legis-

* The two Orāons who first started this Association in September, 1909, are Rungtu Oraon and Bandiram Oraon.

lative and executive measures to remedy other grievances and improve their lot in life. And, as we have said, it is not unreasonable to expect that the time is not immeasurably distant when the Orāons will be able to compete on equal terms in the race of life with their Hindu and Muhammedan neighbours. And that consumation, when it comes about, will be one of the noblest of the innumerable noble achievements of the British Government in India in the cause of humanity and civilization.

CHAPTER V.

The Village Dormitories, and the Training of Youth.

We have seen in the last chapter how hard and persistent is the struggle for material existence,—for mere food, raiment, and shelter,—that the Orāon has to maintain throughout life. Even his children, as we have seen, have to participate in this struggle as early in life as they can. Under such conditions of life, it is no wonder that the Orāon should have remained in the same low level of culture for centuries upon centuries. It is only within the last few years that under the fostering care of the British Government and the stimulating example of Orāon Christian converts that a desire for educating their children on modern lines and thereby improving their material condition has sprung up amongst a number of non-Christian Orāons. But they possess no written language of their own, their industrial arts are as yet few, and even these areonly in a rudimentary stage of development, and the fine arts—unless their rude style of music and dancing be dignified by that name—are practically unknown ; custom is the only code of morality they recognize, and erroneous ideas as to the causes of natural phenomena and 'superstitious' beliefs as to the nature and powers of the supernatural world do duty respectively for science and religion.

I. The Bachelors' Dormitory.

The only indigenous institution for the training of youth that the Orāons possess to this day is one that appears to have been evolved at a stage of Orāon society far more primitive than it is at present. This institution of the 'Jōnkh Eṛpā' or 'Bachelors' Hall', as it is called,—though it must have served an useful purpose in the savage stage of society when hunting was the principal occupation of the people—is now in many respects an anachronism. It is an abomination which is of interest only as a survival of savagery.

(a) Its object.

In the 'Jōnkh-Eṛpā'—better known to us under the Hindi name of 'Dhūm-kūṛiā' or 'Dhāngar-kūṛiā', the hut of the dhāngars or young men,—we catch a glimpse of a very archaic form of economic, social, and religious organization. It must have been in its time an effective economic organization for purposes of food-quest, a useful seminary for training young men in their social and other duties, and an institution for magico-religious observances calculated to secure success in hunting and to augment the procreative power of the young men so as to increase the number of hunters in the tribe. Although several of the institutions, customs, and beliefs of the Orāons of our times appear to be resultants of a mixture of their own ideas and practices with those of their neighbours the Mundās, and although Hindu ideas are, to some extent, and Christian example is, to a smaller extent, exercising disintegrating influences on some of their own ideas and practices,—the institution of the Dhumkūṛiā appears to be a genuine and unadulterated product of 'primitive' Orāon culture. The tradition of the Orāons, too, speaks of this institution as having been brought over by their ancestors from their ancient home on the Rohtās plateau to their present home on the Chotā Nāgpur plateau. And to this day in the greater part of the Orāon country, it is a living institution, though maimed and modified by the hand of Time. Although in many villages of Chōtā-Nāgpur, the public Dhumkūṛiā building has for some reason or other * ceased to exist, the institu-

* In some villages superstitious considerations, and, in others, practical difficulties appear to have led to the disappearance of the public Dhumkūṛiā house. Thus, in one village we were told that long ago a tiger carried off two boys from the Dhumkūṛiā house and since then the house

tion itself is by no means extinct, for the young bachelors of such villages too generally sleep together at night in some spare hut in the village and, more or less, observe the time-honoured practices associated with the Dhumkūṛiā. But it is with the greatest difficulty that an outsider can gather a fairly complete knowledge of all those practices. Such knowledge as we have been able to gather partly from personal observation and partly from information elicited by prolonged careful and persistent enquiries from the people themselves, is given below.

(*b*) The Dhumkuria-House.

The Dhumkūṛiā building, where it exists, is a modest house generally with four mud walls, one door-way and no windows. It is either thatched over with wild grass or is roofed over with tiles. The house consists of a spacious rectangular room or rather 'hall,' where the boys all sleep on a bed of palm-leaf mat annually presented to them by the maidens of the village, with occasionally bundles of straw for pillows. In winter

has been abandoned and allowed to fall into ruins, under the belief that the tiger indicated the will of the gods that the village should no longer maintain a public Dhumkuṛiā building.

nights, logs of wood are kept burning at one end of the 'hall' to keep it warm. Although the interior of the house is usually kept fairly clean and tidy, its surroundings are in a most filthy and insanitary condition. Adjoining the 'hall' and, in some villages, inside it, there is a stinking drain which is seldom cleaned and into which the Dhumkūṛiā boys micturate. In other villages an earthen pot (gāgri) is kept in the 'hall' for the purpose, and the younger boys have to throw away its liquid contents every morning. This human urine is in some villages mixed with the fodder of cattle, in the belief that it imparts strength and vigour to the cattle. Adjoining the Dhūmkūṛiā is the ākbrā or dancing-ground of the village.

(c) Constitution and Management.

Age of the Dhangars.

An Orāon boy is admitted into membership of the Dhumkūṛiā fraternity at about eleven or twelve years of age. It is said that in the olden days, the age of admission used to be a little higher, but that since the marriageable age of Orāon boys and girls has, among the more well-to-do Orāons, been reduced probably in imitation of the custom among local Hindu castes, the age of admission into the Dhumkūṛiā has been proportionately reduced.

Classes of Dhangars. The Dhumkūṛiā boys are divided into three classes or grades (tūṛs), called respectively—(1) Punā Jokhār, or novices, who are dhāngaṛs of the first or lowest grade; (2) Mājh-tūṛiā jokhār, or members of the intermediate class who are dhāngaṛs of the second grade, and (3) Kōhā Jokhār, or the oldest dhāngaṛs who belong to the third or highest grade. The duration of membership of each of the first two classes is three years, whereas the third or highest class of dhāngaṛs are supposed to continue as members only until their marriage; but as Orāon boys are now sometimes married quite young, they now retain their membership, to all intents and purposes, until they have one or two children by their wives. Thus the ages of the Dhumkūṛiā boys range from about eleven or twelve years to twenty years and over.

Supervision and Control. The supervision and control of the Dhumkūṛiā fraternity rests in the hands of a boy who is appointed as the Māhāto or headman of the dhāngaṛs. This Dhāngaṛ-Māhāto, as he is called, is assisted in his work by another boy who is appointed as the Chālābu or Kotwār of the

Dhāngars. The Dhāngaṛ-Māhāto has to instruct the Dhumkūṛiā boys in their social and religious duties; and the Kotwār or Chālābu has particularly to attend to the jātrās and dances and to see that the boys are properly decked with flowers and fineries for the jātrās. He has also to collect flowers for the purpose. He may compel unwilling boys to attend dances and jātrās, and, for that purpose, may punish disobedient members by lashing them with the *bindi* or plaited straw-whip which is the insignia of his office. In fact, something like military discipline is enforced. Even the Dhāngaṛ-Kotwār is liable to be fined by the Dhāngaṛ-Māhāto if a boy is found absent from a dance without sufficient cause. In a large village consisting of more than one tolā or hamlet, as many Dhāngaṛ-Māhātos and as many Dhāngaṛ-Kotwārs are appointed for the Dhumkūṛiā as there are tolās in the village. These officers are known as the Mukhiās or leaders of the Dhumkūṛiā fraternity, and are changed once every three years. About half a dozen flags and flag-staffs, three or four nāgerās (large drums), two or three dhōlōks (small drums) and, in some villages, a narsinghā (brass horn) or a jhānj (brass cymbal) or both, form the property of the Dhumkuriā, and are used at dances, festivals, hunting expeditions and *jatras*.

Election of Dhangar Mukhias or headmen.

The formalities connected with the appointment of these *Mukhias* or headmen of the Dhāngaṛs are very simple. In the month of Chait or Baiśākh (April), (and,in some villages, in Māgh) the village-headmen through their messenger, the Goṛāit, send round information to the villagers that on a particular day the *Mukhia-handi* ceremony (the drinking of rice-beer in honour of the *Mukhias*) will be celebrated, and they must brew rice-beer (*handi*) for the occasion. On the day thus appointed, one female member from each Orāon family of the village takes a pot of rice-beer to the place fixed for the ceremony and leaves it there. This ceremony is generally held on an open space close to the village *basti*. There the men of the village assemble and take their seats on palm-leaf mats. No women may attend the meeting except old women. When any old women happen to attend, they sit a little apart from the men. The Dhumkūṛiā boys serve rice-beer in leaf-cups to all present. The village-headmen and the other elders of the village now hold a consultation amongst themselves as to which of the Dhumkūṛiā boys should be elected Māhāto and Kotwār respectively. An elderly Orāon is also selected for the office of Pelō-Kōtwār or watchman of the unmarried girls. His duty is to look after the conduct of the unmarried Orāon girls, and to supply them with flowers to deck themselves out with for the *jatras*. He is also responsible for any improper relations between a *dhumkuria* girl and a non-Orāon young man or an Orāon youth of prohibited degrees of relationship. When at length their selection is made, the selected Māhāto, and Kotwār (or Māhātos and Kotwārs, where more than one are elected), and the Pelō-Kotwār are called out by name and made to sit down in a line before the village-elders. In some villages they are adorned with flowers. Now the outgoing Dhāngaṛ Māhāto, and Dhāngāṛ-Kotwār and Pelo-Kotwār each hands over to his successor a leaf-cup filled with rice-beer. When the newly-elected Māhāto and Kotwārs have drunk this rice-beer (the drinking itself constitutes them respectively Māhāto and Kotwārs), the outgoing Dhāngaṛ Kotwār makes over to the new Kotwār his *bindi* or plaited straw-cord. Before parting with this insignia of the Kotwār's office, the out-going Kotwār takes care to give two lashes with it on the hip of his successor. The original idea that gave rise to this custom was probably to make a magical transference of his own power and authority to his successor. After this the outgoing Kotwār again hands over two leaf-cups of rice-beer to the newly appointed Kotwār. Finally the new Kotwār salutes each member of the assembly and resumes his seat. The outgoing Māhāto in making over charge of his office to the new Māhāto addresses him as follows:—"Take care that no one may find fault with you or with the boys. When an offence is committed by any of the boys, deal out even justice to all parties concerned; and when you feel perplexed as to what to do in any matter, refer the matter to the village-Māhāto. When relatives of any Orāon family of the village come to the village see that they do not find cause to complain of deficient hospitality. When presents of sacrificial or other meat (*sandes*) have to be distributed to the villagers or sent to other villages, see that the *dhangars* do their duty properly, *etc.*, *etc.*"

(d). Admission into the Dhumkuria.

Once every third year new boys are admitted into the Dhumkūṛiā. On the day of the new moon in the month of Māgh (January-February), the Dhumkūṛiā boys go out after breakfast to some neighbouring jungle, with their bows and arrows, their axes and spears, their sticks and cudgels. Towards evening they return to the outskirts of their village with such

Sandhi-sendra or the New Moon Hunt in Winter.

game as they may have secured. There, the younger boys clean an open space and dress the meat of the animals or birds killed in the chase. In the meanwhile, the older boys hold a consultation amongst themselves and determine which boys of the village may be newly admitted into the Dhumkūṛiā. When they have come to a decision, they keep apart for each boy to be newly admitted a few small pieces of flesh closed up in an envelope made of *sal* leaves stitched together with splinters of wood. The rest of the flesh is either roasted or fried and is eaten by the party. They then enter the village and at the house of each boy to be newly admitted to the Dhumkūṛiā, leave a leaf-envelope contianing meat and intimate their decision as to the admission of the boy. The eating of that meat by the boy appears to be the first step towards effecting an 'union' of the boy with the members of the Dhumkūṛiā.

'Era-Mokhot' or the 'Goat Eating' ceremony.

This 'union' is completed a fortnight later when on the day of the full-moon (purna-māsi) in Māgh, the boy is formally admitted into the fraternity by being allowed to eat in company with the members of the Dumkūṛiā the meat of a goat sacrificed that day to Chāndi—the spirit who presides over hunting and war. This sacrifice is made by the bachelors at noon that day. All the bachelors remain fasting from morning until the *puja* or worship is over and then they partake of the sacrificial meat. The *puja* consists in the bachelors throwing handfuls of rice on the Chāndi-stone, after the Dhangar-Pāhān has stripped himself quite naked of his clothes and brought a gourd-ful of water from the sacred spring of the village and bathed the Chāndi-stone with that water and, if possible, with milk,—and put three marks of vermilion over the stone. For the purpose of washing it, the Chāndi-stone is taken out of the ground where it ordinarily remains half-buried. The sacrifice of a black she-goat that has not yet borne a kid, and the sprinkling of its blood over the stone and into the hole formed by the portion of the Chāndi-stone which ordinarily lies embedded in the ground, complete the ceremony. It may be noted that although ordinarily only a goat is sacrificed to Chāndi on the Māgh Purnimā day,—in a year in which new dhāngaṛs are admitted a pig is also killed in the village on the Māgh Purnimā day. The flesh of the pig is brought to the Chāndi-tanr and cooked there. It is further worthy of note that as for the goat sacrificed to Chāndi, its head is chopped into small bits and roasted separately from the rest of the meat, and it may not be sauced with turmeric in any shape; and that it is the bachelors alone who may eat the meat of the head of this goat. It is only after the bachelors have finished eating the head, that the rest of the flesh may be eaten by the married young men. But it is different with the meat of the pig, which is served first to the older boys, then to the younger boys, and again to the older boys.

That evening, the newly-admitted boys formally take part in the dancing at the ākhṛā, and then sleep in the Dhumkūṛiā together with the older boys. And this completes their 'unification' with the Dhūmkūriā fraternity.

During the three years of novitiate of each boy, his family has to supply annually a certain quantity of *karanj* (*Pongamia-glabra*) fruit from which oil is extracted for lighting the Dhumkūṛiā house. Generally a Bhuinhār family has to supply for each of its boys ten seers of *karanj* fruit for the first year, fifteen seers for the second year, and twenty seers for the third year, and a non-Bhuinhar has to give for each boy five seers for the first year, ten seers for the second year, and fifteen seers for the third year. A *seer* is equivalent to about two pounds. For purposes of a 'fire-place' to keep the Bachelors' Hall warm during the cold months, the bachelors of the lowest grade have to collect fuel, and may 'steal' it from the houses of any Orāon of the village, and the latter has no right to remonstrate.

Tuition Fees.

(e) Religious and Magico-Religious Observances.

The avowed objects of the religious and magico-religious observances of the Dhumkūṛiā boys are, as we have said, to secure success in hunting and to ensure the multiplication of male progeny, and otherwise to 'make men' of them. From the day following their admission into the Dhumkūṛiā, the novices are given instructions in their social and religious duties.

The magical jug of water.

Every dhāngar has on his admission to provide himself with three new earthen jugs. The night following his admission, each newly-admitted boy has to go stark naked with his earthen-jugs (*chuka*) in his hands to the spring (*dari*) of some neighbouring village. There he stealthily fills his jugs with water mixed with mud from the *dari*. He also picks up and puts into his jugs one or more torn bits of *sal*-leaves which are always found in and about village-springs; for, whenever a new bride or the mother of a new-born babe first goes to a spring to draw water from it, she must go there with a *sal*-leaf containing vermilion diluted in oil to daub the stone of the spring with. The reasons assigned for taking water, mud, *etc.*, from the spring of another village instead of from their own village-spring, are that this will enable them (apparently through sympathetic magic) to secure game from beyond the limits of their own village, that game from other directions will come towards them, and that at the great tribal hunts they will be able to steal an advantage over huntsmen from other villages. Leaves of mango-trees which have not yet borne fruit (*dinda* or 'virgin' leaves) are also put into the jugs. When their earthern jugs are thus filled, the boys go back to their own village, and each boy keeps his jugs concealed in a place known to himself alone, to avoid the evil eye of mischievous persons falling on the jugs. Should any person come to know where they are kept, the boy loses no time in removing his jugs to some other hiding-place. Every night he examines his jugs to judge from their contents if *Chandi* is pleased with him. The Dhāngar-Māhāto himself similarly examines the jug of each boy once a week to see if the boy has been earnest in his 'sewa' or service.*

* Apparently the idea of 'service' has been borrowed from Hinduism. The Orāon's normal attitude towards his deities is that of a human being towards other human beings more crafty and powerful than himself; and control through magic, and not propitiation by service, is the ideal method of dealing with his gods.

The criterion by which this is found out is whether the jugs are full to the brim or not and whether any animal (such as a rat) or any insect (such as a cockroach) has entered them and died there. If a rat or a mouse or a lizard or an insect or other creature is found lying dead in the jugs, it is a sure sign that the Chāndi spirit is pleased with the owner of the jug and the owner will prove a successful huntsman. If it is a dead rat or mouse or similar other animal that is found in any of his jugs, he will be successful with big game; but if it is a dead insect, he will have plenty of small game. A boy in whose jugs no such dead animal or insect is found, or any of whose jugs shows that its water has diminished, is believed to have been remiss in his service (*sewa*) and he is warned to be more diligent and careful in the future. This process of ceremonially filling his jugs with water from the *dari* of a neighbouring village, taking every possible care of his jugs as if they were secret treasures and submitting them to the Dhāngar-Māhāto for examination at the end of the week, is repeated week after week.

Towards the beginning of the following month (*Phagun* or March), one midnight the Dhāngar-Māhāto with the other boys of the Dhumkūṛiā goes to the *tanr* or plot of upland where Chāndi is represented by a stone. There the novices offer up the contents of the earthen jugs—water and all—to the Chāndi spirit. The water in the jugs is poured over the stone, and the *sal*-leaves as well as the dead animals and insects in the jugs are buried underneath the Chāndi-stone. It is believed that this serves to rouse the Spirit into activity. There the Dhāngar-Māhāto proclaims to the boys that the *Phagu-Sendra* or the hunting excursion of the month of *Phagun* (March) will be undertaken on that day week.

The spring Hunt or Phagu-Sendra.

For three consecutive days preceding the day fixed for the Phāgu-Sendrā, the members of the Dhumkūṛiā in a body shout out every morning "Sendrā-sendrā—hārō !"—"The hunt—the hunt—Eh !" On the evening before the appointed day, office-bearers for the hunting expedition are elected in the following manner. A boy of 'mediumistic tendencies' (of *halka chhai* or 'light shade') is blind-folded. The bachelors are seated all around the hall, absent bachelors being represented by small pieces of stone. The blind-folded boy standing at the centre of the hall sets a *lorha* (a round stone used in grinding curry-spices) rolling,* his

* It is believed however that the *lorha* moves of itself and takes the medium along with it to the boy chosen by Chāndi.

own hands slightly touching the *lorha* as it moves. The boys throw grains of rice on the *lorha* saying,—"If thou beest the real Sikāri Chāndi (Hunting Chāndi) that ridest this *lorha*, find out thy flag-bearer." And the boy at whose feet the *lorha* stops is elected as the flag-bearer or Jhāndi-dharoā for the hunting excursions of the year. By the same process they now elect the *Nindaru* or 'sleepeer' whose business is to pretend to fall asleep on the jungle path. Some Orāons, say that the Nindaru lies down in this way to decoy animals ; according to other Orāons the Nindāru lies down in this manner so that deer and other game may, by sympathetic magic, be found lying asleep in the jungle when the party arrive there. The *Khandua* whose duty is to carry on his shoulders (kāndhā) the game killed by the hunters—a duty which is often taken to have been discharged if he carries on his shoulders at least the first animal killed by the party, the *Chekhel Uina* whose duty is to place on the road stones which are supposed by a magical process to intercept all means of escape for the animals, the *Chandi Pahans* or priests for the propitiation of the different Chāndi-spirits,—*viz.*, the Hunting (śikāri) Chāndi, the Mountain (Pāhār Pāt) Chāndi, and so forth,—of the village,—are all similarly elected. In many villages election by the magic sūp* or winnowing-basket process is in use and it is only the priest for the propitiation of the goddess *Chandī* who is elected by the *lorha* process described here.

For three successive nights preceding the hunting expedition, each Chāndi-Pāhān goes out stark naked at midnight, bathes at the village-spring and from there carries water in a pumpkin-gourd and proceeds to the particular Chāndi-stone which he has to propitiate. The other boys follow him at some distance. Arrived at the Chāndi-tānṛ, he washes the Chāndi-stone with the water in his gourd, and puts three parallel vermilion marks on the stone. Then he returns to the Dhumkūṛiā where he puts on his clothes again. In some villages, where one of the Chāndi-stones is comparatively small and portable, it is carried as a fetish by the hunters in every hunting expedition to bring them luck in the chase. This reveals the real magical character of religion at this stage of culture.

The formalities connected with the Spring Hunt are the same as in the Summer Hunt which will be presently described. This Spring Hunt of the Orāons commences eight days before the Phāgu festival in March and continues from day to day generally up to the day of the Phāgu festival. The hunters start for the hunt every day after breakfast and re-

* See *post*, p. 2 4

turn home in the evening. The day after the Phāgu festival, they celebrate the Dhūret Sikār which is but a continuation of the Phāgu Sikār. An essential feature of the Dhūret is that early in the morning one or more men from every family must take their ploughs to one of their fields and ceremonially drive the plough at least one or two times all over the fields. This is known as 'raising dust.' After this is over, the hunters start for the Dhūret Sikār, and, as usual, return home in the evening. Early next morning they go out again for what is known as the *Jarjari Sikar*—the final hunt of the Phāgu Sikār. This time the hunters return home by noon. That day every villager must religiously abstain from ploughing his field. After the hunters have returned home and taken their midday meal, the animals and fowls killed in the hunt during all these ten days and disembowelled the very day they were killed, are brought out, skinned and dressed, and the meat is distributed amongst the Orāon families of the village. The hunter who actually killed a particular animal or fowl is given one of its legs as his extra share.

In some villages where the Sarhul ceremony is ordinarily held much later than in other villages, new flowers and fruits of the season are ceremonially gathered for the first time during the Jarjari Sikār, taken to the village-Pahān's house, and there in the presence of the village-elders are offered by the Pāhān to the deity Chhālo Pāchcho or Sarnā Buṛhiā. These offerings are then distributed to all the villagers. By this ceremonial offering of the first fruits to the deity, the usual tabu against gathering or using new flowers and fruits of the season until the celebration of the Sarhūl festival, is removed.

The Summer Hunt or Bisu Sikar.

In the month of Baiśākh (April-May) the Orāons have their greatest hunt of the year. This is known as the Kohā Sendrā or Great Hunt, and also as *Bisu sikar*. Information is sent round beforehand on market-days to the different market-places. It is the *Kotwar* of the Pārhā who carries the information from village to village and is paid one *anna* or so by every village for his trouble. He goes with his drum (nāgera) and proclaims that it is the order of the Pārhā Rājā that the Orāons of the Pārhā are to start on their annual Bisu-śikār excursion on such and such a day. This method of sending round information to different villages is known as 'circulating the twig' (dahūrā).* People of several *Parhas* with flags and drums (*nagera*) and bugles (*narsingha*) go out

* Formerly, it appears, the usual method of sending messages was through a messenger carrying a *sal* or other twig. The name (dahurā bhulānā) now remains though the method of sending messages has changed.

together to some distant forest or hill-range, armed with their bows and arrows, their spears and swords, their axes and their clubs of various shapes and sizes. A few hunters take trained dogs with them which they hold in leashes. It is believed that if the party while starting for the hunt happen to come across a corpse or dead animal they will have remarkable success in hunting. No woman is permitted to go about with pitchers for drawing water while the hunters start on their excursion. Before the hunters leave the village, the women must have returned home with water from the village-spring or stream, or else they may not go out for fetching water until the party have left the village. If any of the hunters happen to have with him any coin while going out for the hunt, he is sure, so the Orāons believe, to fare ill at the hunt. So all pieces of coin they may wish to take with them are made over to the bearers (bhāriās) who carry the rations of the hunters. The huntsmen leave home on a Thursday evening and return to their villages generally on the Tuesday following. During all these days not only do the men of the party, but all the members of their families left behind in their villages must observe strict sexual continence. It is believed that if this tabu is disregarded by any Orāon, male or female, his or her fellow-villagers or at any rate the members of his or her family who may have joined the hunt, are sure to have ill success at the hunt. Another tabu which the stay-at-home Orãons of such villages have to observe is that they must not kill, beat, or even purchase any eatable fowl or animal so long as the hunters are away from home.

An interesting feature of this Summer Hunt is that so long as the men are out hunting, the Orãon women of the village behave like men. Several of them dress like men, go about with men's *läthis* or sticks in their hands, and use the jargon of the males. As for instance, they say to each other 'guchã hõ bechã ho!' (come along, let us dance)—as men say while talking to each other, instead of saying 'guchãe bechãe ho!' as women ordinarily say to each other. The women also pose as men before strangers coming to or passing through the village, and realise drink-money from them by threatening to poke them with their *lathis*. Orãon women of such villages are by common consent allowed at this period perfect liberty to behave in this way, and even alien landlords and Police-officers submit to their demands for drink-money. The utmost license of speech is also permitted to these women, and they may with impunity abuse any man they meet in the filthiest language they choose.

During these days, the women also set up an *ākhrā* or dancing-ground for themselves in the village. This ākhrā is called the *chhot* or minor *ākhrā*, and here the women sing and dance till a late hour of the night in the manner of young men. If during these days, any Orāon woman refuses to join the dances at the *Chot äkhrà*, the other women pour water over her head, poke at her with their *lāthis*, and finally drag her by force to the dancing-ground. The idea seems to be that to omit the village-dances during these nights bodes ill for the village,—and perhaps for the hunters too. Two motives appear to lie at the root of this custom,—first, an anxiety to let the outside world know that everything is going on as before in the village so that enemies may not know that the fighting people of the village are away; and, secondly, and principally, the superstition that if the people in the village are merry, the hunters also will, by sympathetic magic have cause to be merry. After they have finished their dances at the ākhrā, the women approach the houses of such men as have not joined the hunting-party, poke their *lathis* at the doors of their huts, taunt the men (except of course old men and young children) as womanly cowards and abuse them in the filthiest language they can think of . Before proceeding to the *akhra* they generally drive away these stay-at-home men temporarily from the village, unless they have themselves already taken care to keep themselves out of their way.

To return to the Bisu-Sikār party. The day before the party start on their expedition, office-bearers of the expedition are elected in the following manner. The wife of the Village-Pāhān goes to theā khrā with a jug-ful of water, a little cow-dung, and some rice on a winnowing basket. Arrived there, she clears a small space towards the centre of the *akhra* with cow-dung and water. A fresh twig of a sāl tree is now split at one end so as to form a fork, and the winnowing basket is fitted into this forked end. A boy of known mediumistic tendencies is now blind-folded and the sāl twig with the magic *sup* fitted into its fork and lightly touching the ground is put into his hand. The bachelors are all ranged round the ākhrā,—absent ones being represented by pieces of stone. As the medium and his magic *sup* move on, the boys throw handfuls of rice on the *sup*, saying, "Choose the right person for performing the dāndā-kāttā ceremony." As soon as the *sup* touches the feet of any of the bachelors, that particular bachelor is selected as the priest who is to officiate at the Dāndā-kāttā ceremony in connection with the projected hunt and his feet are washed by one of the young bachelors. In the same manner the other functionaries,—the flag-bearers, the sleeper (nindāru), the carrier (khānduā), *etc.*, are selected. In some villages, the selection is made by the *lorha* process.

The day before the hunters start on their expedition, each family offers a black (or reddish) fowl or goat to the goddess Chāndi. The spot on which the *semar* or *erendi* trees of the Phāgu festival were ceremonially burnt is selected for the sacrifice. The bachelors then clean the spot with the water of their mystic jugs. On the spot thus cleaned, the weapons of the hunters are arranged in a row, and when the sacrifices are offered, the blood of the sacrificed goats or fowls is sprinkled on these weapons. A portion of the vermilion and rice-flour (*aripan*) used at the sacrifice is also sprinkled on the weapons to add to their strength and effectiveness. The Dhum-kūria boys of the three grades collect tobacco from their houses and make them over to the Dhāngār-Māhāto for the use of the party during the hunting expedition. Next morning the hunters leave their village before day-break so that they may not be seen by other people. The reason for this precaution appears to be the anxiety for avoiding the 'evil eye' of others, which may stand in the way of a successful hunt. When the men of the different villages of each Pārhā are assembled at the appointed forest, the Kotwār of the Pārhā, inquires which village of his Pārhā is represented and which not, and makes his report accordingly to the Rājā and other principal office-bearers of the Pārhā. Should any village happen to be unrepresented, the hunters on their way back from the chase generally pass through such village and, as of right, kill and carry away one or two pigs belonging to the Orāons of that village.

All the animals and fowls bagged by the hunters of a particular Pārhā are divided in equal divisions between such of the villages of that Pārhā as have joined the hunt. The Kotwār of the Pārhā is given a handful of meat out of each such division, and the hunter who has actually killed a particular game gets a leg of such game. As each division of the meat is taken up, the man who takes it up receives from the Pārhā-Kotwār a stroke of his stick. This is probably meant to impart strength to the person by a process of magic transferrence of *mana*.

When the hunters from each village approach the limits of their village, they subdivide their division of game into as many shares as there are families of Orāons in the village. Even families whose members consist of only women and old men and children who could not take part in the hunt, are given their respective shares. The dogs, too, that assisted at the hunt, are each given a share of the meat.* Now the hunters enter their village with their flags gaily flaunting in the air and their drums and bugles sounding triumphal music. As soon as the hunters enter their respective houses, the Orāon women of the village, each carrying a plate filled with water, go about from house to house washing the feet of the hunters and making their salutations to them as to heroes arrived home in triumph after a glorious victory. And, as a matter of fact, these hunting expeditions are even to this day sometimes attended with fights between different villages amongst whom disputes arise as to the rights to take a particular game. And if these disputes remain undecided even after such fights, or inspite of the mediation of the elders of the Pārhā who attend a hunting expedition as umpires, the quarrel is carried on to the great inter-pārhā dancing-festivals known as Jātrās. On several occasions we have known or heard of such fights at the Jātrās in the course of which grievous hurt has been caused and even lives have been lost. † One

* As for the division of game in the informal one-day hunts, *vide* pp. 156-157, *ante*.

† When however, the matter comes to the Courts, the murder or grievous hurt is generally attributed to some private

curious feature about these fights is that the weapons employed are mostly pieces of stone that are carried about in purse-like bags slung at the shoulders, and are flung with unerring aim with the help of a sling made of a long string doubled up. This warfare with stones reminds you of the description in the Rāmāyana of the *Vanaras* fighting their enemies in the same way.

After their feet have been washed and they have been refreshed by a cup or so of rice-beer at their own houses, the hunters go about from house to house and help themselves to one or more cups of rice-beer at each house. For, every family has brewed one or more jars of rice-beer for the occasion. As the hunters thus go about from house to house, they make over their shares of meat to the families of widows and others who could not join the hunt.

In the month of Jeth (June, July), when, in consequence of the rains, deer and other game generally collect in certain sheltered spots in the jungles, the Orāons of each Pārhā go out in a body to hunt in some big jungle. The office-bearers of the hunt are elected in the same way as in the Summer-

grudge borne by a particular individual or individuals, and the rest of the offenders generally escape punishment. The police-officers are generally ignorant of the custom and so cannot find out the real facts

Hunt. In such a hunt, the hunters stay away from the village for a week or more, and so it is also known as a *Basa-sikar* or a hunt in which the hunters camp out.

It is worthy of note that no Orāon may kill any wild animal in the months of Sāwan and Bhādo (middle of July to middle of September.) The reason for this hunting tabu appears to be the fear of injury to the growing paddy-crop, which may, through sympathetic magic, follow the slaying of the beasts and birds of the forests.

Chandi as the giver of progeny.

It is not success in hunting or in war alone that Chāndi the chief deity of the hunting stage of primitive Orāon culture is believed to confer on Orāon youth. Through appropriate magic rites, Chāndi may be made to impart sufficient strength to the procreative powers of the young men so as to enable them to indefinitely increase the number of huntsmen in the tribe. Among such ceremonies for the multiplication of male progeny may be mentioned the *Puja* or propitiation of Mūtri Chāndi, celebrated shortly after the Sarhūl festival. For three successive nights, while the unmarried young men and women dance at the village ākhrā, the young bachelors rob the ens of their ear-ornaments called *bindios*. A little after sunset on the fourth day all the Orāon youths of the village assemble at the ākhrā. From there the unmarried boys proceed to the tānr or upland where the Mūtri Chāndi is represented by a stone half-buried under a tree. A boy *pahan* or priest who has been selected at the ākhrā by the *lorha* method described above, digs a hole at the foot of the Chāndi stone, sacrifices a black fowl and consigns its blood and severed head into the hole, together with the *bindios* looted from the ears of the village maidens. While all these offerings are being thrown into the hole, the boys all shout in one voice : "*Kukkoe khaddar ghaträ-nekä, kukko khaddar bärhnà nekä,*" "May female children decrease, (and) may male children increase." After this, all the bachelors micturate into the hole, which is then filled up with earth. After the hole is thus covered over with earth, the boys proceed to a short distance from the Chāndi stone and from there pelt clods of earth at the tree so that the clods may come down and fall just over the filled-up hole. As the object of this micturation appears to be to magically strengthen the procreative powers of the young men, so the object of this pelting of clods of earth at the tree is probably to secure by a magical process an infallible aim at birds or animals in the chase. From the Mūtri Chāndi *tanr*, the boy-priest is carried on the shoulders of the other boys to the house of the village-priest (Pāhān). Arrived there the boys leave the boy-priest in the middle of the village-priest's kitchen, and the former begins forthwith to put his hands into the cooking-pots and help himself greedily to whatever remnants of food he may find there. The females of the Pāhān's family now come out with plates and cups filled with water, and throw the water at the boy-*pahan*. The other boys, in the meanwhile, go on pelting clods of earth at the walls of the *Pahan's* house. Thence the boy-*pahan* and the other boys all proceed to the ākhrā, and dancing and singing go on till a late hour of the night.

Magical augmentation of procreative energy.

Besides magical accession of procreative energy from the deities, such magical augmentation of procreative vigour may also be derived from capable men and from such powerful natural objects as the *sal* tree. Such a belief is probably evidenced by the following Orāon custom. Twice in the year, once about a week before the Phāgū festival in March, and again about a week before the Sarhūl festival in April or May, the boys of the Dhumkūṛiā are led forth by the Dhumkūiṛā Mahāto to a suitable secluded place some way off from their village. Each pair of boys carry on their shoulders a *bahinga* or wooden pole from each end of which is slung a *sika* or carrying-net with a basket in it. The Dhumkūṛiā Māhāto carries a new thin *sal* stick and also a *sal* (*shorea robusta*) sapling in which a slit has been made to resemble the female organ.* When they have reached a suitable spot in a jungle or on some waste upland, the boys fill their baskets with red ferruginous earth (*panjri khajj* or *lalmati*). When their baskets are filled to the brim, the boys besmear one another all over the body with red earth. The Dhumkūṛiā Māhāto has in the meanwhile planted the *sal* sapling firmly on the ground. The boys of the two upper grades now spit into the slit in the sapling. The boys of the lowest grade have now to strip themselves absolutely naked, and each boy in turn has to insert his organ into the saliva-filled slit. All the time, the boy-Māhāto stands beside the *sal* sapling with the new *sal*-wood stick in his hand. And as each boy is about to step back after performing the magic operation, the Māhāto

* In some of the Dhumkūṛiās you may see a similar slit in the central post supporting the roof. And in one Dhumkūṛiā we found the central post rudely carved into a human figure with a slit representing the female organ Such a wooden post is familiarly known as the mistress (*dubri*) of the Dhumkuṛiā bachelors. Besides its other uses, it serves to scare away young boys seeking to pry into the secrets of the Dhumkuṛiā.

strikes the boy on his thigh a little below the groin with his *sal* stick. After the ceremony is over, the novices place their clothes on their carrying-poles and carry to the ākhrā the baskets of earth slung in nets suspended from the ends of the poles, and return to the ākhrā quite naked. The boys of the two higher grades follow them with their clothes on. Arrived at the ākhrā, they all go round the dancing-ground three times. After this ceremonial circumambulation they all sit down on the ground with shouts of "Ho! Ho! Ho!" Then the red earth in the baskets is poured over the ākhrā-ground and the boys go home. In the evening, the boys of the lowest grade gather dry leaves which they pile over the heaps of red earth, and set fire to the leaves so as to make the earth redder still. The ashes are then blown away with a winnowing fan and the pulverised earth is spread out over the floor of the ākhrā. Here,as in several other customs of the Orāons, we see a persistent endeavour to gain an accession of power through alliance with the powerful forces of Nature and of man. The saliva of efficient young men and contact with the powerful *sal* sapling and the *sal* stick, are evidently supposed to promote fecundity. And the object of the ceremony seems to be a magical accession of power to the procreative organs.

(*f*). Training in Social Duties.

Besides qualifying young men for the work of procuring food for the family, and of maintaining the stability of the community by increasing its numerical strength, the Dhumkūṛiā organization is further designed to make the young men otherwise useful and serviceable members of the community. When there is a wedding or other feast in the house of an Orāon of the village, it is the young men of the Dhumkūṛiā who have to dress the animals and fowls killed for the occasion and to act as cooks and otherwise look to the comforts of the guests. When guests visit an Orāon's house, where there is no adequate accommodation, they are accommodated in the Dhumkūṛiā, and the younger members of the Dhumkūṛiā have to shampoo the legs of the guests. Besides this, they have to regularly shampoo the legs of the older boys of the Dhumkūṛiā as also of such Orāons of the village as may go to the Dhumkūṛiā of an evening to have their limbs shampooed. In most Dhumkūṛiā houses you see hundreds of wooden scrapers of the shape of shoe-horns hanging in rows from the central beam. With these the younger boys scrape the soles of the elder boys' feet to remove dried-up bits of scarf-skin. If any villager is in need of the services of labourers for thatching a house or for some other similar purpose, he applies to the Dhāngar-Māhāto and strikes a bargain with him. At the bidding of the Dhāngar-Māhāto, the Dhumkūṛiā boys go in a body to do the job. The wages received are generally spent in the purchase of some new musical instruments or other requisites (such as cloth for making flags) for the Dhumkūṛiā. When a fine is imposed by the village-panchāyat on a young man for some sexual offence, and pigs *etc.*, are purchased with the fine, portions of the meat are distributed to every village of the Pārhā, and it is the Dhumkuṛiā boys who have to carry the meat to the different villages of the Pārhā. Such meat is known as Khāonrō or *sandes.*

Treatment of the younger boys by the older boys.

As we have already said, something like military discipline is enforced in the Dhumkūṛiā. It is the younger boys whose lot is the hardest of all They have to fag for the older boys, run their errands, keep the Dhumkūṛiā house well-provided with fuel, and to keep the hall clean and tidy. If a dog or other animal or bird happens to dirty the house and the younger boys do not clean it before it comes to the notice of theolder boys, the younger boys are made to press the excrement with their own hands, make it into small balls, and finally throw away the balls. Should a young boy happen to wet his bed, the older boys stick a hair-pin into the soiled ground and spit upon this hair-pin, and then the offending boy is compelled to take up the pin from the ground with his own teeth. Should he refuse to undergo this punishment, his family has to supply the Dhumkūṛiā fraternity with one pot of rice-beer, one fowl and one gourdful of *urid* pulse (*phaseolus Roxburghii*) by way of fine. The most demoralising errand, however, on which the younger boys are employed by the senior members of the Dhumkūṛriā, is to bring them girls from the girls' dormitory (*pel-erpa*). Should the younger boys show any disinclination to obey, their legs are pressed by the older boys with wooden pincers until they do what they are bidden. When the girls who are sent for come near the Dhumkūṛiā, each of the older boys retires with the girl of his choice to some straw-stack or other sheltered place in the vicinity. Should a girl refuse to come when sent for, a number of young boys are despatched to bring her by force. When she is brought, should she refuse to elect a mate, a number of the older boys, we are informed by several Orāons, violate her one after the other, until she names the boy she would have for her mate. Generally, however, most young bachelors have their respective favourites among the maidens, and the liking is reciprocated. In fact, the older girls decide beforehand which boy will suit a particular girl and in this choice the wishes of the younger girls and of the boys concerned are considered. The wishes of the boy are generally signified by his wearing a particular flower or other thing which a particular girl habitually wears. And we have been told by young Orāon boys that shortly after their admission into the Dhumkūṛiā, most of them fix upon particular girls as their respective future sweet-hearts. During the first three years of Dhumkūṛia life, however, a boy is not permitted to have intimacy with a girl. If a girl does not agree to have a mate from amongst the boys of the Dhumkūṛiā, she is 'cut' by the older girls who refuse to dance with her or otherwise mix with her, until she agrees to do what she is told. Such illicit companionship of a boy with a girl goes on, it is said, till after the young man or young woman has been married, and sometimes until a child has been born to either of them. But such companionship seldom ends in marriage. Marriage between boys and girls of the same clan (*gotra*) is strictly prohibited, and even when the boy and the girl are of different clans, a marriage between a boy and a girl of the same village is not considered desirable. Community of clan is, however, (in practice, though not in theory) often no bar to premarital intercourse. Cases of abortion, though they seldom come to light, are not rare. To prevent conception, an Oraon maiden either reverses her loin-cloth for the nonce by wearing it with its front side to the back or ties to his loin-cloth just over the abdomen the false plait of hair sometimes worn as a coiffure. When, notwithstanding such precautions, inconvenient consequences follow such pre-marital connexion, the girl is given a glass or two of *phuli* or Mohuā-liquor to drink, and this, it is said, generally serves to cause abortion. If however this fails of the desired effect, the help of a *Kusrain* or midwife (generally of the Ghāsi caste) is sought to cause abortion through medicines. In a very few cases, this course is not adopted, but either the affair ends in a marriage if the boy and the girl belong to different clans; or, if they happen to belong to the same clan, they live together as husband and wife. In the latter case, the young man has to provide a feast to his co-villagers to legalise the union and avoid excommunication. Sons by such a marriage inherit their father's property. It may be noted, that by ancient Orāon custom, it is not permissible for grown-up girls to enter the boys' Dhumkūṛiā-house. It is believed that should a girl do so the inmates of the Bachelors' Hall will for the time being lose their eyesight. This belief is, however, gradually losing ground. The supporters of an older 'group-communism' theory will probably see in these Dhumkūṛiā practices re ics of the stage when 'group-communism' might have been, according to them, the rule amongst this people. In the villages where the Dhumkūṛiā no longer exists, things are some-what better.

Rule of fidelity.

It is after the nocturnal dances at the Akhrā are finished and before they go to sleep in their respective dormitories, that such of the young men as choose to do so, retire with their respective sweet-hearts to such secluded places as a deserted hut, a straw stack, a bush, or a ditch. There appears to exist amongst these Orāon bachelors and maidens a well-recognised rule of fidelity. In case a Dhumkūṛiā boy is found to go with a maiden who is known to be the sweet-heart of another boy, and a complaint to that effect is made to the Dhāngaṛ-Māhāto, the latter on being satisfied of the truth of the complaint, imposes a fine of a rupee or so on the offending boy.

The farewell feast.

The dissolution of the tie binding a young man to his old companions of the Bachelors' Dhumkūṛiā and of the Maidens' Dormitory appears to be signalized by something like a farewell feast. On the day of the marriage of a Dhumkūṛiā boy, his parents hand over one *kat* (about 60 lbs.) of rice to the maidens of the village. The girls pound the rice, boil it and make it into small round cakes. The day following the return home of the bridegroom and his party, the maidens make over these rice-flour cakes to the Dhumkūṛiā boys in five leaf-cups. Each of these leaf-cups must be capacious enough to fit into the head of a man like a cap and reach down to his neck. The bachelors fry these cakes in oil supplied by the parents of the newly-married young man. Then one of the leaf-cups is filled with cakes and is handed back to the maidens of the village, and the rest of the cakes is distributed amongst the members of the Dhumkūṛiā.

(g.) Other Duties and Privileges of the Dhumkuria Bachelors.

Among other duties and privileges of the inmates of the Bachelors' Dormitory, the following may be noticed :—

Gathering Karanj fruit.

(1) The Dhumkūṛiā boys are privileged to gather once in the year fruit from all the Karanj (*Pongamia glabra*) trees of the village, * to whomsoever they may belong. In large villages where

* Now-a-days, however non-Orāon owners of such *Karanj* or *Mohua* trees, when they are on bad terms with the Orāons of the village, occasionally seek revenge against particular Orāons by prosecuting them in the courts as thieves, and the men thus accused generally deny having taken the fruit

there are lots of such trees in different parts of the village-jungles or uplands, they appoint different days for plucking Karanj fruit in different parts of the village. The *Karanj* fruit thus collected are dried in the sun, packed in straw-bags (*moras*) and made over to the charge of the Dhāngar Māhāto. According to the needs of the inmates of the Dhumkūṛia, portions of this *Karanj* are from time to time pressed into oil for lighting lamps (*deorakhi*) with which to illuminate the *akhra* during dances in dark nights.

Gathering Mohua flowers.

(2) By ancient custom, the Dhumkūṛiā boys enjoy a similar license with respect to Mohuā (*Bassia latifolia*) trees in their village and village-jungles. After the *Phagu* festival in the beginning of March and before the Sarhūl festival in April, the Dhumkūṛiā boys fix a day for gathering Mohuā. After evening meal they start in procession, with their drums and bells and cymbals, and go on gathering Mohuā, often till the evening of the following day. The owners of the trees abstain

at all,—for they know that the courts are generally ignorant of such a custom and will not believe in its existence, and the law will not allow such interference with what is now looked upon as private property although, in the eyes of the Orāons, they may still appear as communal property for certain purposes. In some villages the custom is dying out.

from gathering Mohuā so long as the Dhumkūṛia boys have not finished. The Mohuā, thus collected is dried, packed up and made over to the custody of the Dhāngar-Māhāto. When the Dhāngars of the village call a *bhaiari* or *panchayat* of the Dhāngars of the Pārhā, this *Mohua* or a portion of it is taken by the *dhangars* to the nearest grog-shop and the owner of the shop has to allow them to distil liquor from it. He gets no price for it but a present of a fowl and some rice, pulse, and other ingredients sufficient for a good dinner. Sometimes as many as ten or fifteen large earthen jars (*gharas*) of liquor are thus prepared and secretly taken to a village. Should the owner of the shop refuse to accede to their request, the Orāons of the neighbourhood would generally combine and refuse to be his customers unless he makes amends.

Penalty for absence from Jatras.

(3) When the young men of any village have been in the habit of joining the *jatra* held in a neighbouring village in a particular month every year, should such young men omit to attend such *jatra* in any year, the young men of the village in which the jātrā is held would visit the absentee village on the morning following the evening of the jātrā, and, as of right, kill and carry away a pig from that village. It is the Dhāngar Māhāto who has

to make good the loss thus caused to the owner of the pig, for it was the duty of the Dhāngar-Māhāto to have seen that the boys under his charge had joined the jātrā which by ancient usage they were bound to join.

The Dhangars' duties at weddings.

(4) When the bride-price (dāli-tākā) for an Orāon girl of the village is brought by the would-be bridegroom's people, the latter have to pay from four *annas* to a rupee, according to circumstances, to the Dhāngar-Māhāto as the representative of the Dhumkūṛiā boys. And it will be the duty of the Dhumkūṛiā boys, on the occasion of the wedding to act as cooks in the house of the bride's parents. It is only the meals of the bride and bridegroom that are cooked by the members of the family. On the day of the betrothal-feast (kohā-pāhi or barkā-kutmāiti), the members of the family cook the meals for the friends and relatives of the future bridegroom, but as for the other guests it is the Dhumkūṛiā boys of the village who have to cook for them.

Driving away cattle diseases.

(5) An interesting magical ceremony that the Orāon bachelors are required to perform is the driving away of the spirit that causes cattle-disease. When cattle-disease appears in any village in the district, a day is fixed for driving away the disease-spirit. The

village-Kōtwār informs all the villagers of the date so fixed, and in the evening of the appointed day every family leaves one or more old earthen vessels in front of their huts, and as soon as their evening meal is finished all except the bachelors keep indoors and maintain strict silence. At about midnight, when not a breath is to be heard in the village, the young bachelors assemble at the village-ākhṛā, strip themselves perfectly naked, and each takes up a cudgel in his hands. The village cow-herd too is there with a wooden cow-bell (*tharki*) suspended from his neck, (or, sometimes, from his waist). At a signal, the naked bachelors give him chase, with shouts resembling the bellowing of cattle and on the way go on striking with their cudgels all the earthen pots and pans exposed before the huts of the village. Should they happen to meet on the way any person, whether a villager or a stranger, they forthwith belabour him with their sticks; and they are likewise privileged to deal blows with their cudgels on any one who may be heard talking or making any manner of sound. Thus they run on making a show of chasing the cow-herd. On reaching the boundary of the village, the cow-herd advances a few paces into the limits of the adjoining village, quickly drops down his cow-bell and beats a hasty retreat. His pursuers too go up to the spot where the cow bell, which seems to represent the disease-spirit, has been dropped by the cow-herd, and there leave their own cudgels too and return to their village perfectly satisfied that the disease-spirit is now safely chased out of their village. The men of the village to which the disease-spirit has thus been transferred will, in their turn, send it on by the same process to the village next to their own in the direction opposite to that of the other village; and thus it goes on until the disease-spirit has been altogether chased out of the district. In such a case, it is not so much the fear of physical force as the pressure of the cumulative *mana* or spiritual energy of the batch of naked bachelors that is believed to compel the disease-spirit to take its flight.

Bird-driving or Ora-khedna.

(6) In December every year, a day or two before the annual hārborā (bone-burial) day, *dhangars* of all the three 'tūṛs' or classes go out in a body after breakfast with their nets and dogs and drums and flags to ceremonially drive away and, if possible catch birds that eat up paddy grains. As the party go about from field to field, shouting and clapping their hands, they gather some paddy grains from every field they pass through. They also catch as many birds as they can. In the evening they return and thresh the

paddy on some rocky place (tāngrā). In some villages this paddy is set apart for meeting the expenses of the Chāndi puja in the month of Māgh. In other villages the rice is sold, and the proceeds go to the funds of the *dhumkuria*.

Mandar-sala

(7) In some villages, generally in villages where a jātrā is held, the *dhangars* have what are known as Māndar-sālās. These consist of two or more clay pillars of the shape of small pyramids erected side by side on a bit of fallow up-land. One of these is higher than the others. The higher one measures from eight to twelve feet in height and the lower ones from about five to eight feet. Every year on the day of the annual village-*karbori* or other jātrā-day the dhangars bring *potni-mati* (a kind of whitish clay with an admixture of lime) to paint the māndar-sālās with. They first add fresh earth mixed with water, and, in some villages, mixed with their own urine, * to the *Mandar-salas* so as to repair any breaches made by rain water during the rains, then plaster the *Mandar-salas* over with the *potni-mati*, and also besmear their own bodies with the same earth. Then they go to some stream, wash them-

* In the villages with Mandar-salas to which I have been, only water is now used but I am credibly informed that in some villages human urine is used and not water.

selves, change their clothes, and seize a few chickens belonging to the villagers and make them over to the village Pāhān for the Jātrā-Puja to be held next day. Then the boys take their breakfast, and with their flags and drums, their nets and their dogs proceed to drive away birds and, when possible catch them. They first go to the Mandar-sala tāṅṛ, circum-ambulate it three times and then proceed to 'drive away birds' from the fields. The village Māhatō and village Pāhān remain fasting the whole day. Paddy is gathered from every field, and used as described in the last paragraph.

Kohra-Mokhna. (8). In some villages the day after the *Pus-jatra*, the dhāngaṛs assemble on a rocky place. Each dhāngaṛ brings one *Kohnra* (pumpkin) to the headmen of the Dhāngaṛs. Each dhāngaṛ also brings some *chiura*. The Kōhrās are boiled by the Dhāngaṛs. All the villagers are informed, and they assemble there to discuss all the important affairs of the year. Then they are feasted with the Kohṛā and chiuṛā.

Mice-catching. (9). In some villages from the month of Kātik each of the Dhumkūṛiā boys goes on catching mice which are dried up after being killed, skinned, and disembowelled. One day in the month of Māgh, at an appointed place all the dhāngaṛs assemble, each with the mice collected by him. There each boy puts down his mice on a small plank of wood. The *mukhias* weigh the mice collected by each boy. If this falls short of the required measure, the boy has to pay a fine. Mice that fall out of the plank are not taken into account. The boy is given back one leaf-cupful of the mice, and the rest are taken charge of by the *mukhias*. When all the mice have been weighed and fines realised, the mice are roasted, and liquor purchased with the fines realised, and all the villagers have a merry time of it. This feast, like the feast of chiuṛā and kobṛā would appear to be survivals of what were once sacramental meals.

Bhaiyari.

(10). Once in a way you witness the very interesting spectacle of a *bhaiyari* or friendly gathering of the Dhumkūṛiā young men of two or more villages. Generally, the occasion for such a social gathering is the formal present to another village of a flag, bearing a particular device, by the young men of a village which has hitherto used the particular device as its own exclusive property. On a day appointed beforehand, generally in the afternoon, the young men of the former village approach the latter village with music. At the sound of the music, the young men of the latter village go out to welcome their guests with jugfuls of water, handfuls of *arua* rice, and with bundles of leafy mango-twigs. As soon as they meet their guests, they wash their feet, sprinkle *arua* rice on them and throw the benedictory mango-twigs at them. Then they all make obeisance to one another, and dance together. In the evening, the guests are billeted in batches to the houses of the different Orāon families in the village. It is on this occasion that the young bachelors of the village have to enter into the 'sangi' from of friendship with the young bachelors of the other village. The socio-political significance of this artificial alliance will be referred to in sub-section III, below. After their evening meal, they all dance together often until the following morning. At about 10 A.M., they are escorted to some open space, where they all sit down, clean their teeth with wooden tooth-brushes (dātun) supplied by their hosts, wash their mouths, and discuss topics that interest them. In the after-noon, a feast is provided with the funds, if any, of the Dhumkūṛiā or with money raised by subscription in the village. The *Mukhias* or headmen of the Dhumkūṛiā supervise the feast. And now when the time for giving them farewell is at hand, the flag or other ensign is ceremonially handed over by the headman of the Dhumkūṛiā to the leader of the guests.

(11). When a village Panchāyat imposes a fine on any Orāon young man of the village for some sexual offence—such as the abduction of a married Orāon girl, intrigue (leading to inconvenient consequences) with a girl of the same clan or with a girl of forbidden degrees of relationship,—portions of the meat of pig, *&c.*, purchased with the fine are sent through selected Dhāngaṛs by the Dhāngaṛ Māhāto of the village to the Dhāngaṛ-Māhātos of the other villages of the Pārha for the Dhāngaṛs of those villages. * Such presents of meat are known as Khaoṛō or *Sandes.*

Khaoṛo.

II. The Maidens' Dormitory.

Here it will not be out of place to briefly notice the sister institution of the Maidens' Dormitory (*Pel-Eṛpa*) and its relation to the Bachelors' Dormitory.

* In justice to a growing section of non-Christian Orāons eager for the moral, intellectual and material improvement of their tribe, we must make it clearly understood that in villages in which their influence has penetrated the objectionable practices mentioned in this chapter are being abandoned. Among Christian converts, such practices are out of the question. And in many non-Christian villages too the village dormitories no longer exist, and the practices connected therewith are more or less falling into disuse.

Constitution and Management.

The dormitory for Orāon maidens is not, like the bachelors' dormitory, a public building, and its location is not supposed to be known to any one except its inmates and to those of the Bachelors' Dormitory. There are no office-bearers attached to the Maidens' Dormitory, but an elderly male Orāon is appointed Pelō-Kōtwār by the elders of the village to act, as the supervisor of the girls during the village-dances at the ākhrā and the tribal jātrā-dances. This Pelō-Kōtwār is held responsible for any scandal that may occur in connection with the village-maidens, and is fined by the village elders for his remissness. As his perquisite he receives one *anna* (one penny) from each girl when the year's jātrās are finished. It is generally the most intelligent among the oldest maidens, however, who is regarded as the natural leader of the other maidens. She is sometimes called the Baṛkā Dhāngṛin. She, in consultation with the other girls of her class, directs and controls the inmates of the maiden's dormitory. As in the boys' dormitory so also in the girls,' three years is the term of novitiate during which the novices have to do all the drudgery connected with the institution. Once in three years a fresh batch of maidens are admitted into the Pel-eṛpā. The maidens are, like the bachelors, divided into three tūṛs or grades according to age.

Duties and privileges of the maidens.

Among the duties and privileges of the Orāon maidens, the following may be noticed :—

The maidens' presents of mats to the bachelors.

(1). During the three years of her novitiate, each Orāon maiden is required every year to plait a strip of pātiā or palm-leaf-mat about six inches wide and as long as the length of the Bachelors' Hall. All the strips of mat thus plaited every year by the maidens are made over to the dhumkūṛiā boys who stitch together the different strips of mat into two or more mats covering the entire width of the Dumkūṛiā hall. These mats made by the maidens serve the Dhumkūṛiā bachelors for beds for one year, at the expiration of which they are renewed by similar presents of strips of mat from the maidens.

The maidens' presents of barley-shoots to the bachelors.

(2). In the month of Bhādō (August), seven days before the Karam festival, the Orāon maidens of the village carry two basketfuls of sand to their own dormitory, deposit this sand on the floor of their dormitory, scatter over this sand a few handfuls of barley-seeds, and cover them over with a thin layer of sand. Every night up till the Karam festival on the eleventh night of the moon, the maidens sprinkle water over the sand and sit up late at night singing songs and watching the seeds germinating. On the morning following the Karam festival, the maidens take up the seeds with shoots sprouting out of them, and distribute these germinated barley-seeds to the young Orāons of the village who all assemble at the village-ākhrā at the time and also to such other Orāons of the village as may happen to be present at the ākhrā at the time. When the young men have received these mystic presents, the youth of both sexes dance together at the ākhrā. Although the meaning of this rite is no longer remembered by the people, it looks like a magical ceremony designed to improve the fecundity of the young people, and also perhaps to stimulate the growth of the standing crops of the fields.

Preparation of wedding cakes.

(3). The services of the maidens are indispensable at Orāon weddings. The chief of these services is to pound rice and boil the pounded rice and make it into small balls which are dignified with the name of wedding-cakes (*pithas*). One evening, the Orāon maidens of the village are called to the māṛoā or mud-pulpit erected for the marriage-ceremony. The mistress of the house brings out a basket filled with *arua* rice. Now one of the maidens stands behind the bride or bride groom, as the case may be, and closes with her hands the eyes of the bride or bridegroom. The latter with closed eyes and the palms of the hands joined together takes up three or five handfuls of rice from the basket and throws them into another basket. This rice becomes the perquisite of the maidens. Then the mistress of the house puts into the basket as much rice as may be required to prepare cakes (*pithas*) sufficient for the benedictory *karsa* to be used at the wedding and for distribution to all friends and relatives who may attend the *Karsa-uthana* ceremony which is a necessary preliminary to the wedding. To these maidens is allotted a separate hut in which to prepare the cakes. There they take the rice and leave it steeped in water. After evening meal, they pound the rice. This rice-flour is now mixed up with water and kneaded. The dough is rounded into small balls which are then boiled in water. When these are sufficiently boiled, the water is thrown away and the rice-flour cakes are ready for use. Throughout these operations, which continue almost till daybreak, the maidens go on singing song after song of love and marriage. And many a merry jest and much hearty laughter enliven them in their tedious work. Next morning three young bachelors are called to the courtyard (āngan) of the house to select, out of a bundle of paddy-sheaves, suitable ears of paddy for the *Karsa* which is meant to bless the wedded pair with prosperity. This 'Kārsā' consists of a crown made of selected ears of paddy and wound round an earthen pitcher which is carried on the head by one of the women dancing the benedictory marriage-dance. The maidens hand over to each of these three young bachelors one dōnā or leaf-cup filled with wedding cakes and then one dōnā of cakes to each of the village-elders—the Māhāto and the Pāhān,—and to the wife of the Māhāto and the wife of the Pāhān, as also to the village Gōṛāit, and finally one dōnā to each of the assembled guests. Of the cakes some are of larger size and called 'bāinā-lāddu' and are meant for those related as elder brothers or elder cousins of the bridegroom. The surplus cakes are kept carefully apart. When all the marriages of the year are finished, the surplus cakes of all the houses are taken to the Dhumkūṛiā boys assembled at a fixed place, and the cakes taken from each house are placed a little apart from the cakes from the houses of others. The maidens prepare a number of small cups of sāl leaves, and as many large leaf-bowls as the number of the different boys of the village married during the year: Each of these leaf-bowls is as large as the head of one of those boys. The cakes from each house are measured with the leaf-bowl that represents the head-measure of the young man of that house who was married during the year. Seven such measures form the share of the Dhumkūṛiā boys, and the balance forms the share of the Orāon maidens of the village. Out of the boys' share, however, one small cupful has to be given to each Orāon family in the village.

The Gairahi Karsa.

(4). In some villages, after the annual bone-burial (hār-bōṛi) ceremony in December when the bones of all the Orāons of a village who have died since the preceding sowing season are ceremonially disposed of, cakes are prepared by the maidens in the same way as for a wedding and a *Karsa* is similarly prepared with ears of paddy selected by young bachelors. This *Karsa* is known as the *gairahi-karsa* or the common 'kārsā', and is ceremonially carried on the head by one of a group of maidens who go all about the village dancing and singing as at a wedding. This kārsā is similarly carried on the head by one of the women dancing at what is called the Hāṛbōri-jātrā or the dancing festival in connection with the bone-burial ceremony. This jātrā or dancing festival takes place on the day after the Hārbōri ceremony of the village, and it is only after this ceremonial dance with the *gairahi* kārsā that any marriage may be celebrated in the village. *Gairahi-karsas* are similarly prepared and carried to the *Magh-jatra* and other jātrās by Orāon women of villages where jātrās are held.

(5). The maidens as well as the young bachelors of a village where a bridal procession is expected, go in a body up to the boundary of the village singing and dancing to greet the bridal party. When the actual wedding ceremony is over and the bride and bridegroom are being anointed with oil and turmeric, the maidens of the village come to them in a body. The bridegroom's party make a present to them of a quantity of rice-flour which the former have brought with them from their village. One of the maidens dips one of her fingers into the rice-flour to see if there is enough for them all. If the quantity is not considered sufficient the maidens will have to be satisfied by the bridegroom's people by paying them the approximate price of the balance of rice-flcur demanded.

Other duties of the maidens.

(6). As Orāon who requires the services of the maidens of his village to reap his paddy-crops, applies to the Barkā-dhāngṛins (the senior maidens) for 'pachā' service. At the bidding of the Barkā-dhāngṛins, all the maidens go in a body to reap the paddy. By way of

Maidens' Pacha.

remuneration they are given one goat or pig once in three years besides their meals for the days they are thus employed. Besides this, whenever the maidens require rice-beer (hānṛiā) for their festivals, such as at the Karam festival in which the girls have to provide the bachelors with one pot of beer for their trouble in guarding the sacred Karam-branches,—it is from such people as habitually employ their pāchā-labour that the maidens look for the required pot of rice-beer.

Women's (Jani) Sikar or Mukka-sendra.

(7). Once in twelve years, Orāon maidens, with generally a sprinkling of married women, go out on a pretended hunting expedition, armed with *lathis* (sticks), spears and axes, and wearing *pagṛis* or turbans on their heads, and *pechouris* or cloth-sheets wound round their bodies in the manner of men. One female from each Orāon family must join the 'hunt'. Arriving at the village next to theirs in a particular direction, they go to the ākhrā of the village where they dance for a while. The wife of the village-Goṛāit accompanies them with a nāgerā or drum. Then they chase a pig belonging to some Orāon of that village. And if they cannot or do not kill a pig, the men of the village make up the price of a pig by raising a subscription amongst themselves and pay the amount to the female 'hunters'. If a pig is killed by these female 'hunters', the money thus raised is paid to the owner of the pig by way of compensation. The women of the village where the pig is killed, in their turn proceed in similar guise to the village next to theirs in the same direction as the direction of their own village from that of the female hunting party who just visited their village.*

Driving away Public calamities.

(8). The 'women's hunt' does not appear to have been in its origin, as it is not indeed in its present form, a real hunting expedition. It rather appears to belong to a class of ceremonial expeditions undertaken with the object of transferring, by magic, real or fancied calamities from the country. To this class belong the two varieties of the Rōg-Khednā expedition, one undertaken by men and the other by women—generally married women.

When a rumour is somehow set afloat that in a certain village at one or other extremity of the country—no one knows where—some unusual misfortune has occurred to cattle,—as, for example, a cow has given birth to a pig, or plough-cattle

* It is sometimes supposed on the strength of a Hindi song that this hunt (Jani-sikar) was started by a Raja of the Nagbansi family. But there appear to be strong reasons against accepting this interpretation of the song.

have refused to work and have been found invariably lying down on the ground when taken to the fields,—it is the men who have to undertake the 'Rōg-khednā' expedition; when, on the other hand, the rumoured calamity refers to child-birth—as, for instance, a human mother giving birth to animals or fowls or to monstrous human children,—it is the duty of the Orāon women to undertake a similar expedition. Before the party start for the next village, the women of every Orāon family sweep the floors and court-yards of their respective houses and clean them with cowdung and water. The sweepings are then carried to the nearest stream or pool of water and thrown away. Then the women return home, bathe, and, in some villages, the Pāhān or Pāhānāin burns incense (the gum of Sāl tree) at the village-Pāhān's house. Then men or women as the case may be, go out from house to house in their own village, carrying one or two bamboo-baskets, a brass *lota*, and a few mango twigs, and receive a handful of rice or māṛuā from each house. Then they proceed to the next village in the direction opposite to that in which the calamity is said to have occurred. As soon as they enter the next village in that direction, they go from house to house with their baskets and at each house receive a handful of rice or maṛuā. Then they proceed to the second village in the same direction, and collect doles of rice, maṛuā, *etc.*, in the same way. Thus, after finishing three villages including their own, they retire at mid-day to some selected spot on the outskirts of the last village they visited, boil as much of the rice or *marua* as they require for their mid-day meal, and eat the food thus prepared. Then they sell the balance of the rice and māṛuā, and with the sale-proceeds buy liquor with which they cheer up their spirits, and then return home. Next day the men or women, as the case may be, of the villages visited the preceding day start on a similar expedition in the same direction. And thus the calamity is driven away from village to village till it is altogether driven out of the Orāon country. In such an expedition, the meń go under the lead of the village Pāhān and a few other village elders, and the women under the lead of the wife of the Pāhān and a few other elderly women of the village. It is now sometimes asserted that through the penance of begging and the 'merit' of giving alms, the 'Sin' which brought on the calamity is removed. But clearly these ideas of 'penance' and 'religious merit' are imported from Hindu beliefs, and the original idea (even now entertained by the majority of the Orāons) behind the practice is a magical transference of the calamity. The better informed Oraon will tell you that such a monstrosity is born only when some Orāon woman has had sexual intercourse within forbidden degrees of relationship or with a man of another tribe ; and such breach of sexual tabu by an individual woman of the tribe is sure to be visited on the tribe as a whole, unless such an expiatory expedition is undertaken.

And, in this connexion, we may notice another class of supposed calamities for which such a 'Rōg-khednā' or 'disease-driving' expedition is undertaken. Should a woman happen to drive the plough, even for a minute, the whole village would be thrown into consternation, as drought and famine would be apprehended as the consequence. The offending woman's family, in such a case, is fined by the village Panchayat ; and the offending woman it is said, is, or at any rate formerly used to be, yoked to the plough she handled. But, in any case, a 'Rōg-khednā' expedition has to be undertaken by the village. Recently such an expedition was even undertaken by the Orāons of a village where a non-Orāon resident—a Muhammadan—had in a fit of drunkeness accused his wife of laziness and forced her to drive the plough for a short while only. The touch of a woman, it is believed, impairs the strength and effectiveness of a plough and of certain other implements and weapons. If an Orāon cultivator while driving the plough feels thirsty and asks his wife or daughter or some other female to hand over a cup of water to him, he must for the nonce leave hold of his plough to take the cup of water, in order that a female may not come in contact with the plough. Similarly a sword or a shield is believed to lose its sharpness and effectiveness through the touch of a woman. The rule prohibiting a woman to thatch a house appears to be based on a similar consideration. Should a woman be found getting up on the thatch of a house, disease and death to some inmate or inmates of the house and misfortune to the village in general are apprehended, and a 'Rōg-khednā' expedition has to be undertaken. In former times, it is said, one of the ears of the offending woman used to be cut off. But in our days it is only when a dog or a goat gets up on the roof of a house that one of its ears is cut off. It is believed that the sight of the blood of the severe dear serves to appease the wrath of the offended spirit.

III. Dances.

For the inmates of the Orāon village dormitories, songs and dances appear to form the chief items in the ordinary programme of their night's business. In summer and winter nights, young people of both sexes may be seen dancing and singing at the village ākhrā from evening till midnight and, often, much later. And on occasions of their important religious festivals you generally find them dancing and singing whole days and nights.

Time, place and management.

Ordinarily, it is after their evening meals, that the young men assemble at the ākhrā and begin to dance and sing. This is the signal for the girls to come out of their houses and join the dances. And in less than half an hour's time you see the young men and women all at their respective places on the dancing-ground. On moon-lit nights, you may occasionally find a few spectators seated for a while on the stone-slabs that generally lie at one end of the ākhrā. The Dhāngar-Kōtwār attends to the training of the dhāngars of the lowest grade in the secrets of the various styles of dancing and singing, and so too the Baṛkā Dhāngṛin—the leader of the maidens—takes care to see that the younger girls properly imitate the older girls in the various steps of the dances and the different tunes of the songs. In villages with a small Orāon population, the young men and boys are arranged in one and the same line, the smallest boys standing at one end of the line and the oldest and tallest at the other end, and the rest in the middle. And so too the girls stand in one line arranged according to the descending scale of their respective heights. But in the larger villages, where the number of boys and girls is large, the younger boys and girls are arranged in two or three rows behind the older boys or girls as the case may be.

Object.

Thus, singing and dancing, which were in their origin spontaneous rhythmic movements of the human voice and feet under the weight of strong emotions, soon became even with such rude peoples as the Orāons, arts directed to a definite end. That end, so far at least as Orāon dances are concerned, appears to be not merely the delight which the exercise itself affords, but, as we shall presently see, pantomimic representations of such incidents in their own lives as excite intense feelings of pleasure. Although such pantomimic representations may have had their origin in the pleasure and excitement they afforded, they soon came to have a magical significance attached to them. It came to be believed that by the law of sympathy such dramatic representation or imitation would help in some cases in bringing about the state of things imitated just as it is believed by the Orāon that the ceremony of dramatic rain-making is sure to be followed by actual rain. Dances and songs are also believed to bring happiness and prosperity and a stimulation of the helpful forces of Nature, so that the earth may be fruitful and the Orāon may be blessed with an abundance of animal and vegetable food, and the fertility of man and of the rest of creation may increase.

The Winter and Spring-Dances.

The most important incidents in the life of an Orāon are love and marriage, fighting, hunting, and agricultural operations. As every season of the year has its appointed work for the Orāon, so too has every season its appropriate dances and songs. The Orāon's year begins after the harvesting of his lowland rice in November-December. The period from the paddy harvest till the next Phāgu festival in March, when operations for growing the next paddy crop have to be thought of once more, is the merriest season of the year for the Orāon. This is the season when the Orāon's granary is generally full, and he has comparative leisure from work in the fields and it is now that Orāon young men and girls turn their thoughts seriously to love and marriage. This is, in fact, the season *par excellence* for Orāon weddings.* There are ghostly weddings in the beginning, real human

* Not long ago, when adult marriage was the rule amongst the Orāons, and their young people themselves used to choose their partners in life, this was also the season for courtship.

weddings in the middle, and a divine wedding at the end. The season is ushered in by the 'great marriage' (*koha-benja*) of the dead, is continued with the marriage of the living, and is ended with the marriage of Nature with God—of Mother Earth herself with the Sun-god. Until the 'marriage of the dead' is celebrated, no human wedding of the year may take place. The main features of this 'marriage of the dead' are briefly as follows: As soon as all the villagers have finished harvesting their winter paddy and stored it in their houses, the 'marriage of the year's dead' is celebrated. From the sowing season until the harvest is over, the Orāons may not cremate their dead; and thus until then the corpses of all Oraons dying during this period remain buried at the village burial place (*masan*). After the winter paddy has been harvested and garnered by all the villagers, the corpses of all the buried dead are disinterred and cremated on a day appointed beforehand, and the bones are then ceremonially gathered by the women, anointed with oil and turmeric, as brides and bridegrooms are anointed, and, with music, carried in procession to the stone-*kundi* by the side of some stream, pool or water-course where the bones of the dead Orāons of the 'village-family' are always deposited. Along with the procession, the benedictory *karsa*-pot is carried to bless the union of the souls of the dead with those of their predeceased ancestors. That night, boiled rice, pulses, *etc*, are left at the *kundi* to provide a wedding-feast for the Orāon denizens of the land of the dead. Thus do the Orāons celebrate the union of the dead Orāons of the year with their pre-deceased relatives. And a dancing festival known as the 'Hārbōri (bone burial) jātrā' follows this wedding. It is only after this great marriage (Kōhā benjā) of the dead that human marriages may begin for the year. The dances of the season rudely imitate the pleasant occupation of seeking a partner in life. A principal feature of the customary dances of the period known as the 'Jadur' dances is the long line of maidens with their arms interlaced retreating backwards as the young men advance towards them with measured steps to the sound of drums, and anon, as the young men in their turn step backwards, coquettishly advancing towards them with the most captivating movements of the feet the girls know. At the termination of each Jadur song and before another song is commenced you hear a loud burst of voices shouting in chorus-'Le-le-du-r-r-r'—an exclamation indicative of intense yearning and eager pursuit. The tribal consciousness appears to have perceived the same yearning for union throughout nature at this season; and this is perhaps why at the end of this season, at the great religious feast known as the Sarhul, the Orāons annually celebrate the marriage of Mother-earth with the Sun-God. From the Phāgu festival in March till the Sarhūl festival in April, all human weddings are suspended, and songs are sung, dances performed and rejoicings made in honour of this Divine union, symbolised by a ceremony of marriage of the village-priest and his wife, representing the Sun and the Earth respectively. Until this union is celebrated, the Orāon may neither use nor even gather the new vegetable roots, fruits, or flowers of the season. Even manuring his fields is not permitted to him before the Sarhūl, for, says the Orāon, up till then Mother-Earth has remained a virgin, and how can it be permissible to fecundate her before she is duly married? The Sarhūl dances appear to mark the transition stage between the Jadūr dances and the Khāṛiā dances and appear to partake of some of the characteristics of both.

The Summer dances.

By the time of the Phāgu festival, the weddings of the year have almost all been celebrated. Most of the marriageable boys and girls have now been wedded, and the dances known as the Jātrā Khāṛiā' dances, that are now taken up, appear partly to symbolise the bliss of wedded love. Unlike the Jadūr dances in which the young men are arranged in a group separate from the girls, and the style of dancing is expressive of a longing for union of one group with the other, in the Jātrā Khāṛiā dances the male and female dancers are generally intermixed and arranged in a column one behind the other, each dancer clasping with his or her right hand the left hand of the dancer standing behind and extending his or her left arm forwards to be clasped by the dancer standing in front who holds the clasped hands akimbo. And the chorus of exclamation that terminates each song is 'hur-r-r' or 'hir-r-r'—an exclamation expressive of overflowing joy and supreme staisfaction. But this is only one aspect of the Khāṛiā dances. Now that young Orāons are married, it will not do to spend all their time in soft dalliance. The hard realities of life have to be faced. The quest for food has to be taken up again. Men have to go out a-hunting and women have to go to the jungles to gather edible roots and fruits. This is, in fact, the Orāon's season *par excellence* for hunting excursions. They have the Phāgu Sikār or Spring hunt at its beginning, the Bisu Sikār or summer hunt at its middle, and the Jeth-Sikār or rainy-season hunt at its end. And besides these great hunting expe-

To face p. 281.

The war-dance of the Oraons.

Oraon women dancing at the *Chhorakhra* while the men are out hunting.

ditions in which Orāons of several Pārhās go out together, the Orāons of each village now and again go out on informal hunting excursions known as Dourāhā Sikārs. In the dances of the season, we accordingly find a pantomimic representation of hunting. In these Khāṛiā dances, the men no longer carry musical instruments to attract the other sex as in the Jadūr dances, but they carry clubs and sticks as they do in hunting expeditions. The movements of the Khāṛiā dances are not so sprightly and playful as in the Jadūr dances, but martial and business-like. The dancers march on with quick steps and now and then appear to be running, as they would do in a hunt. They are ordinarily arranged not in lines but in columns, though occasionally they spread out in a line. This too appears to be imitative of the movements of hunters.

War-Dances.

Tradition speaks of frequent warfare in the past between the Orāons of one Pārhā and another. And a fruitful source of these inter-Pārhā wars was disagreement as to the right to game. And at the Jeth-Jātrās, even to this day, the Orāons celebrate the memory of those times. Often as the young men of each Pārhā enter the Jātrā-arena, they dance a war-dance waving their long tapering pārhā-flags high up in the air and brandishing their sticks and clubs as in actual warfare. Actual warfare over the right to game, which must have been a thing of frequent occurrence in the stage of social culture in which hunting was the main occupation of the tribe, is not altogether unknown even in these peaceful days of British rule when agriculture is the principal occupation of the Orāons. Occasionally the war-dance at the Jātrā is only the prelude to an actual fight. When, during one or other of the great hunting excursions of the Orāons in which members of many Pārhās go out together, a game claimed to have been first chased or first shot at by some member of one pārhā is captured or taken by the members of another pārhā, and the quarrel that ensues over it is not settled by an armed fight at the śikār-land (hunting-ground) or amicably settled by the elders of the pārhās concerned who act as umpires during these hunts, on the approach of the next of Jeth-Jātrā, the members of the aggrieved Pārhā have a flag made with the same design as that of the distinguishing flag of the offending Pārhā or village. As the young men of the aggrieved Pārhā enter the Jātrā-arena carrying this flag of another Pārhā and dance the war-dance, the members of the latter Pārhā take it as a challenge, and, if attempts at arbitration fail, proceed to snatch away the flag by force. And now ensues a regular fight in which the different

To face p. 283.

An Oraon in War-dress at a Paiki-dance.

villages usually take sides. In these fights more use is made of stones than of sticks or clubs. Jāl-khāris or net-bags containing small pieces of stone are suspended from the shoulders of each combatant. These stones are each flung at the enemy with a sort of sling consisting of a doubled-up string with a knot at one end where the stone is lodged. As the sling is rapidly whirled round, one of the strings is deftly loosened, and away flies the stone with great force, and strikes the enemy. Cases of death have been known to have occurred in this way even in recent times. But as soon as death or grievous hurt is caused to any party, the Jātrā breaks up for fear of the police.* Besides the war-dance at the time of these Jātrās, the Orāons have also a sort of mock war-dance known as the *Paiki*-dance which is performed when a wedding-procession arrives at the precincts of the village of the

* And when a case is instituted in court, the real cause of dispute is carefully suppressed by both parties, some private grudge between individual members of the two parties is put forward as the cause of the fight, and the fight too is represented as one in which the dead or wounded persons alone formed one party and a few selected persons on the other side are named as having formed the assailing party. The reason for this suppression of the real facts appears to be the anxiety to save their time-honoured tribal customs and institutions from being abolished by the Government authorities.

bride or bridegroom as the case may be. A few men on each side are dressed like warriors, one or two of them carrying swords and shields (generally made now-a-days of wood or bamboo) and a few others carrying only sticks. And a mock-fight accompanied by dancing ensues, at the end of which (when it is the bride who has been brought to the bridegroom's village for the wedding) the bride is, as if forcibly, taken to the bridegroom's house. This is clearly a survival of the ancient custom, now abandoned, of marriage by capture,—as the songs full of indecent abuse sung by turns by the females of both parties during a wedding appear to be another surviving remnant of the same custom.

The Rainy-Season Dances.

After the Jeth Jātrā in June, the Jātrā Khāṛiā dances are given up and the Karam dances are taken up and continued till September. The peculiar feature of the Karam dances is the graceful stooping posture of the youthful dancers. As the Orāons appear to have learnt the art of agriculture from other peoples, so the Karam festival as well as the Karam dances and songs which are appropriate to the cultivating season appear to have been borrowed from Hindu or rather Hinduized peoples. After the Jeth-Jātrā, in June, agricultural operations proceed in full vigour; and

To face p. 285.

A form of the Karam Dance.

in these operations, there is, as we have seen, a distinct division of labour between Orāon males and females,—any infringement of the rule being liable to punishment by the *Panch*. Karam dances performed during this season are rude representations of the occupation of the people. Now that most of the marriageable young men and women have been married and have entered the life of householders, the tumult of youthful passion has to some extent subsided, and men and women are anxious for a successful paddy crop. As in their work in the fields so in their dances during this season, the men and women are not intermixed but are arranged in separate groups. The posture of the dancers is very graceful and the movements slow. The young men at times kneel down and each girl stooping low sways one arm backwards and forwards, as if in imitation of reaping paddy-crops. This movement of the hands may not improbably be intended as a magical operation calculated to ensure an abundant harvest. The young man who leads the dance, and also other young men who care to do so, carry *sailos** or *chawars* made of the wild date-palm which they wave over the ground, as if coaxing the earth to bear abundant crops. The chorus of exclamation with which they begin

* Sometimes yak's tails are similarly used.

a Karam song and Karam dance, is 'bhālè bhālè-ho!' (fairly, fairly, oh!) which sounds like a 'fair entreaty and sweet blandishment' whereby it is sought to induce Mother-Earth to bear abundantly.

Autumn Dances

From the second half of Aswin (September-October) the paddy crops begin to be ripe. The days of anxious expectation are over. The ripening sheaves of paddy that now wave with the breeze and adorn the bosom of Mother-Earth, gladden the hearts of the old and the young,—and men and women once more prepare to work merrily side by side. But even the rose has its thorns. And before the paddy crops are fit for the sickle, wild hogs and deer and other animals often seek to eat them up. And the Orāon has to keep guard over his fields, and now and again to wield his sticks and clubs to ward off or kill these thievish animals. The tabu against killing wild animals which the Orāons have to observe during the month of Bhādo (August-September) is now removed. And, appropriately enough, the Khāṛiā dances in which the men carry sticks and clubs are again taken up at this season. This division of the Khāṛiā dances are known as Chirdi (Aghan) Khāṛiā dances which differ from the Jātrā Khāṛiā dances only in the tune of the songs. As men and women join hands in the reaping operations, so do they dance together in one and the same row in the Chirdi Khāṛiā dances.

Social-Dances.

Besides the dances at the ākhṛā, the Orāons have a magico-religious dance known as the marriage-dance (Benjā-nālnā) which is danced at marriages, and a social dance known as 'chāli bechnā' (court-yard-dance) which is danced only by the girls in private houses and in the lanes and not at the public ākhṛā. Besides these regular dances, there are a few dances that the Orāons appear to have borrowed from their Hindu or rather Hinduized neighbours. These are the Māthā, the Jhumar, and the Lujhri dances. For the Jhumar and Lujhri, there are no fixed seasons, but these dances may be danced at any time. The Māthā is danced by girls generally in the months of Aswin (September-October) and Aghan (November.)

We shall now proceed to give a short account of the essential features and technique of each of the principal dances of the Orāons.

Common Features of the Dances.

As for the essential features common to all Orāon dances the following may be noticed :—In all Orāon dances at the ākhṛā, the dancers must complete the circle of the ākhṛā from left to right ; in all the dances the right foot must be advanced before the left foot, and all the dancers must move their feet simultaneously. Some Orāons say that the reason why the dancers must move in a circle is that as they go round and round their minds are wholly taken up with the dance, and their enthusiasm and delight go on increasing. In fact as you watch an Orāon-dance at the village ākhṛā, you perceive an atmosphere of ecstatic delight being gradually induced, and occasionally at the Karam dances you see one of the dancers,—generally a sensitive young woman—all on a sudden vigorously shaking her head round and round,—a phenomenon which your Orāon friends will explain by saying that some deity or spirit come as an invisible spectator of the dance became so transported with delight that in his endeavours to take part in the dance, he has entered the body of this sensitive dancer.

The Orāon has no notion of the movements of his circular dances representing either the infinite or the rotation of the heavenly bodies. He will generally refer it to ancient custom. Except in the Jātrā Khāṛiā dances, drum-beating is an invariable accompaniment to the Orāon dances. The other dances have their appropriate musical instruments. Thus the Māndal and the Nāgerā are appropriate to the Jadūr dances; the Māndal, Jhānj, Soikhō, Runj, Theskā (but in no case the Nāgerā) may be used at the Karam dances; the Nāgerā (but not the Māndal) may be used at the Chirdi Khāṛiā dances and the Gūgūchū is played upon at the Angan dances.

The peculiarities of each of the principal dances are given below.

(1) The Jadur Dances.

A Jadūr dance begins with the formation of one or more lines by the girls who stand at one side of the *Akhra*, which is a circular plot of ground—often a circular earthen platform. A number of young men stand at a little distance from them on the ākhrā in two or three rows. Between these young men and the girls stand two or more young men who carry Nāgerā and Māndal drums. The young men all stand facing the girls. In the central and western parts of the Orāon country, the girls stand with arms crossed in such a way that each holds her right-hand neighbour's right hand with her own left, and conversely her left-hand neighbour's left hand with her own right hand; and the hands thus joined are held a little forward. But in most villages in the eastern parts of the plateau, the girls stand in line (as in the Jadūr dances of the Muṇḍās) each with her right arm passed across one neighbour's back so that her hand rests upon the latter's shoulder, and with her left arm round her other neighbour's waist. The young men first begin a song. As soon as they have sung the first portion of a song, the girls repeat the lines. If the girls sing the lines correctly, the drums are sounded and the dance begins. If, however, the girls fail to sing the lines correctly the first time, the lines are sung by the young men again and again until the girls correctly reproduce the tune. Now the young men with a simultaneous yell of 'Lé-lé-dūr-r-r', sing the second half (called the *kirtana* or *charhaon*) of the song in accompaniment to their drums, and then sounding their drums in a higher key advance two paces towards the girls, almost running. The girls take up the *kirtana* song and recede three steps, singing as the young men advance. Then the young men who came up to within one pace of the girls go three steps backwards, and the girls, singing all the time and facing the young men, again advance two steps towards them, as the latter recede. In this manner the two parties alternately advance and recede until the girls have finished the second half of the song. Then the young men sing the first lines of the song, and the girls repeat them as before. And then, as before, the young men sing the second half of the song and advance towards the girls who thereupon

To face p. 291.

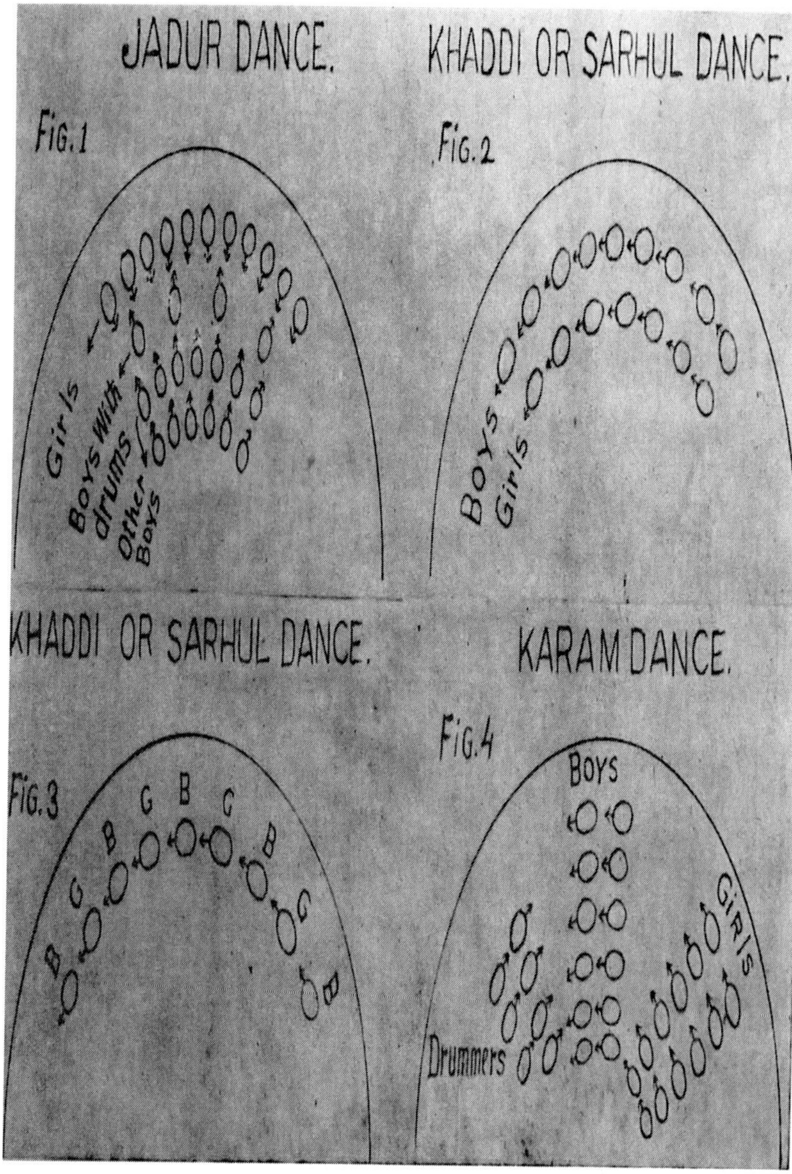
JADUR DANCE.
FIG. 1
Girls
Boys with drums
Other Boys
KHADDI OR SARHUL DANCE.
FIG. 2
Boys
Girls
KHADDI OR SARHUL DANCE.
FIG. 3
B
G
B
G
B
G
B
G
B
KARAM DANCE.
FIG. 4
Boys
Girls
Drummers

step backwards singing the 'Kirtānā' or second half of the song. And again and again as the boys recede, the girls advance and *vice versa*. All the time the rows of girls slightly move towards their right so as to complete the circle in due time. Throughout, the most perfect rhythm of foot and voice is maintained, the dancers keeping time with the drums. And in this way when one Jadūr song has been sung three or four times, the dancers shout in chorus 'Lé-lé-du-r-r-r'. And now that one song is finished, another is taken up. After a song has been repeated three or four times, it is again sung and re-sung with a slightly varied tune. The accompanying figure (*figure 1*) shows the usual arrangements of the dancers in a Jadūr dance.

(2) The Khaddi or Sarhul Dance.

The Sarhūl dances, as we have said, partake of the characteristics of both the Jadūr and the Khāṛiā dances, but more of the latter than of the former. The Orāons who live nearer the Mundā country consider the Sarhūl dances as a subdivision of the Jadūr; other Orāons consider it as a subdivision of the Khāṛiā. In one variety of the Sarhūl, the arrangement of the boys and the girls is practically the same as in the Jadūr. Now and again the girls unclasp each other's hands and clap their hands rhythmically. In another variety of the Sarhūl dance, the boys and girls are arranged in two parallel columns advancing in the same direction, as shown in the accompanying figure (2). In this way they dance round and round the ākhrā. In a third and a more common variety, the boys and girls are arranged together in one column, as in the Khāṛiā dances, the boys and girls alternating as far as possible, and making circuits round the ākhrā, as in figure (3). In the Sarhūl dances the steps are slower than in the Jadūr, and the boys generally carry sticks on their left shoulders.

In the Sarhūl dance, one party (when the young men are arranged in a separate group, then their party) begins the first part of the song, the other party repeats it; and after this portion has been thus sung and re-sung a few times, you hear a simulteneous shout of 'Hūr-r-r or 'Hir-r-r.' Then the first party again sings the first portion of the song, and both parties commence dancing in unison, and when this portion of the song is finished, you hear the same startling yell again. Now the second, party takes up the song (the first portion again) and both parties dance in unison and end with the same yell. Then the first party sings the second half of the song, and all dance in union.

To face p. 293.

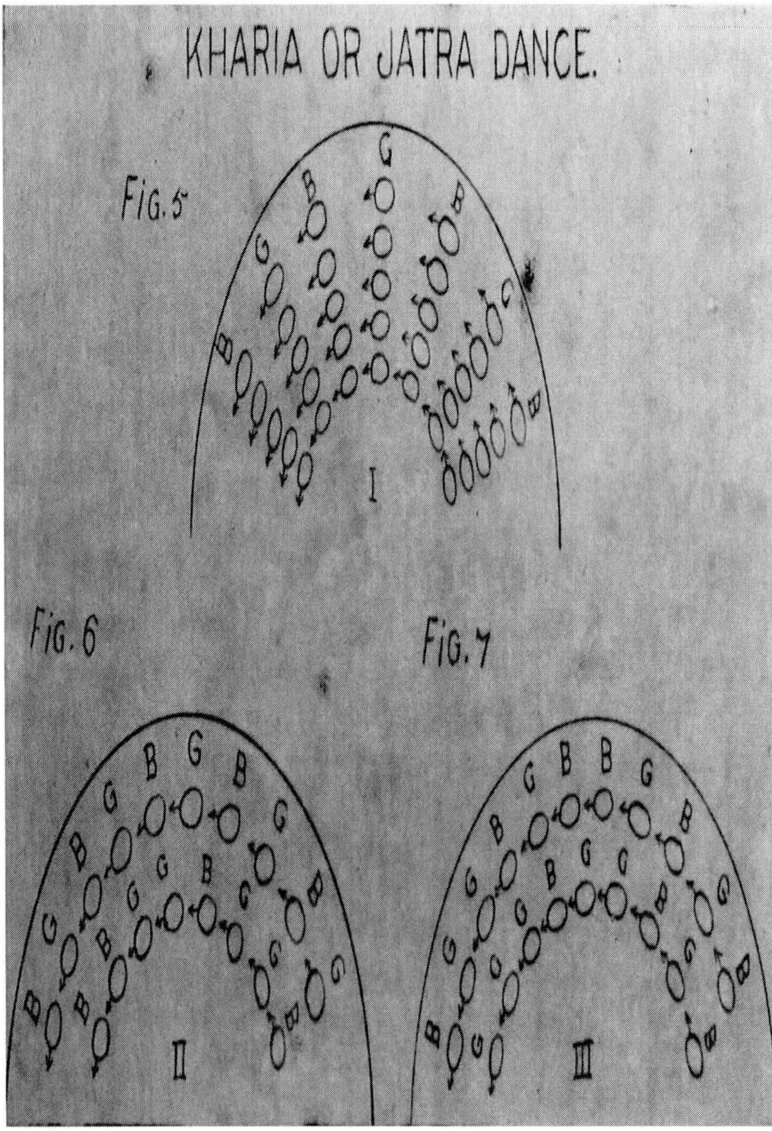

With the last words of the song and a simultaneous yell of 'Hūr-r-r' all jump up and stamp their feet on the ground. Now it is the turn of the second party to lead the song. And so the second party first sings the first half of the song and the first party repeats it after them. Then the second party sings the second half of the song, and all dance in unison. As soon as the last words of the song are sung, they again simultaneously cry 'Hūr-r-r' and with a sudden jump they come down on the gound with a resounding stamp of the feet. And anon you hear the same yell again, and with, unabated energy, the young men and women begin the song and the dance over again in the same fashion.

(3) The Kharia Dances.

The Khāṛiā dances are what the Orāons call bhejjā' (intermixed) dances in which young men and women are arranged in an orderly mixture. In these dances, the boys carry sticks on their left shoulders. The dancers move in parallel columns, each dancer facing his or her neighbour's back. They divide themselves generally into two parties who sing by turns. The style of dancing and singing is similar to that of the Sarhūl dance described above. As the dancers in a Khāṛiā dance are arranged in columns (as in figures 5, 6 &

7), at the termination of a song or a portion of a song the dancers with a half turn spread out in a line, come to a halt, and after one long leap, two short leaps and a high jump, stamp their feet vigorously down on the ground, and at the same time shout in a deafening chorus 'Hir-r-r' or 'Hūr-r-r.' Once more they form into columns as before, and, go on dancing, or rather marching soldier-like,—now walking and now running,—as before. The Jātrā Khāṛiā and the Chiridi Khāṛiā dances, as we have said, differ only in the tunes of their songs.

(4) The Karam Dances.

In the Karam dances, the boys and girls dance in separate lines (as shown in fig. 4) but they all sing the same songs together in one voice and not by turns. Unlike the Jadūr and the Khāṛiā dances, which are 'standing' dances, the Karam dances are what are called 'stooping' dances—both boys and girls stooping very low, head forward. The boys carrying drums and other musical instruments and 'jhāls" or peacock-feathers, yak's tails, and 'sailōs' or bunches of date leaves, form the foremost group; then follow other boys who are arranged usually in two rows, and then, a little apart, the girls in one or two rows. The boys in the first row carry either

To face p. 291.

The arrangement in one from of the Khāṛiā Dance.

Blowing *bhers* or trumpets.

chawars or yak's tails or 'sailos' or peacock feathers in their right hands, and with their left hands clasp the hands of the boys of the second row. And similarly the girls of the first row clasp the hands of the girls of the second row when there are two rows; or, when there is one row, each girl places her left hand on the shoulder of the girl next to her on the left and keeps her right hand free. The boys carrying musical instruments stand facing the boys who dance. Often the drummers as well the boys who dance form one line and the girls the other line. The drummers move backwards and forwards, but more backwards than forwards. The boys who dance slowly move in a circle so as to make a circuit of the ākhṛā in due time; but now and again they quickly advance and recede, waving their 'chawars' and 'sailōs' in the air now upwards and downwards and again forwards and backwards and at times fanning the earth as if coaxing her to bear abundantly. Now the drummers and the boys kneel down, and anon they squat on the ground, and, once in a way, you see one or other of the drummers turning a somer-sault, with his drum suspended from his neck. The girls go on dancing in a stooping posture swinging their right hands backwards and forwards. Both the male and female dancers, as we have said, sing together. Each song commences with a simultaneous cry of 'bhālé-bhālé.' The dancers do not stamp their feet on the ground as in the Khāṛiā dances. In the Lujhki variety of the Karam dance you see the girls dancing with a peculiar limping gait and now and then wheeling round and clapping their hands. In another form of the Karam dance known as the Hūtūngiā Karam, each girl clasps her neighbour to the left by passing her left arm round the latter's waist and placing her right hand on the shoulder of her neighbour on the right. The most interesting of all Orāon dances is the variety of Karam dance known as 'Kesari Kāppā' (gathering *kesar* fruit growing in tanks and marshes). In this dance the girls kneel down and the drummers squat on the ground facing them. The hair of the girls is dishevelled and they go on shaking their heads and thumping the ground with their hands (in imiation of *kesar* gatherers). In this posture they advance singing songs to the sound of music. Gradually their heads begin to shake more and more violently and the music sounds louder and louder until one or more of the girls show signs of 'spirit-possession' : such a girl appears to partially lose her external senses, her cloth gets loose at the waist, and the head moves frantically from side to side. Finally she has

To face p. 297.

The Courtyard Dance of Orāan women. (One form of the Jadur dance has the same arrangements.)

to be brought back to her senses by some young man pulling her hair or kicking her in the back.

Minor Dances.

(i) The Court-Yard Dance.

In the month of Aghān (November-December), Orāon girls dance the Chāli-bechnā or Angan dance. As it is not danced, like the other dances, at the village ākhrā, but in the āngans or courtyards of people's houses and in the village-lanes, it is called the Angan (chāli) dance. In this dance, girls alone take part. They arrange themselves in two parallel lines, one line facing the other. Every girl clasps the girl standing next to her on the left by passing her left arm around the latter's back on to her left shoulder. As one line of girls advances towards the other line, the latter recedes, and as the former recedes, the latter advances towards it. A song is sung by each party alternately and not simultaneously. The party not engaged in singing sound the earthen pipe called *guguchu.* No other musical instruments are played upon.

After the winter harvest, Orāon girls go from house to house dancing the *angan* dance and from each house get one sūp (about a *seer* or two pounds) or so of paddy. When paddy has been collected in this way from all the houses, they thresh the paddy, and grind it into flour. Of this rice-flour they make a kind of cake, a portion of which is presented to the village-Pāhān and the village-Māhāto, and the rest the girls divide amongst themselves.

(ii) **The Wedding-dance.**

The Benjā Nālnā or Wedding Dance is a benedictory dance performed by women, at an Orāon wedding ceremony. After the wedding, you see a most interesting dance performed by a few women each with her own feet touching each other. Each of the women carries one or other of the benedictory things used in the wedding to bring luck and happiness to the wedded pair. Thus, one woman carries on her head the *Karsa-hanria*, another the 'nāchuā' or basket containing wedding cakes, a third carries on her head the curry-stone on which the bridegroom stood, and another carries the yoke on which the bridegroom was made to sit, and still another holds in her hands the bundles of straw that were placed over the yoke. And with these they dance, with feet together, a most interesting dance intended to bless the wedding. . The drums, called dhāk, dhōl, and nāgerā, the horn called narsinghā, the sāhnāi flute and the *bher* trumpet may be sounded at these dances. In the months of Aghān and Pūs, young girls practise this dance and learn the farewell songs supposed to be sung by an Orāon bride to express her grief at leaving her parents' home. In one form of the dance, the girls form a ring holding each other's hands, move from right to left and again from left to right and at intervals exclaim 'ōōi,' 'ōōi.'

(iii) The Jhumar.

The Jhūmar dance has been borrowed by the Orāons from their Hindu or Hinduized neighbours. There is no fixed season for this dance, and it is not connected with any religious feasts, social ceremonies, or agricultural operations. It is danced by females alone. A few men stand in front of the dancers and act as drummers. The dancers arrange themselves in a column, each dancer facing the back of her neighbour, and clasping with her left hand the right hand of the girl behind her and with her right hand the left hand of the girl to her front. The hands thus clasped together are raised upwards as the girls leap up in unison at the termination of each song or group of songs.

(iv) The Jarga and the Matha.

The Jārgā, like the Jhumar, is a borrowed dance. It is generally danced by Orāon females, but sometimes a few young men also take part in the dance. The dancers form a column as in the Khāṛiā dances; each dancer stand facing his or her neighbour's back, clasping with the right hand the left hand of the neighbour in front. The hands thus clasped are not raised upwards as in the Jhūmar nor held downwards as in the Sarhūl dance, but rest at the sides close to the waist. When there are male dancers, it is they who lead the column. The column of dancers while moving forward to complete a circle round the ākhrā, now and then move sideways to their right and again sideways to the left. The Jārgā dance is somewhat similar to the Karam and the Jadur. In it the dancers form two parties and the drummers stand between them. The drúmmers sing a line or two twice and the girls repeat the lines after them. After two such repetitions, the party of men advance two steps rapidly dancing towards the girls who recede bending. Then the girls advance two places towards the men with one foot extended forward a little above the ground, and the men recede before them. The girls hold each other's hands as in the Māthā, and now and then whistle together.

Such are the different dances of the Orāons. As you watch them in their dances, hour after hour walking and running, bending and bounding, strutting and tumbling, with remarkable agility and tolerable grace, what impresses you most is perhaps the uncommon exuberance of life and animal spirits in the dancers. You are delighted to find that their exceptionally hard lot in life has not succeeded in drying up the sap of life that ever wells up from within as from a perennial fountain and gaily courses through every limb of the Orāon young man and woman.

IV. Songs.

Different classes of songs.

The Orāons have songs appropriate to each different class of their tribal dances. These different classes of songs are distinguished from one another chiefly by the differences in interval, rhythm, and modulation of the voice, and also by the peculiar vociferation with which a song or portion of a song is introduced or ended. It would seem that all Orāon songs were primarily meant to be sung in accompaniment to dances. And the different classes of songs are named after the different kinds of dances they accompany. The names of the persons who composed particular songs are not remembered ; and no singer may claim proprietary right in his songs. There are no professional singers amongst the Orāons, though some young singer (pāṛu) here and there sometimes acquires a local reputation as a perfect singer. Men, women, and children may sing the same songs, with the exception of marriage-songs and āngan songs which are sung generally by women and little girls respectively. A few Orāon songs are traditional, many are old, and some are modern. Improvised songs are not unknown.

Structure of the songs.

Both as to matter and form, the songs of the unlettered Orāon are necessarily very simple. Each song ordinarily consists of two distinct portions—generally of two lines each. The first portion is known as 'dāndi-chō'dā' (the 'lifting up' or beginning of the song or rather of the tune) which roughly corresponds to the 'dhūā' of Hindi songs; and the second portion is known as the 'dāndi-ārgā' or 'chaṛhāon' ('turning the song over' or 'raising the song'). Unlike the Jadūr and Khāṛiā songs which are sung alternately in parts by two parties, a Kaṛam song which is always sung by all the dancers together begins with the 'chaṛhāon' or 'arga' generally of two lines; this is followed by the 'dhūā' or 'dāndi chō'dā' generally of one line, and again we have a line or two of 'charhāon' and then a line or so of 'dāndi chō'dā.' You perceive an attempt, often futile, to make the number of syllables in the different lines of the same song uniform. The failure of such attempt, however, is sought to be remedied by lengthening out the vowels in singing, and by the feeble aid of expletives. A few words and phrases not understood by the Orāons, and apparently borrowed from the Hindus and transformed in the process, are used in the songs. Hindi words too are freely used in Orāon songs to supplement the Orāon's poor vocabulary. The use of a few onomatopoetic words and phrases expressive of particular sounds, movements, *etc*, is another peculiarity of what may be dignified with the name of Orāon 'poetic diction'. Simple similies and metaphors occur in many Orāon songs; and a number of love-songs, or, to be more correct, songs about premarital intrigues, are rude allegories—often too thinly veiled to conceal their indecent suggestions. The lines of the songs do not ordinarily rhyme, but you perceive in Orāon songs a dim appreciation of the suitability of rhyming words and phrases in the beginning of two or more successive lines to express the idea of harmony. The suitability of the *cæsura* or pause in the middle of a line appears to be understood. The first portion of a song is sung while the singers are standing both before and after a dance, and the second portion is sung and re-sung while the singers are actually dancing. The second portion of the song is either an answer to the first portion or an amplification or variation of the same, in which you meet with a reminiscence or repetition of the main idea and often a return to the characteristic phraseology of the first lines: In this way does the Orāon poet secure unity to the whole song. Thus does the Orāon seek to satisfy the requirements of the artistic sense of which he too has his humble share. The inability of the unlettered Orāon to give adequate verbal expression to his feelings is sought to be made up for by a continuous repetition of the first portion of his song. The entire song, too, after it has been sung a few times is re-sung in a slightly varied tune. With every repetition of a song, the singers appear to get more and more enthusiastic. In fact, the Orāon singer appears to revel in what he considers the 'rich' melody of his songs, and pays little heed to the poor language of the songs.

Matter of the songs.

When we turn from the outer form of the songs to their matter—the inner ideas and feelings they embody,—we meet with the same simplicity. Each song springs from a single thought or emotion. It is either an expression of a simple thought or a passing feeling excited by some natural or artificial object, an interesting incident or situation.

The joys and sorrows of love naturally form a chief theme of the Orāon's songs. His apprecia-tion of beauty of form, colour, and movement in man and Nature finds expression in a large number of songs. The well-developed and muscular figure of the healthy young man or woman, the agile movements of a young man or girl dancing at the village ākhrā, the red embroidery of a young woman's clothes or her brass ear-ornaments with their shining pendants gleaming in the sun, appeal to his sense of beauty and give the Orāon poet appropriate themes for song. The sight of 'vernal bloom',—of the *mohua* tree in fruit, the waving yellow mustard or *surguja* crops on his fields, the luxuriant green herb of the jungles, the gaudy or fragrant flower in jungle or field,—gives him delight and the Orāon expresses his delight in simple songs. The joys of fishing, hunting, fruit-gathering and of reaping the paddy-harvest, form the theme of some of his songs. And even the delight of drinking rice-beer is not left unsung. The Orāon youth's greatest delight is in dancing and singing, especially at the Jātrās, and these afford the theme for a large number of his songs. The animal world interests him no less than natural objects. To the Orāon the whole of Nature and of the animate world appear to be more kin to him than they appear to the more civilized man. The Orāon often endows birds and beasts as also trees and rocks and streams with life and even with will, feeling, and intelligence. The buzzing of bees, the chirping of birds, the bellowing of cattle, excite some pleasing thought or emotion in the Orāon and furnish themes for some of his songs. As for songs of purely human interest, the Orāons have, besides songs of love and friendship, a number of songs relating to the domestic affections including even the mutual attachment of an Orāon servant to his Orāon master. The Orāon's altruistic feelings,—his love for young children, his pity for distressed orphans, his hospitality to friends and relatives, his charity and habit of alms-giving,—find expression in a few songs. The necessity for, if not the dignity of, Work is also emphasized by the Orāon in song. There are a few Orāon songs in appreciation of bravery in man as well as in woman. Light sarcasms against the lazy young man or woman occur in a few songs. The terrors of his native jungles and of his hill-streams in flood, the dread of the scourge of drought and famine, the misery caused by the loss of cattle by disease, afford themes for several songs. The Orāon is, however, essentially jovial by nature. He generally preserves his buoyancy of spirits and always enjoys a good joke. In a number of his songs, you hear of the exchange of light-hearted jokes and jests, chaff and banter, between bachelors and maidens, young husbands and wives. On the other hand, in a few songs apparently inspired by the example of his Hindu neighbours you meet with an attempt at serious reflection—usually about the decay of youth and beauty. As for historical songs, the Orāons have very few to boast of. One of them, the 'genesis-song' of the Orāons appears to commemorate the primitive time when the Orāons lived in cave-dwellings described in the songs as 'crab-holes' (song No. 5 in Appendix). In another song (No. 1 in Appendix) we hear the Orāons still fondly remembering their palmy days on the Rohtās plateau. And a third song (No. 6) celebrates the memory of two Orāon heroes who fought and died in the 'Kol Rebellion' of 1832.

V. The Jatras or Inter-Parha Dancing Meetings.

No Orāon institution has perhaps greater attractions for the bachelors and maidens of the village-dormitories than the inter-pārhā dancing-festivals known as the Jātrās. Many are the songs in which we hear the Orāon youth eagerly welcoming a Jātrā festival where they may choose their partners in life. Thus in the following dialogistic song we hear the young bachelors and maidens of a village expressing their admiration respectively for the maidens of villages Lendo and Lundri and the bachelors of villages Jaigi and Jōnjrō, and yearning to meet them at the forth-coming Māgh Jātrā :—

Boys : Lendo-Lūndri pelō, bairenghāé !
Jūṛi Jūṛi mānō dé.
Girls : Bhālā, Jaigi-Jōnjrō jokhārim, bairenghāé !
Pati pati mānō dé.
Boys : Bairenghāé bairé ! Kahā dūrū māno dé,
Jūṛi jūṛi mānō dé ?
Girls : Kahā dūrū mānō dé, pati pati mānō dé ?
Boys : Baidenghāe bairé ! Māghe chāndō jātrā lāggō,
Jūṛi jūṛi mānō dé.
Girls : Māghe chāndo jāterā lāggō
Pati pati mānō dé.

[TRANSLATION.]

Boys : Girls of Lendo Lundri, oh my friends !
Will be partners [meet for us].
Girls : Boys of Jaigi Jonjro, oh my friends !
Will be partners [meet for us].
Boys : Oh friends, my friends ! How will it be
That we shall fitting partners make ?
Girls : How will it be that we shall form the
[dancing] lines ?
Boys : Oh friends, my friends ! In month of Magh
a jātrā meets :
[We] shall fitting partners be.
Girls : In month of Māgh the jātrā meets :
[We] shall form the [dancing] lines.

As the Dhumkūṛiā institution, where it exists, still serves to regulate the premarital sexual relations between the young people of an Orāon village, so do these seasonal jātrās still afford them opportunities for choosing their partners in life from clans and villages other than their own. This choice, however, is subject in the first instance to the approval of their parents, and, finally to the absence of unfavourable omens. It is not unlikely that the Dhumkūṛiā institution had its origin at a stage of Orāon culture when endogamy and mother-right were the rule, and the jātrās originated when at a later stage clan-exogamy superseded clan-endogamy.

The genesis-tradition of the Orāons, as we have seen, refers to a primitive stage of society when they lived in cave dwellings in small family groups composed of a man and woman who were near kinsmen ('bhāyā-bahin' or 'brother-sister', as the tradition puts it), and presumably their female children and minor male children.

Formation of Totemic clans or 'gotras'.

We have not come across any definite tradition amongst the Orāons as to the steps by which in course of ages these small family groups came to coalesce into the friendly aggregate of a clan and each such clan came to have a distinctive totem-name. An Orāon tradition (or rather what is apparently an *ex post facto* theory transmitted in the form of a tradition) about the formation of totemic groups, tells us that people who occupied river-valleys took either the tortoise or some species of fish for their totem, whereas those who lived in tiger-infested forests had the tiger for theirs, while those who dwelt on wooded uplands had birds for their totems. Another tradition goes into details apparently inferential or imaginary and says that the Tortoise clan originated on the banks of the Subarnarekhā river, the Tiger clan at Hundru Ghāgrā* and Arsipokhra,* the Crow clan at Dārndā Tigrā,* the Kujur clan at Silāgāin,* the Minj Fish clan at Lundri,* the Dog clan at Mānpur* and so on. Whatever might have led to the totemic organization of Orāon society, in course of time the totemic clan would seem to have overshadowed the natural family. All the members of a totem clan came to regard themselves as 'of one blood', and knit together by the mystic bond of the totem. Before the Orāons took to agriculture and established villages, each small clan group thus formed would move about from one piece of forest land to another as their temporary home and hunting ground which they would jealously guard against the aggressions of neighbouring clans. One or two men believed to possess magical powers over nature and at a later time over supposed supernatural

* These are names of places on the Chota-Nagpur Plateau.

agencies,—powers in a measure denied to the rest,—would come to be regarded as the natural leaders of the clan. To this day the village-Pāhān or Priest is regarded as the real head of the village.

The Orāons have a vague tradition that a growing aversion to permanent sexual union within the clan led to clan-exogamy. Probably the society of women (more attractive for their novelty) occasionally captured from other clans in the course of the frequent hostilities between neighbouring clans helped in fostering this aversion to clan-endogamy. The men began by preference or perhaps through scarcity of women in their own clan-group, to seek permanent mates by capture from clans other than their own. And the oft-repeated practice came in time to be the law of the people. The clan came to be looked upon as an extended family-group. And the tabu against sexual union within the family-group came to be extended by a natural analogy to unions within the larger group of the clan.

Probable origin of the Jatras.

In course of time, probably in part through the influence of those very captured women and in part through the gradual softening of manners as well as through motives of an 'enlightened self-interest', neighbouring clans would, when practicable, meet at convenient centres to settle disputes about game or about captured females. When amicable settlement failed, they would come to blows. In time, a 'bride-price' came to be accepted as a sufficient compensation for the transfer of a girl to the group of her captor or lover. To this day a simulation of capture forms a preliminary to an Orāon wedding, and the payment of 'bride-price' forms an essential condition of an Orāon marriage except in a few instances where the would-be husband goes to live with his future bride's parents as 'eṛpāeon khaddi' or 'ghar-dāmād'.* Such periodical meetings of neighbouring clans gradually came to be organized as a regular institution. They came to be regularly held at convenient centres at the beginning of each changing season of the year, and helped in welding the various intermarrying clans into a regular tribe. It was at these Jātrās, that the young men of the tribe came to choose their mates from amongst the girls of clans other than their own; it was there that outstanding disputes about game

* This exception would seem to be in accord with Mr. Sidney Hartland's opinion that the change of residence depended on the payment of bride-price. (*Primitive Paternity*, Vol. II. pp. 96-99). In the case even of the Orāon 'ghar-dāmād,' however, descent of his children is now reckoned on the father's side.

were settled ; and it was then that the customary dances and songs of the outgoing season were formally exchanged for the dances and songs appropriate to the incoming season. And to this day it is at these Jātrās that new dances and songs are similarly taken up, and disputes about game are settled by arbitration or by fight. Nor is it unusual to find, even to this day, attachments formed between young men and girls of different villages during these seasonal jātrās, ending, if other considerations permit, in marriage. As during a Jātrā month there is a regular round of such dancing-meetings held one after another in several neighbouring villages, the young men and girls have repeated opportunities of coming together. Besides this social aspect, the Jātrās have also their socio-political and religious aspects which will be referred to in the next chapter. Here we shall content ourselves with a brief account of the proceedings of an Orāon Jātrā.

The Procedure of the Jatras.

The Orāon Jātrās are usually held once in Aswin (Dasārā Jātrā) or Kārtik (Sōhōrāi Jātrā), when the rainy season is over and the Karam dances and songs are exchanged for the Chirdi Khāṛiā dances and songs,—again in Aghān, Pūs or Māgh when the lowland paddy crops have been harvested and the Jadūr dances have to be taken up, and finally in Jéṭh when the Jātrā Khāṛiā dances taken up after the Sarhūl festival have to be exchanged for the Karam dances. The Jeth Jātrā is considered the most important of all the Jātrās as it is held after the hunting expeditions of the year are over. This appears to be the most ancient of the Orāon Jātrās, as the Khāṛiā style of dancing is said to be the oldest form of Orāon dance—in fact, the only genuine Orāon dance. About a week before the date fixed for a Jeṭh Jātrā, rice-beer is set a-brewing by every Orāon family of a village which intends joining the Jātrā. Three or four days before the Jātrā-day, the pots of rice-beer are brought to the ākhrā where the Orāons of the village are assembled. The Dhāngār-Kōtwār and the Dhāngāṛ-Māhāto are first given five leaf-cups of rice-beer each, and then rice-beer is served to the rest of the assembly. It is interesting to note that the first few drops of liquor from each pot of rice-beer are always offered to the deceased ancestors of the family that brewed it, just as the first few grains of rice are offered to his deceased ancestors by every orthodox Orāon householder while taking his daily meals. After all have drunk rice-beer, the youngest dhāngars hand over to the Dhāṇgar-Kotwār flowers brought by them for the occasion. The Dhāngar-Kōtwār inserts flowers into the hair or over the ears of each dhāngar and

To face p. 315.

The Orāon's mode of salutation (johār). The younger man bends lower than the elder in saluting each other.

of other Orāons present and makes obeisance (Johār) to each one as soon as he is thus decked with flower. Then the Dhāngar-Kōtwār calls upon all present, not even excepting the old men, to join in a dance. Should any one decline to join he is threatened with a beating. In the village where the Jātrā is to be held, a few chickens are sacrificed on the Jātrā-ground by the Pāhān of the village to the village-deities on the forenoon of the day preceding the Jātrā day. It is either before a long wooden post called the Jātrā-Khūnṭā or before the Māndar-Sālās that these sacrifices are offered. After midday meal the young men of the village look up their flags and other village-badges and in the evening set them up on the Jātrā ground. And the whole night is spent in singing and dancing either on the Jātrā ground or at the village ākhrā, by the young people of the village and also in some cases of one or two adjoining villages who come on invitation and are ceremonially escorted into the village. If the pārhā has any unsettled dispute about game with any other pārhā the line of action to be adopted is decided upon at this meet ing. After midday meal on the Jātrā-day, the Dhāngar-Kōtwār and the Pelō-Kọtwār of each village, their straw-whips in hand, respectively lead the young men and the girls of their village to the Jātrā. If the Jātrā village is at some distance, the young people generally carry their Jātrā-dresses in bundles, and put them on when they are nearing the village. Now as they enter the Jātrā village, the bearers of the standards and other emblems lead the procession and are followed by a few young men in war-attire and then by the main body of dancers. The Dhangar-Kotwār takes with him some *tund* (*Diospyros melanoxylon*). twigs, and the Pelō-Kōtwār a number of *gulaichi* flowers. These flowers are distributed to the young people and the *tund* twigs to the boys before they enter the Jātrā-ground. The different village-parties at first dance and sing outside the Jātrā ground; and when all the dancing parties are arrived, they enter the Jātrā-ground one after the other and circumambulate the Jātrā-arena and then each village-party place their flags and musical instruments at an appointed spot, and occupy their accustomed place called 'buhi' in the Jātrā-arena, and display their utmost skill in dancing. The women of the village in which the Jātrā is held carry the benedictory 'karsa' used in weddings. As these women advance in a phalanx, dancing the 'marriage-dance,' they present a very interesting spectacle. After some time, a few elders of the Jātrā-village come and invite one or two representatives from each village to a spot close by, where a jar or two of rice-beer, supplied by the village-elders, have been taken. The Dhāngār-Kōtwār of the village distributes this rice-beer in leaf-cups to the representatives of the different villages. At the larger Jātrās, such as that of village Mūṛmā, the villagers raise a subscription with which a quantity of liquor is purchased for the purpose. After they are thus regaled with drink, the representatives of the different villages discuss social matters of common interest to the tribe or to the Pārhās assembled. If any village of a pārhā has brought to the Jātrā a flag or other device resembling that peculiar to another pārhā, the representatives of that village are remon strated with. If the latter do not agree to forego the use of such flag, the particular village is generally excommunicated; thenceforth no Orāon of such a village will be permitted to join an inter-pārhā hunting excursion or Jātrā dance. If the plea of wrongful looting of game by another pārhā is put forward, they are either told that they should have settled the matter at the śikār-dānr (hunting-ground) by appeal to arms or to arbitrators, or the matter is now decided by these assembled representatives,. Often however the decision is not accepted, and fights take place, on the Jātrā-dānr.

The use of the Jatras.

Just as the success of an inter-pārhā hunting expedition in the month of May (the Biṣu-śikār) is believed to induce an abundant paddy-harvest, so it is believed that a successful Jeṭh-Jātrā in which there is a large gathering of Orāons foretell an abundance of paddy-crops. It may also be noted that it is not permissible for an Orāon to execute a dance or sing a song not appropriate to the season, and should he be found doing so in any village, the elders of the village would impose a fine upon him ; for, such untimely songs or dances bode ill for the village, as, it is believed, in consequence of this either the crops will fail or an epidemic break out among men or cattle. In some of the more important Jātrās, such as those held in village Jaigi (*thana* Kuru), and Bhaskō (*thana* Lohārdāgā) Orāons of a very large number of Pārhās assemble to this day. In fact, the Jātrās of old would seem to have been the great Social Congress of the Orāons,—the first and the last attempt to secure and maintain the solidarity of the tribe. The use of the benedictory 'Kārsā,'—an invariable accompaniment of a marriage ceremony—and the dancing of the marriage-dance may appear to point to the origin of these Jātrās in a recognized necessity for tribal union. At any rate this custom would seem to support the supposition that it was at these jātrās that originally young men would choose and take brides from clans other than their own. The suppòsed magical influence of the tribal dances over crops and game has been referred to in a previous section. The sticks and clubs carried by the young men at the Khāṛiā dances in imitation of hunters appear to be designed to secure, by a process of homœpathic magic, success in hunting. And similarly the gaudy tufts of peacock feathers, the bushy tail of the yak, and the leafy twigs of the wild Khijūr palm, waved about by the male dancers at the Karam dances in imitation of ears of corn waving in the breeze, and also perhaps the tufts of feathers sticking out of the chignon of the female dancers and looking like ears of corn shooting out of the standing paddy stalks, appear to be intended to ensure good crops. Although at the dances at the village-ākhrā you do not see these sticks and clubs, 'sailos' and chāwars being regularly used by the dancers,—at the tribal dances on occasions of the Jātrās, which have for one of their main objects the magical control or stimulation of Nature for the benefit of the Pārhās or villages concerned, you see hundreds of young men carrying sticks, on their shoulders as they dance the Khāṛiā dances, and hundreds of young people—some waving sailōs and chāwars in their hands and some wearing tufts of feathers on their heads—all making a brave show as they dance the Karam dances.*

The observant visitor to one of the more important Orāon Jātrās gets some insight into the socio-political and magico-religious life of the Orāons, just as at an Orāon village-market he gets an idea of their economic life. Besides the *parha* flags with their socio-political importance, the wooden animals and other emblems with their magico-religious significance, and the council of Pārhā elders discussing topics of tribal interest,—he may notice here a Nāg-māti or snake-charmer with his numerous following of young Orāon disciples playing with an apparently venomous snake or passing an iron rod right through the cheeks of a young disciple, there an Orāon Bhagat and his devoted followers invoking some spirit with whom one of

* The female dancers at the Karam dance who thump the ground to imitate *Kesar*-gatherers apparently aim at securing success in fruit-gathering. Col. Dalton appears to have been mistaken in supposing that they thus 'pat the Earth' to make her fruitful. According to Oraon ideas it is the proper function of men and not of women to 'fecundate' the Earth. And this appears to be one of the reasons why the sowing of seeds (and now-a-days the ploughing of the ground too) may not be undertaken by women. As men propagate the human seed so it is they alone who may plough and sow corn-seeds to any purpose. As, however, it is the proper function of the women to nurse human babies, so it is their proper business to transplant young paddy-seedlings after they have been grown by the men.

his sensitive disciples is erelong 'possessed'; and amongst the crowd may be seen batches of two, three, or more Orāons with their bodies painted all over in grotesque colours moving about from stall to stall in studied muteness and carrying in their hands a wooden pestle or a winnowing basket or both. On enquiry, the inquisitive visitor learns that these men have for sometime past been suffering from some persistent malady, and the object of this strange behaviour is said to be to make laughing-stocks of themselves so that the disease-spirits may take flight from their bodies out of very shame. To this older idea, the higher idea of penance appears to have been since superadded; and these men, as they go from stall to stall, accept such 'alms' in the shape of a handful of rice or other grains, sweets, vegetables, tobacco, or a piece of copper coin, as the stall-keepers or others may choose to give them. In fact, the pestle and winnowing-fan they carry are now taken to signify an appeal for alms of grains, although it is not improbable that the original idea was one of blowing away the disease-spirit with the magical winnowing-fan and crushing it out with the pestle. Another interesting sight that will not fail to attract the notice of the observant visitor is that of an Orāon mother with a baby at her breast carrying a short stick in her hand. Inquiry will reward you with the information that such a stick is carried as a menace to the evil eye or to evil spirits so that they may not harm the babe.

Conclusion.

Such are the main features of the village-dormitories, the village-dances, and the Jātrā festivals of the Orāon youth. These take us back to an early stage of human society which the Orāons have otherwise outgrown. The sight of Orāon women eagerly running about from house to house and washing the feet of the hunters returned home with the slain deer, the different Orāon families of the village eagerly going in for their shares of the game, and even the dogs joyfully sharing in the spoil,—brings before you the vision of the hunting stage of Orāon culture, when great must have been the rejoicing of their women and children as the men returned home with the eagerly expected food that was to save their families from starvation. To this day the belief persists that the ill success of an Orāon village at the great annual summer-hunt bodes famine and starvation for that village. And to ensure a plentiful paddy crop, bits of flesh of the deer bagged at the Biṣu-Sikār are minced and dried in the sun and carefully preserved in many an Orāon family, and, at sowing-time, this meat boiled with pulses is eaten as a sacramental meal by many an Orāon on the day that he first sows paddy in his fields. In some places, bits of this dried up meat are mixed with the paddy-seeds to be sown in the fields. The ceremonial fishing, bird-chasing, mice-catching, and fruit-gathering customs described in this chapter, would also appear to be survivals of the same early stage of Orāon culture when the art of agriculture was practically unknown and the wild fruits and roots of the forest and the spoil of the chase formed the Orāon's chief means of subsistence. They are, indeed, like the hunting expeditions of the present day as well as the seasonal dances, the survivals not only of their tribal occupation in the remote past but also of the magico-religious rites performed in those days to secure an abundance of food and to neutralise the dangerous mystic powers inhering in certain kinds of food. The odd offerings to the Chāṇḍi-spirit for the increase of male children and decrease of female children, and the magical observances of the young men designed to augment their procreative powers and secure success in hunting —these and other customs and practices described in this chapter introduce us to an archaic world of thousands of years ago.

CHAPTER VI.

Social Organization and the Regulation of Tribal Life.

The present social organization of the Orāons is the archaic organization of the ancient Orāon hunting communities adapted to the needs of the more complex agricultural village-communities of later days.

I. Totemism.

Totemism which was the basis of the social and political organization of the Orāons in what may be roughly called the hunting and pastoral stages of Orāon culture, still forms the fundamental feature of their social organization in so far as kinship, marriage, and relations of the sexes are concerned. For purposes of exogamy the whole tribe is to this day divided into a number of clans or *gotras*. Individual totems, sex totems, or associated totems are unknown. The fauna and flora of their past and present habitats naturally supply the bulk of the totem names. With the acquisition of a knowledge of agriculture and the use of metals, a few new totem names have been since added. The existing Orāon totems so far as known to us may be classified as follows :—

(i) BEAST TOTEMS.

1. Addō (Ox)
2. Allā (dog).
3. Bāndō (wild cat).
4. Barwa (wild dog).
5. Chidrā (Squirrel).
6. Chiglō (Jackal).
7. Ergō (Rat).
8. Gāṛi (Common monkey).
9. Halmān (Baboon).
10. Khoeā (wild dog).
11. Kiss or Suār (pig).
12. Lākrā (tiger).
13. Osgā (field rat).
14. Rūndā (fox).
15. Tig (a species of monkey).
16. Tirki (young mice).

(ii) BIRD TOTEMS.

1. Bākulā (paddy-bird).
2. Dhechuā (a small black bird with a long tail).
3. Garwā (stork).
4. Gede (duck).
5. Gidhi (vulture).
6. Gislihi (a species of bird).
7. Khākhā (raven).
8. Kerketā (hedge-sparrow).
9. Kōkrō (Cock).
10. Orgōrā (hawk).
11. Tirkuār (the Tithio charai bird).
12. Tōppō or Lāng tōp-pō (a species of long-tailed bird).

(iii) FISH AND OTHER AQUATIC TOTEMS.

1. Aind (a subdivision of the eel.)
8. Kosuār (a species of fish).

2. Beāh (a large fishwith thorns on the back).
3. Ekkā (tortise).
4. Gōdō (crocodile).
5. Ken (a species of fish).
6. Khālkhō („ „)
7. Kinduār („ „)
9. Kūsuwā („ „)
10. Lindā (a subdivision of the eel).
11. Litā (a species of fish).
12. Minj („ „)
13. Sāl („ „)
14. Tirū („ „)

(iv) REPTILE TOTEMS.

1. Khettā or Nāg (Cobra).

(v) VEGETABLE TOTEMS.

1. Bākhlā (a species of grass).
2. Bārā or Bar (*Ficus Indica*).
3. Bāsā (a kind of tree).
4. Gōndrāri („ „)
5. Kāndā (sweet potato).
6. Kāithi (a curry vegetable).
7. Kendi (a kind of tree.)
10. Khes (paddy).
11. Kindā (date palm).
12. Kūjūr (a kind of fruit).
13. Kūndri (a curry vegetable).
14. Mādgi (the mohua tree).
15. Mūnjniār (a kind of creeper).
16. Pusrā (fruit of the kūsūm tree).

* In the list given in Sir Herbert Risley's 'Tribes and Castes of Bengal,' a few of the totem names are given twice over, once in Oraon and again in their Hindi forms. Thus, 'Lakra' and 'Bāgh' are given as two different names, and similar mistakes are made with regard to 'Dhan' and 'Khes', 'Ekka' and 'Kachua', 'Khetta' and 'Nagbans', *etc.*

8. Keōnd (a kind of fruit).
9. Kheksā (a curry vegetable).
17. Pūtri (a kind of tree).
18. Rōri („ „)
19. Angal tōppo (a kind of bush).

(vi) MINERAL TOTEMS.

1. Pānnā (iron).
2. Bekh (salt).

(vii) PLACE TOTEMS.

1. Bāndh (an embanked reservoir of water.)
2. Jūbbi (a marsh or surface-spring).

(viii) SPLIT TOTEMS.

1. Amri (rice-soup).
2. Kispōttā (pig's entrails).

Traditional origin of particular Totems.

The Orāons retain very few traditions as to the origin of particular totem names. Such traditions as they have do not reveal any belief in the descent of men from their totems. All that they indicate is that the totemic animal or plant is believed to have helped or protected the human ancestor of the clan, or been of some peculiar service to him. Thus, it is said that while an Orāon had fallen asleep under a Kūjūr plant, a flexible twig of the plant entwined round his body and protected him from molestation. Accordingly the man took the Kūjūr plant for his totem, and his decendants now form the men of the Kūjūr clan.

Some legends, on the other hand, refer the origin of a few clan-names to some help or protection extended by a man to some animal or plant. Thus, it is said, that while a certain Orāon of olden times was about to catch a tortoise, the latter exclaimed—"I am your jāt (caste-fellow)." And so the man desisted from catching it, and his descendants came to form the Tortoise clan. The origin of the Kis-Pōttā (Pig's entrails) clan is stated to be as follows. An Orāon killed a pig and ate its flesh, but threw away its entrails. The life of the pig ramained in the entrails, so that the slain pig was soon afterwards found moving about in actual bodily form. Thenceforth pig's entrails became tabu to the slayer of the pig and his descendants, and they came to constitute the Kispōttā clan. More matter-of-fact is the account given as to the origin of the Khālkhō Fish clan. An Orāon was fishing in a stream. A Khālkho Fish which was caught in his net managed to escape. Thenceforward, the Khālkhō fish became tabu to the man and his descendants who came to be called men of the Khālkhō clan.

Totem tabus: Sex-tabu.

Although the members of an Orāon clan do not believe in their actual descent from their totem animal or plant, they regard themselves as descendants of a common ancestor, and, as such, blood-relatives between whom marriage or sexual intercourse is not permissible. Although an Orāon will strongly protest that such an union is an incest (a 'brother-sister union' as he calls it) which can never be permitted, the geneological method of inquiry will occasionally reveal an instance here and there of such endogamous union. But in each of the few instances of this sort of union that you may come across, you are sure to find on inquiry that some premarital intrigue leading to inconvenient consequences resulted in a permanent union which was ultimately sanctioned by the village and the Pārhā to which the man belonged, only on the latter having paid a fine and provided a feast to the 'Pārhā brethern.' After the offending pair are thus formally readmitted into the tribe, and their union thus legalized, their sons are considered as good as legal heirs born of lawful wedlock. But of every case of such union, if the parties are no longer in the land of the living, you will be told that, such an union 'could not endure' and that 'as was but inevitable' one of the pair died within a few years of the union. Instances, though rare, have occurred in which a man has married a woman of his own clan in ignorance of her real gōtrā, but when the real facts were discovered the pair were excommunicated, and had to gain readmission into the tribe by a fine and a feast to the members of the Pārhā. As totemism is now a dying institution amongst the Orāons except in its relation to marriage. you will find many Orāons of the present generation ignorant of the gōtras of such near relatives as their mother's father and the husband of either their mother's sister or father's sister. Although an Orāon may not marry into his own totem, he may marry into the totem of his mother. *

Food-tabu and other tabus.

As a general rule, an Orāon must abstain from eating or otherwise using, domesticating, killing, destroying, maiming, hurting or injuring the animal or plant or other object that forms his totem; nor must he use anything made of it or obtained from it; and, when practicable, he will prevent others from doing so in his presence. In the case of tree-totems, the men of the clan will neither go under the shade of the tree nor cut or burn its wood nor use its produce in any shape. When, however, the totem is an animal or plant or other thing which forms an indispensable article of diet or household use, considerations of necessity or expediency appear to have introduced a modification of the tabu against using it. Thus, instead

* While collecting pedigrees of a number of Orāons, we found that our attempts to note the clan of each collateral member of the table would never succeed unless all the villages with which a family was connected by marriage could be visited.

of abstaining altogether from the use of paddy, Orāons of the 'Khes' or Paddy clan abstain only from eating the thin scum that forms on the surface of rice-soup when it stands unagitated in a cool place. Similarly, instead of avoiding the use of salt altogether, Orāons of the Salt clan have only to abstain from taking raw salt unmixed with any food or drink, but may take food or drink to which salt has been added in cooking or in which even raw salt has been mixed beforehand. In the same way, men of the Iron clan have only to abstain from touching iron with their lips or tongue, but may use iron in any other way they like; and men of the Pig clan may eat all parts of the pig except only the head. Men of the Bārā clan may not eat the bār fruit by splitting it up in two but are allowed to eat it whole.

Split totems.

From similar considerations, some of the class of totems that Dr. Frazer* calls 'split-totems' may have arisen. Such are the 'Kis-pōttā' (Pig's entrails) and the 'āmri' (rice-soup) clans. Some may have arisen, as Dr. Frazer suggests, by 'the segmentation of a single original clan which had a whole animal for its totem into a number of totems, either of

* *Totemism and Exogamy*, Vol. I. (1910) p. 10.

which took the name either of a part of the original animal or of a subspecies of it.*

Mutiple tabus.

If in the cases of certain clans, the totem-tabu has been thus modified to suit the convenience of men of the totem,—in a few cases, on the other hand, the tabu has been extended by the law of similarity to other obects that have a real or fancied resemblance to the totem or may happen to bear the same or even a similar name as the totem's. Thus, men of the Tiger (Lākrā) clan, besides the various tabus they have to observe in connection with the tiger and the wolf, have also to abstain from eating the flesh of the squirrel inasmuchas the squirrel's skin is striped like the tiger's. Men of the Kerketa (hedge-sparrow) clan, in addition to the usual tabus with regard to the 'Kerketa', observe a similar tabu with regard to the Dhichua or King-crow which has also a long tail like the kerketā. In some localities, again, an Orāon of the Tiger (Lākrā or Bāgh) clan may not marry in the month of Māgh (December or January) inasmuchas the word 'Māgh' rhymes with 'Bāgh'—the Hindi name for a tiger. Similarly, men of the Monkey (Gāri) clan besides observing the tabu against killing, hunting, domesticating, or eating the flesh of a monkey, have also to abstain from sitting under the shade

* *Ibid*, P 54.

of a tree bearing the same name (Gāri) or cutting or burning its wood. And men of the Khākhā (Raven) clan besides observing the usual tabus with regard to the raven or the crow, has further to abstain from touching with their lips or their tongue the foam of a river,—for such foam is also called 'Khākhāmāndi' in Orāon. Men of the Tig (Baboon) clan, besides observing the usual tabus regading the baboon, have also to observe similar tabus with regard to mice (Chūtia-mūsā) because they resemble the Tig in its colour. We have come across one instance in which the members of an Orāon clan have even to observe a four-fold tabu : The men of the Young Mice (Tirki) clan in addition to the usual tabus against eating, hurting or killing mice, may not look at any young animals (such as young dogs, cats, etc) that have not yet opened their eyes after birth, in asmuchas in this respect they resemble young mice who do not open their eyes until a few days after they are born. Orthodoxy requires that an Orāon of the Tirki clan must not even look at his own children unless they are wide awake. Further, an Orāon of the Tirki clan has to abstain from sitting under the shade of, or cutting or burning the wood of the 'Sonnārkhi' (*B ndarlouri*) plant. The Orāons explain this last tabu by saying that this plant stands related to them as 'bhāisur' (husband's elder brother). And this is how the relation is said to have arisen. The wife of a man of the Tirki clan gave birth to a son under the shade of a 'Sonnārkhi' or 'bāndar-lōuri' plant while she went to gather fuel in the jungles. She left the after-birth suspended on a 'Sonnārkhi' bush, and returned home with her new-born babe. The elder brothers and cousins of the woman's husband who had been out hunting, saw on their way home, the after-birth lying on the 'Sonnārkhi' bush, and mistaking this for the entrails of some animal, took it home, roasted and ate it up. When the mistake was discovered, the 'Sonnārkhi' plant became tabu to the clan. To this day men of other clans taunt the men of the Tirki clan as having the 'Sonnārkh' plant for their 'bhaisūr' (husband's elder brother). We sometimes hear a variant of this legend, according to which a man of the Tirki clan* whose wife was in labour pains asked his brother to get him some flesh to eat, but at the same time warned him not to bring home a dead animal or return home without flesh. The brother considering the errand on which he was sent impossible of literal accomplishment, directed the female members of the family not to dispose of the

* According to another variant it was the woman who asked her brother to get some meat for herself.

after-birth in the usual way but to leave it on a 'Sonnārkhi' bush close by. And this was done as directed. The brother, on his return home after a fruitless quest, took this after-birth to the new-born babe's father who, now caught in his own words, had to eat this curious meat. Thenceforth the 'Sonnārkhi' plant became tabu to men of the Tirki clan. Some of these tabus, again may be the result of what Dr. Frazer calls a fusion of clans.*

Transformation of Totem names.

In a few cases a double totem appears to have arisen from the anxiety felt by a particular totem to change a totem name, now considered opprobrious, into a more respectable name. Thus in a few villages, we have found members of the *Kispotta* (pig's entrails) clan, when asked as to their *gotra* or *clan* give their gotra-name as 'Kasāi' (a kind of tree); and, on enquiry, we found that while observing the customary tabus with regard to pigs, they observe in addition further tabus with regard to the 'Kasāi' tree, under which they do not sit, whose branches they do not burn, and whose fruit they do not eat. usion of clans may also be a possible explanation for such a transformation of the totem name.

* *Ibid*, p. 60.

Other incidents of Totemism.

Tradition testifies to the former recognition by the Orāon clans of the principle of collective responsibility as illustrated by the law of the blood-feud. But, at the present decaying stage of totemism, practically the only trace of the old solidarity of the clan as a whole exists in the recognition by every member of the clan of his duty to welcome as a brother any member of the clan, however unrelated, who may happen to require his hospitality. Individual Orāons have no totem-badges or tabu-marks, nor any difference in dress or in the mode of wearing the hair, to indicate their totem. Nor is there any division of labour between the different clans. They perform no ceremonies for the multiplication of the totem nor indeed is it considered the particular duty of a clan to seek to multiply its totem. The Orāons do not observe any totemic ceremonies in which the flesh of the totem animal or the fruit of the totem tree may be eaten. There are indeed no traces amongst the Orāons of any custom of eating the totem—a custom which, Dr. Frazer suggests, might have preceded the custom of abstaining from it. A man is not believed to have any particular influence over his totem; but a tiger, it is said, would in olden times, abstain from killing or harming a man of the Tiger (Lākrā) clan. But when men departed from their primitive habit of truthfulness and any one meeting a tiger sought to escape by pretending to belong to the Tiger clan, tigers grew suspicious of the veracity of men and ceased to spare even an Orāon of the Tiger clan for the simple reason that a genuine *Lakra-gotra* man could not be distinguished from the mere pretender. A man is not regarded as partaking of any of the qualities of his totem. An Orāon wife retains the totem of her father and has to observe the customary tabus in connexion with it. Although she has further to observe the usual tabus relating to her husband's totem so long only as she actually resides in her husband's village, she is not required to observe these latter tabus when she goes, even on a visit, to her father's village or elsewhere. Any unintentional breach of the totem-tabu by an Orāon, though regarded with social disapproval, is no longer generally believed to entail any serious consequences. But the older people will always tell you that such an infringement is not safe. Thus, it is believed by them that an Orāon of the kūjūr clan will fall ill if he rubs over his body oil made of the kūjūr fruit; and similar beliefs are entertained with respect to the other totems.

Although the general attitude of the Orāon to his clan-totem is that of a man to his equal,—to his friend and ally,—there is a practice still existing which appears to be a survival of a period when at any rate a few of the more powerful among the totems were evolving, if not into actual deities, at any rate into fetishes believed to bring success in hunting or war. Here and there, at an Orāon Jātrā, you see the young men of a village carrying on their shoulders a wooden plank on which stands a tiger, or a pig, or an ox, or other animal, or a bird, made of wood or clay, or perhaps a wooden tortoise or a fish made either of wood or of brass. And you are apt to dismiss it from your thoughts as a fanciful device which the village has arbitrarily chosen to serve as its distinctive badge or emblem at the Jātrā. But if you accompany one such Jātrā-party from their own village up to the Jātrā-ground, you will find that these supposed fanciful emblems are actually treated almost as deities and propitiated with sacrifices. Before such a Jātrā party leave their own village, you see the village-priest religiously putting vermilion marks on it, sacrificing a chicken and offering a little rice-beer to this figure of a tortoise or bird, tiger or some other animal.* On their way from their own village

Religious aspect of Oraon Totemism.

* In some villages a chicken is ceremonially fed on aruā rice and set apart as a vow to be offered in sacrifice after the Jātrā-paty return home with success in any fights that may ensue on the Jātrā-tānr.

to the Jātrā-ground, in whatever village the party happen to halt for a while, they take down this wooden or brass figure at the ākhrā of such village, and the men of such village make offerings of rice-beer and chickens to it. These chickens are, however, not killed but are tied up to the plank supporting the figure; and, on their return home, the chickens are released and they may be taken away by anybody. Now and then you see people carrying merchandise to the markets for sale, offering a little of what they are carrying to these wooden tigers, tortoises *etc.*, to bring them 'luck,' so that they may secure a good sale for their merchandise. These wooden or other emblems are either kept in a hut specially constructed for the purpose, or in some villages they are kept in a hut or shed in the Pāhān's house. These huts or sheds are not however regarded as actual shrines. If you ask the people the significance of these wooden, clay or brass figures, they can only tell you that they are the ancient emblems of the village. On further inquiry, however, you find that in some, though not in all, cases, the figure represents the totem animal of the Bhūinhārs or first Orāon settlers of the village. Thus, the Bhūinhārs of village Jāmgai in thānā Lohārdāgā, and of village Prāyāgu, in thana Māndār, belong to the Tiger clan, and wooden tigers are the emblems that each of these villages carry to the Jātrās. The Bhūinhārs of village Amboā in thānā Lohārdāgā belong to the Tortoise clan, and two wooden tortoises besides a wooden pig are carried by the young men of this village to the Jātrās. The men of village Būṛhā Khūkrā (in thānā Māndār) of which the Bhūinhārs belong to the khālkho fish clan, take to the Jātrās, a brass fish. However, where the wooden figure of a horse (as in village Kudārko where the Bhūinhārs belong to the Tirki clan), or of an elephant (as in village Dighiā where the Bhūinhārs belong to the Paddy clan), is the emblem used, enquiry shows that the emblem was adopted within living memory. On these wooden horses and elephants people are allowed to ride, but this is not allowed in the case of the tigers which are regarded as the guardian deities of the villages concerned. In a few other cases, although the emblems are said to have been in use from time immemorial, the origin is not so clear,—as, for example, in village Biāsi (thānā Māndār) where the Bhūinhārs belong to the Minj fish clan, but the emblem used is a wooden ox which is carried to the Jātrās. On a consideration of all the circumstances, it appears certain in some cases and probable in several other cases of the older emblems that they represent the totems of the first Orāon settlers of the village, and that they were in process of evolution into totem deities when further progress in that direction was arrested. In a few cases (such as that of the ox) perhaps the original settlers may have become extinct or been displaced by later settlers who preserved the ancient emblem which had come to be regarded as the patron spirit of the village. In the river Koel that flows past village Kānjiā (thānā Māndār), crocodiles may be seen, and it is said that a particular crocodile lived for a long time in the river just below the village and was looked upon with religious awe till it disappeared sometime ago. The men of this village carry to the Jātrās four wooden crocodiles. The wooden figure of a tiger bending over two wooden figures of elephants that form the emblem of village Bānāpirhi (in thānā Rānchi) is perhaps a representation of some memorable incident in the history of the village. The men of village Tūmbā Pūriō (thānā Ranchi) carry a peculiar emblem to the jātrās. This is a huge cylindrical cloth-covered frame called 'tōpor', and inside it you see a live red fowl. The Bhūinhārs of village Kinbiṭhā (thānā Māndār) belong to the Toppo bird clan and carry to the Jātrās as the badge of their village a 'Tengrā Khūṭṭā' (triple umbrella) which consists of a bamboo pole to which is attached three bamboo umbrellas set one above the other and covered over with feathers of birds. The belief that these emblems serve to bring luck to the village is perhaps further indicated by the following incident that occured sometime ago in village Chūnd (thānā Māndār). The emblem of that village formerly consisted of four wooden oxen and a wooden human figure supposed to represent a cowherd. A Bhūinhār of the village saw in a dream that the oxen were flying from the village. On the dream being reported to the villagers, they were all perturbed in mind, held a consultation and decided that if the dream came true, 'luck' would leave the village; and so they cast aside the wooden figure of the cowherd which was apparently neglecting its duty, and, in its place, constructed two wooden yokes, and each pair of wooden oxen was yoked to one of these yokes, so that the oxen might not leave the village and thus take away its 'luck'.

Parha Flags.

Even the distinctive flags (bairākhi) carried by each village to the Jātrās, appear to be regarded as living powers,—almost as deities. To them, as to the wooden emblems, the village-priest offers a chicken and a libation of rice-beer before the Jātrā party start from the village for the Jātrā-ground. It is believed that when at a Jātrā or at a hunting excursion, there is a fight between two parties, some flag of one or other pārhā occasionally crows like a cock to infuse spirit into the combatants of the pārhā. Stories are sometimes told about the supernatural help rendered by its bairākhi or flag to some village or other. Thus, recently in a fight between two pārhās, a violent storm followed by torrential rain resulted in the dispersal of one party. The other party unquestioningly attributed the storm and rain to the interference of the flag of their own pārhā. It may be noted that a 'bairākhi' is a triangular cloth-flag of unusual length and breadth, and even a moderate breeze makes it flap about with great noise and bustle. Some of these flags are plain white or red, or blue, or parti-coloured. In some villages, the flag is made of many strips of cloth of different colours and shades of colours, sewn together. Most of the flags have pendents of red tassels and crowns either of coloured cloth or of bird's feathers or of mango twigs. In some villages, a piece of coloured cloth with the figure of the moon, a sword and a shield, some animal or bird or the leaf of a plant is sewn up on the flag ; but the connexion of such a figure with the totem animal or plant is seldom apparent. The use of such flags by every village would appear to have in most cases superseded the wooden or brass or clay figures of animals, *etc.*, which commonly used to be the badge of an entire pārhā. At the present day, whereas every village has its distinctive flags it is only a few villages (sometimes only the 'Rājā' or head village of some pārhā) that possess such a wooden or other symbol.*

Such are some of the characteristics of Orāon Totemism. As with the establishment of agricultural villages, each totem clan got scattered in small batches, and villages established by other totem clans became interspersed between villages established by members of a particular clan, the clan, as a whole, lost its solidarity and ceased to be a local group hunting and fighting, playing and dancing, feasting and deliberating together. The changed circumstances gave rise to another combination of the local 'food-groups.' Although the totem clan has remained the basis of the social structure of the Orāons, the pārhā confederacy, of which we shall speak later on, has supplanted the totem-clan as the socio-political unit of the Orāons. The totemic grouping of Orāon society, however, retains its importance to this day in so far as marriage and kinship are concerned.

* It is in some villages in *thanas* Mandar, Bero, Lohardaga and Ranchi only that I have come across such wooden emblems.

II. KINSHIP AND THE PRIVILEGES AND FUNCTIONS OF CERTAIN KIN.

(A) The classificatory system.

The exogamous kinship-group of the clan, as we have seen, still forms the foundation of the social system of the Orāons. The Orāon system of kinship is of the kind termed 'classificatory' by Morgan, and more appropriately called the 'clan' system by Dr. W. H. R. Rivers.* The fundamental feature of this system is, broadly speaking, the application of the same kinship term in addressing most, though not all, persons of the same generation and sex. Thus, the Orāon addresses as 'bā' (father) not only his own male parent but also all whom that parent would call brothers ; and similarly he would address as 'āiyo' (mother) not only his own female parent but also, roughly speaking, all whom his father might marry,—and as 'bābu' (son) and 'māi' (daughter) not only his own sons and daughters respectively but all the males and females who would call him 'bā.' In certain cases, however, a distinction is made in addressing the elderand younger members of the same generation.

* *Kinship and the Social Organization* (London, 1914) p. 71.

Kinship nomenclature.

We give below a table of Orāon terms of relationship and mutual address, obtained by means of genealogies. The terms 'brother' and 'sister' in the following table are used in a classificatory sense so as to include cousins hewever remote.

Father—*is spoken of as*—	'Embās',—*and addressed as*—	'bā'
Father's younger brother .	'Eng Kākās' (also 'sānni embās'=my little father) .	'bā' (or kākā)
Father's elder brother .	'Eng baṛās' (also 'kohā embās'=my great father) ,,	'ba'
Wife's father ; Husband's father .	'Eng Sasrus, .	'bā'
Great-grand-father or great-grand-uncle. .	'Eng baṛās' .	'bā'
Husband's or wife's mother's brother .	'Eng māmu sasrus' .	'bā'
Mother's elder sister's husband .	'Eng baṛās' .	'baṛā' or 'baṛā bā'
Mother .	'Ingio' .	'ayo' or 'ayang
Wife's mother, Husband's mother .	'Eng sāis' .	'ayo'
Father's elder brother's wife .	'Eng baṛi' .	'āyō' (or 'baṛi')
Father's younger brother's wife .	'Eng kākki' .	'kāki'
Mother's elder sister. .	'Eng baṛi' .	'baṛi'
Great-grand-mother or Great-grand-aunt. .	'Eng baṛi' .	'baṛi'

Mother's brother*—*is spoken of as*—'Eng māmus'—*and addressed as*—'Māmu'

Father's sister's husband	"	'Eng māmus'	"	'Māmu'
Father's sister	"	'Eng tāchi'	"	'tāchi'
Mother's brother's wife	"	'Eng tāchi,	"	'tāchi,
Mother's younger sister	"	'eng tāchi,'	"	'mosi'
Mother's younger sister's husband	"	'eng mosā'	"	'mosā'
Elder brother	"	'Engdādās'	"	'dā'
Wife's elder brother	"	'Engjeṭh sārās'	"	"
Wife's elder sister's husband	"	'Eng sarhus'	"	'dā '(or sāṛhu)
Husband's elder brother	"	'Eng bāinālas'	"	'dā'
Elder sister	"	'Eng dai'	"	'dai'
Wife's elder sister	"	'Eng bāināli'	"	'dai'
Husband's elder sister	"	"	"	"
Husband's elder brother's wife	"	'Eng gotni'	"	'dai'

* It may be noted that 'em,' eng' or 'ing' prefixed to an Orāon term of relationship signifies 'my' (*e.g.*, 'embās'=my father, 'Ingio'=my mother) Similarly the prefix 'tān' or 'tāng' signifies 'his' (*e.g.*, tāmbās'=his father, 'tangio'=his mother) and 'ning' signifies 'thy', and 'nāng'—'ours.'

Father's elder sister is also callted 'Baṛi' which is a Hindi term and mother's elder brother is called 'baṛā.' So also is the younger brother's daughter called 'baṛi'.

Father's father or uncle—*is spoken of as*—'Eng ăjjos'—*and addressed as*—'ăjjo

Mother's father or uncle	„	'Eng ăjjos' (or engnānăs)	„	'ăjjo' (or 'nănā')
Father's mother or aunt ; Mother's mother or aunt	„	'Eng ajji' (or Eng nani)	„	'ajji' or 'nani')
Son's wife's father ; Daughter's husband's father	„	'Eng samdhis'		'Samdhi'
Son's wife's mother ; Daughter's husband's mother	„	'Samdo'	„	'Samdo'
Younger brother	„	'Ingṛis'	„	'Bābu'
Wife's younger brother	„	'Eng saras'	„	„
Son	„	'Engdas'	„	„
Younger brother's son	„	'Eng baṛabeṭas'	„	'beṭa'(or 'babu')
Elder brother's son	„	'Engkhlagos'	„	„
Husband's elder brother's son	„	'Engkhlagos'	„	„
Brother's son (of a woman)	„	'Engachos'	„	„
Husband's younger brother	„	'Engerkhos'	„	„
Elder sister's son (of a woman)	„	'mosi beta'	„	„
Wife's elder sister's son	„	„	„	„
Younger sister's son (of woman)	„	'baṛa beṭa'	„	„

Wife's younger sister's son—*is spoken of as*—'bara beta'—*and addressed as*—'beta' (or 'babu.

Daughter's husband	,,	'Eng Jaunkhaddis'	,,	'babu'
Younger sister's husband	,,	'Eng bāinālas' (bahin damad)	,,	,,
Wife's youuger sister's husband.	,,	'Eng sarhus'	,,	'Ko' or 'babu' or 'tangmosa' i.e. 'mosa of my son.'
Sister's daughter's husband	,,	'Eng jaunkhaddis'	,,	'babu'
Elders sister's husband	,,	'Eng bheṭas'	,,	'bhatu' (or 'ana ba')
Wife's brother's son	,,	'Eng bhagnas'	,,	'bhagna' (or babu)
Husband's sister's son	,,	,,	,,	,,
Daughter	,,	'Engda'	,,	'mai'
Younger sister.	,,	'Ingṛi'	,,	,,
Husband's brother's wife	,,	'Eng gotni'	,,	,,
Husband's younger sister	,,	'Engerkho'	,,	,,
Elder brother's daughter (man's)	,,	'Enkhlagi'	,,	,,
Husband's elder brother's daughter	,,	,,	,,	,,
Wife's brother's daughter	,,	'Engbhagni'	,,	'mai' or 'bhagn'

Husband's sister's daughter	—*is spoken of as*—	'Engbhagni'	—*and addressed as*—	'mali' or 'bhagni'
Wife's elder sister's daughter	,,	'mosi beti'	,,	,,
Elder sister's daughter (of a woman)	,,	,,	,,	'mai'
Wife's younger sister's daughter	,,	'baṛi beṭi'	,,	,,
Younger sister's daughter (of a woman)	,,	,,	,,	,,
Younger brother's daughter (of a man)	,,	,,	,,	,,
Husband's younger brother's daughter	,,	,,	,,	,,
Brother's daughter	,,	Eng acho	,,	,,
Child's or nephew's or niece's son or nephew	,,	'Eng nattis'	,,	'natti'
Husband	,,	'Eng metas'	,,	'ana'
Wife	,,	'Eng khai'	,,	'anae'
Son's or brothers' son's wife	,,	'Eng kheṛo'	,,	'khai'
Sister's son's wife	,,	'Eng kheṛo'	,,	'khai'
Younger brother's wife	,,	'Eng bainali'	,,	,,
A co-wife	,,	'Eng melkho'		
(A man's) Elder brother's wife	,,	'Nasgo'	,,	'Nasgo'

Kinship and Marriage. Although marriage, amongst the Orāons, is primarily governed by the rule of clan-exogamy, genealogical or blood relationship up to three generations is now generally considered a bar to marriage even with a member of a different clan.* And as to this, it is worth noticing that in tracing such relationship, the classificatory rule is applied even to members of a different clan,—the terms used by an Orāon for relatives by blood or marriage are applied to certain other people of the same generation with whom personally he has no relationship at all. Thus, if X is related to Y as his sister's son, those whom X calls brothers (X's paternal uncle's sons, for example, with whom Y has no actual relationship) will be regarded as in the same category with X and therefore not eligible for marriage to Y.

* The orthodox theory is that so long as relationship is remembered, marriage is not proper between two families. But as the Oraon's memory as to relationship is particularly short,—some of them even forgetting their grandfather's name,—the three-generation rule in bar of marriage generally fulfils orthodox requirements. The rule usually observed in practice is that when ceremonial visits, mutual invitations and exchange of presents on ceremonial occasions, have ceased between two families related by a marriage in a former generation there is nothing wrong in entering into fresh matrimonial alliances. According to some Oraons the only forbidden degrees of relationship with regard to marriage are, besides persons of the same *gotra*, a person's cross-cousins.

Relations between grand-parent and grand-child.

There appear to be reasons for inferring the former existence amongst the Orāons (before clan-exogamy was instituted) of a system of marriage or union between persons related to each other as grand-parent (or grand-uncle) and grand-child (or grand-nephew or grand-niece)—a system the existence of which has been noticed by Dr. Rivers in the island of Pentecost and by Mr. Hewitt among the Dierri of Australia. The father of a grand-father, as we have seen in our list, is addressed by the Orāon as 'bā'—the same term employed in addressing a father as well as a father-in-law; and, similarly, a great-grand-son is addressed as 'bābū'—the same term that is employed in addressing a son and also a son-in-law. This in itself would not prove much. But when, along with this, we consider the bantering mode of conversation regarded as appropriate between persons related as grand-parent (or grand-uncle) and grand-children (or grand-nephews and grand-nieces), in which the two parties habitually act the part of man and wife, one cannot resist the conclusion that this habit must have had its origin at a period of Orāon society when such union was widely current.* As

* It may be noticed that although certain Hindu castes of Chota Nagpur, like some sections of Hindus in Bihar, are permitted to take liberties with the mother's brother's wife which point to a former social regulation such as Dr.

a sample of an orthodox conversation between an Orāon grand-father of our own days and his young married grand-daughter, we may cite the following short dialogue :—

Grand-father :—An pāchcho, ekāsé rāādi ? (old woman how do you do ?)

Grand-daughter :—Koṛé koṛem rā'dān, pāchgi. (I am well, old man).

Grand father :—Enghāi eṛpā enghon ho mālā kādi ? (Why don't you come to my house even once ?)

Grand-daughter :—Ninghāi eṛpā ender beddā kālon ? (Why shall I go to your house ? [The implication is,—Am I your married wife that I shall go to your house ?])

Grand-father:—En pāchkān āungé engān āmbā biddi ārā mālā kādi ? (Is it because I have grown old that you want to forsake me, and do not want to go to my house ?)

Grand-daughter :—Nin pāchgis gūsān en mālā kālon. (I shall not go to you—an old man [that you are] !)

Grand-father :—Mālā kāloy ! Dhāronki pāsnūm

Codrington has recorded (*Melanesians* p. 38) and Dr. Rivers has discussed (*Kinship* &c, pp. 28-31), such liberties are not permitted by the Oraon.

ho'on ; ningio nimbās ningān engāgé bisyār,— mālā kāloy ? (Won't you go ? If you don't, I shall seize you and take you [home] thrashing you on the way [*i. e.* as a husband beats and takes home a truant wife]. Your parents sold (married) you to me. Won't you go ? [*i. e.* go you must]).

It may be further noticed in this connection that amongst the majority of the Orāons it is still considered a comparatively trivial offence if persons related to each other as grand-parent and grand-child in the classificatory sense are found to have illicit relations, just as a similar misbehaviour of an Orāon with his elder brother's wife is not considered a serious offence. It is not unusual to find great liberties being taken with such relatives without any protest. But it is quite othewise when an Orāon is found taking such liberties, not to speak of having improper relations, with a relative of the opposite sex who stands one degree higher or one degree lower than himself in the pedigree and is therefore considered as related to him as parent or child. Excommunication or in the alternative a costly expiation ceremony together with a feast to the Pārhā 'brethren' is the usual penalty for such an offence. There are, again, certain relatives who, though belonging to the same generation, are, by a social fiction, considered as standing to each other in practically the same relation as parent and child. Between such relations, known by the generic name of 'bāinālas' or 'bāinālī' (according as the person is a male or a female), illicit connexion is considered incestuous. We shall refer to these relations in the next sub-section.

Cross-cousin Marriage.

Again, the facts that the mother's brother and the father's sister's husband are both described by the same kinship-term ('māmūs'), and that the father's sister and the mother's brother's wife are similarly both described by the same kinship term ('tāchi'), coupled with the further fact that in the case of a cross-cousin marriage the relationships of mother's brother and father's sister's husband come to be combined in one and the same person, may appear to indicate the former prevalence of cross-cousin marriage amongst the Orāons. And, for aught we know, the Orāons, like the Fijians and the southern islanders of the New 'Hebrides, * might once have used the same term for the father-in-law. The present term for a 'father-in-law'—'sasrus', which is a saṁskritic term is obviously a later loan-word. At the present day the objection that the Orāons urge against a cross-

* *Ibid*, p. 22.

cousin marriage is that it is not proper for the children of persons who have 'been suckled at the same (mother's) breast' to marry each other. Genealogies show that marriages between children of cross-cousins are still permissible. The Orāons appear to have borrowed from their Hindu neighbours and landlords a custom which is, however, not in much favour in the Orāon community. This is known as the 'gōlāt-benja' or 'circular marriage' in which an Orāon marries his son or nephew and a daughter or niece respectively to the daughter or niece and a son or nephew of another Orāon *

It is significant that such of the Orāon terms of relationship as appear to partake of the nature of descriptive terms, are generally borrowed from Śaṁskritic Hindi. Such are the terms 'baṛā', 'baṛi', 'baṛā-beta', 'baṛā-beti', 'gōtni', 'samdhi', 'sasrūs', 'sāis', &c.

General character of the Oraon system of Kinship.

A consideration of the indigenous and borrowed terms of Orāon kinship-nomenclature, would incline one to think that before contact with the Hindu system of kinship, marriage amongst

* The 'golat benja' (or circular marriage), should not be confounded with the 'golbenja' (from 'gollas', a landlord, and 'benja' marriage) which simply means an expensive marriage celebrated with great pomp like a marriage in the Hindu landlord's family.

the Orāons was regulated almost exclusively by the rule of clan-exogamy, and that further restrictions based on genealogical relationship have been since super-added. Such restrictions strictly include only marriages between the children of a brother and a sister and between the children of two sisters. And to this extent, the Orāon system of kinship may be said to be complex, although the general character of the system has been determined by the social condition of clan-exogamy. The application of the vocative term 'bābū' (generally employed to sons in a classificatory sense) to one's own or one's wife's younger brother as well as to own's own (or one's wife's) younger sister's husband—and of the vocative term 'māi' or 'māiā' (generally employed to daughters) to one's own (or in the case of a woman, also her husband's) younger sister may appear to reflect psychology more than . sociology. In conclusion, we may notice a few general terms of address, though not always of kinship, which may be attributed more to psychological than to sociological causation. Such are the terms 'dē' by which a father as well as any old man irrespective of relationship may be addressed, 'dō' by which a mother as well as all old women may be addressed, 'biā' by which little brothers and sisters are sometimes addressed by way of endearment, 'kōe' (abbreviation of 'kukkoe', girl) by which young girls are sometimes addressed by their elders, 'kō' or 'ānā kō' by which boys may be addressed by their elders, 'ānā' and 'ānāé' by which equals (males and females respectively) may be addressed. Not less interesting are the terms of collective address : Such are the terms 'hārō' by which a man addresses a number of other men or boys collectively, 'khādiō' by which a woman addresses a number of other women or girls collectively and 'khādro' by which a woman addresses a number of boys collectively.

(B)Disabilities, Duties, and Privileges of certain Relatives.

Kinship tabus.

In our table of terms of relationship we have seen that certain relatives, stand to each other in the position of 'Bāenālas' or 'Bāenāli'. A man's younger brother's wives and his wife's elder sisters are his 'bāenālis', and a woman's husband's elder brothers (in a classificatory sense) and her younger sisters' husbands are 'bāenālases' to her, and her husband's elder sisters (in a classificatory sense) and her younger brothers' wives are her 'bāenālis'. The compound terms 'bāenālas' and 'bāe-nāli' are composed of the words 'bāenā,' meaning 'strange', and 'ālas' (man) or 'āli' (woman). As the terms signify, a man and a woman standing to each other as 'bāenālas' and 'bāenāli,' although living in the same house, have to behave towards each other almost as strangers. They may not touch each other, nor sit on the same mat or other seat together, nor utter each other's name, nor even talk to each other except about unavoidable domestic or other affairs. Should one happen to touch the other by chance or even take the other's name under unavoidable circumstances, a ceremonial expiation has to be performed. A jar of rice-beer has to be prepared; and, when it is ready, the husband's elder brother in the presence of the other members of the family has to hand over to the woman the brass vessel filled with rice-beer. The younger brother's wife has to take a little rice-beer from it in a leaf-cup and drink it. She has then to hand back the brass vessel to her husband's elder brother who has similarly to fill a leaf-cup with rice-beer and drink it. Then the latter has to say, "Innāntim neg dastūr mānjā, ēmke imsrā khai." ("The customary rite has been observed, from this day do not touch me again"). And thence forth they become tabu to each other again. Marriage or sexual intercourse even between a widowed 'bāenālas' and, a widowed or an unmarried 'bāenāli,' is strictly tabued, although such relatives necessarily belong to different clans. The husband's elder brother is permitted to touch his younger brother's bride only on the day of her marriage and the day following. And that is why you sometimes see an Orāon bride on the day after her marriage being carried to her husband's house on the arms of her husband's elder brother.

Name-tabus.

Besides the tabu on names of persons related to each other as 'bāenālas' and 'bāenāli', the names of a husband and a wife are tabu to each other. In addressing each other the husband generally calls the wife as 'mother of so-and-so' and the wife calls the husband as 'father of so-and-so.' If, however, the pair is childless, the husband often addresses the wife by some such epithet as 'the deaf one' (bahiri), 'the tall one' (dhōngi) or 'the short one' (nātri); and similarly the wife addresses her husband as 'bahirā' (deaf man) or 'dhongā' (tall man) and so forth,—although, as a matter of fact, neither of them may be deaf or particularly tall or short in stature.* Although this tabu is strictly observed in addressing each other, it may be infringed with impunity where circumstances necessitate the husband or wife being spoken of by name. The names of near deceased relatives, particularly of a deceased wife, may not be taken. The reason for this tabu

* Often, however, the husband in addressing the wife simply says 'anā bār dai,' and the wife in addressing the husband says 'ānā hō'.

appears to be the fear of the spirits of the dear departed turning up at the sound of their names. Now-a-days a breach of any of these name-tabus, except that relating to a 'bāinālas' or a 'bāināli', is considered an impropriety rather than an offence. There is another class of name-tabus which has nothing to do with relationship. These are the tabus on names of certain persons, animals, places or other things : It is believed that some names pronounced at certain times bring ill-luck to the person who pronounces them. Thus, the names of certain villages are not pronounced by the men of certain other villages at night-time, for it believed that some misfortune will befall the man who does so.† Similarly some people's names are considered of bad omen if pronounced within an hour or so after sunrise. In the cases of certain beasts and reptiles, substitutes for their names are used at night. Thus a serpent is called a 'rope', a tiger is called the 'long-tailed' thing (dighā khōlā), a sheep is called the 'wool-covered' 'thing (khāni chutti). These prohibitions are not attended with any social consequences or social disapproval and have therefore nothing to do with our present topic.

† Thus the names of villages, 'Pāli,' 'Nagri,' and 'Gargāon' are not pronounced at night by the Oraons of village Sakra and other neighbouring villages.

Ceremonial Functions of certain Kin.

In the performance of certain social ceremonies, Orāon usage assigns definite functions to particular relatives. The more important of these functions are the following:

(a) During Pregnancy.

When an Orāon female is with child, in some parts of the Orāon country, it is the custom to invite her father or brother to her husband's place to perform the sacrificial ceremony of the 'jodākāmnā' meant to prevent the evil spirits of her father's village from doing her any harm.

(b) At Birth.

It is properly the function of the baby's grandfather, and in his absence of the baby's sister's husband, to officiate as the sacrificer at the 'dāndā-renghnā' ceremony performed after the birth of a child and meant to ward off the evil eye and the evil attentions of malignat spirits from the child. But at ths present day, as the rites and the formulæ connected with them are not known to every Orāon, any Orāon of the village who is acquainted with the proper procedure of the ceremony is invited to officiate at the ceremony.

(c) At Marriage.

At an Orāon wedding, it is the function of the

bridgroom's and bride's married sisters (not having been widowed and each living with her first husband) to besmear the forehead of the bride-groom and of the bride respectively with turmeric and oil and to perform certain other ceremonies believed to ensure happiness and prosperity to the pair during their married life. The father or elder brother of the bride has to draw, from the village-well or spring, water required for the marriage rites. This water has to be brought at cock-crow before any one else has touched the well or spring that morning; and the pitcher has to be dipped perpendicularly into the water with its mouth turned straight upwards. Again, when the actual marriage rites are being performed, it is primarily the function of the brothers and (male) cousins of the bride (when the wedding takes place at the bride's house) or of the bridegroom (when the wedding takes place at the latter's parents' house) to hold a screen round the bride and bridegroom and persons officiating at the marriage so that they may be screened from the gaze of strangers (who may have the evil eye) and of evil spirits. The maternal uncle of the bride or bridegroom has no particular function assigned to him in the marriage ceremonies of his sister's child. When the bride first leaves her parents' home for her husband's, her father puts an iron-headed arrow into her hands. The girl carries it to prevent the evil spirits of her parents' village from following her.

(d) At Death.

At the cremation of a deceased Orāon, it is usually the sons of the deceased who have first to put fire into the mouth of the corpse, after which other relatives do the same.

(e) In Disease.

When a child suffers from boils on the head. the Orāons say that the boils are the offspring of the cervical gland which they call the 'old woman' or 'old mother.' It is only the maternal uncle of the child who can, so the Orāons believe, cure the boils by pressing the 'old mother' (cervical glands) with one of his own finger-rings, this not being removed from the finger,—and by singeing the 'old mother' with the heated edge of a sickle.

Rights and Privileges of certain Relatives.

An Orāon mother is considered to have very little right over her children. The father as the lord of the family has almost absolute right. But in case the mother of his children deserts him and remarries, she generally manages to take away the younger children with her. But when such a son becomes old enough to cultivate his lands, (at about fourteen years) he generally goes over to the father's place, and if the father objects to take him on, the village Panchāyat when appealed to by the son generally make the father give him a share of the family lands.

(a) Mother.

In the recognised right of the mother of an Orāon bride to receive three pieces (or sometimes one piece) of cloth known as "mother's cloth" from the bridegroom as part of the consideration for the hand of the bride, we seem to meet with a survival of mother-kin.

(b) Grand-mother.

If the father's mother is alive at the time, she too, however, receives a similar present of a cloth called 'āji ledrā' (grand-mother's cloth).

(c) Father.

The father, however, gets no presents of clothes. The cash bride-price which he (or in his absence the brother or uncle) receives appears to be a substitute for the cattle formerly given.

We have referred above to the rights of an Orāon father over his children. The father may even give away his son to be adopted by another man as his son. The custom of adoption is, however, falling into disuse. In the few cases in which a boy is still taken into his house by a sonless Orāon as his prospective son-in-law, the boy is regarded as standing in the same position as a son adopted from a different clan. This kind of probationary son-in-law stands on a different footing from the other class of 'ghar-dāmād' described in a previous chapter,* for, in the case of such a probationer, the question of bride-price does not enter into consideration at all. Generally it is only an orphan boy who can be induced to become a probationary son-in-law of this kind. When a boy agrees to become such a son-in-law, the girl's father with a few elders of his own village as 'Panch' goes to the house of the boy. There a few elders of the boy's village too are called as 'Panch,' and in the presence of the 'panches' of both sides, the girl's father promises that on his death all his *rajhas* lands will go to the boy if the latter lives with him in his house, cultivates his fields, and in due time marries his daughter. Another custom which has now practically fallen into disuse further illustrates the right of an Orāon father over his son. We have referred in a preceding chapter to the *Soukhia* system of labour, as it now exists. But the *Soukhia* system, as it existed in full vigour half a century ago, was in reality a mild form of slavery. When an Orāon father borrowed a large sum of money which he hardly expected to be able to repay, he made over one of his sons to the creditor to serve him as his 'Soukhia dhāngar' for an indefinite term,—in reali-

* *Vide* p. 199 *ante.*

ty, for life. Sometimes however a poor Orāon who had many children made over one of his sons as a *Soukhia* dhangar to another Orāon—generally a relative. The young man served him as a labourer without any pay but receiving only food and boarding. In such a case, the 'Soukhia dhāngar' was usually regarded as a member of his master's family —almost as an adopted son but without rights of inheritance ; and he was usually married at the expense of the master, who finally paid him some money to make a start in life. From a paper on 'Chota Nagpur' written by Mr. S. T. Cuthbert, a former Magistrate of the old District of Rāmgarh (which included the Chota Nagpur Plateau), and read before the Asiatic Society of Calcutta in 1841, it appears that a mild form of slavery was in vogue in those days and that even a document was executed for the purpose, apparently when the master was a non-aboriginal. Mr. Cuthbert says,—"There are different species of bondsmen in the pergunah. 1st.—When a person receives a sum of money from another, and executes a deed called Saunak patra, he becomes the person's bondsman or *Saunak* for life and cannot be released from the bond, though he offer payment of the money he received. The deed of *Saunak patra* however does not affect the children. It is expected that the master furnishes his bondsmen with food and clothing; generally he pays the expenses attendant on marriage.

"2nd.—A person who borrows a sum of money from another, stipulating by a deed to serve the latter for a specified time, or until the amount of the principal and interest be repaid. This bondsman has an allowance of a *maund* of rice a month, and one rupee is given to him at the cold season, besides which he is entitled to one bundle out of 21 bundles of the crops at the cutting season.

"3rd.—A person who hires himself for field labour, the period of which service is generally from Magh to the end of Pous; and should the bondsman run away within the period of service, the master is entitled to damages on account of loss of services. This kind of bondsman generally receives six rupees a year and twelve maunds of rice."

In our days, the third form of service known as Dhangrāi is the usual form in use, but happily the master is no longer entitled to any damages or fine except that the absconding dhāngar has to pay back the unearned portion of the wages he may have received in advance. Occasionally you still meet with a form of 'Soukhiā' dhāngar service, which looks like a compromise between the first and second forms of service described above: By this an Orāon who has borrowed a large sum of money makes over his son as a 'soukhia' to the creditor whom he has to serve without pay so long as the debt is not repaid. The *Soukhia* servant lives in the house of the creditor and gets only his food. Finally it may be noticed that an Orāon master treats his servant as a member of his family. It is significant that the terms 'Jōnkh' and 'Dhāngar' applied to servants are also applied to the young bachelors of the family.*

Inheritance and Partition of Property.

(a) General Principles.

The Orāon method of reckoning descent is, as we have seen, patrilineal; and the wife lives in the husband's house where the husband exercises supreme authority over his family. The customary rules that regulate the devolution of property amongst the Orāons, appear to have been determined partly, if not primarily, by their peculiar belief in the state of the human soul after death, and partly by social and economic conditions. The human spirit, after the dissolution of the physical body, is believed to reside in the underworld where the spirits of all the deceased Orāons of the same clan of a village live in shadowy forms and constitute a

* The term *Sounak patra* in Mr. Cuthbert's paper is apparently a printer's mistake for *sewak patra* (deed of service).

closely united group. Many an Orāon has been to these spirit settlements during sleep or illness; and, if you succeed in gaining their confidence, they will describe to you the details of those underworld habitations, the appearance of their occupants, and their occupation with a naive simplicity which will leave no room for doubt in your mind as to their firm conviction in the truth of their assertions. These subtle-bodied spirits are believed to derive nutrition from the essence of the offerings made to them by their male descendants daily before every regular meal, periodically at certain sacrificial feasts, and annually at the great 'bone-burial' festival. If on the night following the 'bone-burial' festival you chance to pass by the side of the 'kūndi' where the bones of the dead Orāons of a village have been deposited, and where boiled rice, pulse and other food have been laid out that evening for all the spirits of the dead, you run the risk of being chased by the spirits who are assembled there to do justice to the viands thus provided by their male descendants. Even if you and other foreigners like you whom they respected and looked up to in their life-time as their superiors be allowed to pass unmolested, a rustic Orāon happening to cross their path can hardly escape scot-free. More than one Orāon have narrated to us their gruesome experiences when chased by such spirits, they ran home for dear life or fell down senseless, and in either case some sickness or other at once overtook them. As their own well-being depends on the possession by their male decendants of sufficient means for regularly providing rice-offerings and rice-beer libations to them, these spirits of the dead are naturally solicitous about the preservation in the hands of their male descendants of the property they have left behind. The spirits of the dead keep themselves in touch with such property. And should even a married daughter of the family stealthily take away to her husband's place any property belonging to her father or brothers, the property is sure to be followed by some spirit of her father's village, and sickness or some other affliction is sure to be caused in her husband's family. So strong is the belief in this attachment of the dead to the property they leave behind them and their zeal for the preservation of the property in the hands of their male descendants or other agnates to the exclusion of persons not belonging to the same exogamous stock that even a *ghar-damad* who lived with his sonless deceased father-in-law during his lifetime and who has since been enjoying the *rayati* lands left by him, will, in the event of any case of serious illness occurring in his own family within a short time of his father-in-law's death, often make over any moveable property (especially iron implements, broomsticks, and winnowing baskets) that belonged to his deceased father-in-law to the latter's agnates.

As the living and the dead members of the same exogamous clan of any particular village together form in a sense one village-family in the eyes of the Orāon, and as daughters by their marriage pass out of this family and are debarred from taking part in the sacrificial offerings and libations made to the ancestor spirits of their father's family, a daughter loses all right to a share in the property left by her father or by any other member of her father's clan. And as a married woman may neither offer any oblations to the deceased ancestors of her husband's family nor join in the worship of the genuine Orāon village-deities, she is not entitled to absolute inheritance of property belonging to her husband's family either. Thus the two fundamental rules that meet us at the the threshold of our subject—the rules that property must not pass out of the clan nor be inherited in absolute right by a woman,—are based partly on a religious and partly on a sociological basis. These rules have been further modified on economic and historical grounds by restricting the devolution of property to the deceased owner's fellow-Bhūinhārs of the same clan and village. We have seen in a previous chapter that the division of administrative and other functions led to the splitting of the Bhūinhārs or original settlers of an Orāon village into two or three Khūnts (*lit*, stocks) —the Khūnt of the sacerdotal head (the Pāhān) and that of the temporal headman or headmen (Mundā or Māhātō or both). Under Orāon rules of inheritance, in the absence of any member of the Khūnt of a deceased owner of property, the members of the other Bhūinhār Khūnts by reason of their common descent, would be entitled to divide the Bhūinhāri lands and other property of the deceased amongst themselves. But under the present changed economic situation of the country, alien landlords generally manage to take possession of such property when there is no member of his own Khūnt surviving him unless the deceased owner happened to execute a deed of transfer during his life-time. * Changes

* This right of transfer, however, has for the present been taken away (temporarily, as it is believed) by the Legislature to prevent Oraons from being defrauded into transferring their lands for an inadequate price. But unfortunately, in many cases the unforeseen effect of this measure has been to benefit the landlord at the expense of the Oraon tenant.

in the economic conditlons of Orāon life have introduced important modifications in the two fundamental rules of Orāon inheritance, enunciated above. We have seen that the idea of private (as distinguished from communal) property in lands had been evolved amongst the Orāons before they settled in ChotāNāgpur, and that except in respect of waste lands, public lands such as the Sarnā, the village-masān, the Bhutāhā lands, and village jungles which all remained the common property of the village community, each Orāon family came to be a property-owning unit of which the father was the patriarchal head. From this it necessarily followed—(1) that on the death of the *pater familias* the property devolved on his sons, or, in the absence of sons, on the nearest family or families of male agnates; and (2) that when a deceased *pater familias* left more than one son, the eldest son would step into his place as the head of the family, and, in the event of a partition, would receive a slightly larger share (*jethangs*) than his other brothers as a recompense for his surrender of the *potestas* or authority in the family to which he had succeeded after his father.

An Orāon owner of lands who has no sons may have recourse to either of two contrivances to make a show of continuing his family after his death : He may either adopt a son to himself or take into his house a 'prospective son-in-law.' If the adopted son belongs to his own clan and khũnt, and has been adopted on the other agnates of the owner agreeing in the presence of the Panch to forego in his favour their claim to inheritance, such adopted son acquires the full rights of a son ; otherwise he is only entitled to inherit the rājhas lands of the adoptive father. A *ghar-dijoa* son-in-law (adopted as such *before marriage*) can, in no case, inherit the Bhũnhāri lands of his deceased father-in-law, although the rājhas lands, by reason probably of the small value that came to be attached to them and in consideration of the labour expended by the *ghar-dijoa* over them, go to him, unless the deceased has left a brother or a brother's son who was joint in mess and property with the deceased at the time of his death. In this comparative indifference to *rajhas* lands we see the influence of changed economic conditions under which the tenure of such lands became (and up till recently remained) quite insecure. Another interesting point in the Orāon code of inheritance and partition is that the sons by a first wife are or rather used to be generally allotted a larger share of the family lands than those by a later wife. But under the influence of Hindu ideas of partition and inheritance and also through the indirect effect of judicial decisions pronounced by officers who in the past had very little opportunities of acquainting themselves with the customary laws of the aborigines and so generally assumed that the same rules applied to them as to their Hindu neighbours, such unequal division of property is gradually falling into disuse. The sons by the younger wife know that they can often successfully claim an equal share of the patrimony in the Courts and so they sometimes defy their own tribal Panchāyats in this matter. Even the customary *jethangs* or larger share to the eldest son is now sometimes regarded with disfavour, and in law-suits such a claim is often ignored, and stands little chance of recognition unless the younger brothers consent to such an extra share for the eldest brother, or the case is referred to arbitration. The absolute authority of the *pater familias* over the family property, though it exists in theory probably as a survival of the *patria potestas* of partriarchal times, is, in practice, modified by the important limitation that it has to be exercised subject to the control of the Panchāyat to which the aggrieved party may always appeal. Thus, although in theory a father may drive out a disobedient or disagreeable son, giving him either no share of the family property or else an unfairly small share, such a case rarely happens ;

and, even when it does, the Panchāyat, on being appealed to, interferes to prevent any injustice. And, in any case, the son may on the death of his father come back and claim his legitimate share, for the Orāon father has not the right to disinherit his son altogether nor even to make an unfair distribution of property amongst his heirs. Indeed, one perceives amongst the Orāons a growing sense of injustice even in the present practice which allows the father to dispose of any portion of the family property without the consent of his sons.* In fact, the present practice would appear to be inconsistent with the Orāon conception that the family and not the individual is the property-owning unit. That this is so, would appear from the recognised right of a married son to demand partition of the family property in the father's life-time in certain circumstances. Although this customary right is not recognized by the Courts it is always recognized by the Panchāyat, when the father marries a second wife or, less often, when the son's wives do not well agree with their mother-in-law or sister-in-law or perhaps when the son is at variance with his father or brothers.

* The present writer has been more than once requested by several Oraons to move the authorities on their behalf for some legislative provision requiring the consent of the sons to any disposal of family property by the father.

Rules regarding Partition of property

Should the father under such circumstances refuse to partition the family property—a contingency which rarely happens—the son convenes a Panchāyat and the father generally submits to its award. In a partition made during the father's life-time, a share equal to that of a son's in moveable personal) as well as immoveable (real) property is allotted to the father. Generally, when a partition is demanded by the sons on the father marrying a second wife, the sons generally take care to have the partition made before a son is born to the second wife, for unborn children, even though in the womb, are entitled to no prospective share. The father's share is on his death divided by the sons amongst themselves according to the rules of inheritance given below. But if the father lived with any of the sons in particular and such son looked after his comforts during life and paid his funeral expenses, he inherits the father's share to the exclusion of the other sons. It almost invariably happens that the father who has married a second wife lives with such wife and her sons and, in such a case, his share goes on his death to the son or sons of the second wife with whom he had been living till his death. The lands allotted by way of maintenance to an Orāon widow, when her sons divide their father's properties between themselves, are on her death or remarriage repartitioned amongst the sons, unless she has lived in joint mess and cultivation with a particular son, – the latter, in such a case, being entitled to his mother's lands, provided he alone has borne her funeral expenses. If a regular partition has been effected during the life-time of the father no fresh partition of the same lands (except the share of the deceased father) is permissible.

As to other customary rules governing partition, they follow the customary rules of inheritance. These rules are given below in the form of a code* such as might be laid down by the Orāon Panchāyats :—

The property of a deceased Orāon shall be distributed as follows :

Customary Law of Inheritence.

(a) **Where he has left lineal male descendants :**

When the last owner has left a lineal male descendant and a widow, suitable maintenance consisting of lands (not more but) generally less than that which a son will receive, shall be allotted to the widow, and the balance of the property shall be divided as follows :—

* The arrangement and phraseology of the Indian Succession Act (1885) have, so far as possible, been followed in drawing up the following code of Orāon Customary laws of Inheritance and Succession.

1. Where the deceased has left surviving him a son or sons, born of an Orāon wife or wives but no more remote lineal descendant through a deceased son, the property shall belong to the surviving son if there be only one, or shall be equally divided among all his surviving sons, except that (i) so far as lands are concerned, the eldest son shall get a small area in excess of his regular share, and (ii) if the surviving sons are born of different mothers, the sons by the first wife of the deceased shall each receive a larger share than the sons of the second or a later wife.

Sons.

[Note : This custom of unequal division is falling into disuse in some parts of the Orāon country, and therefore in each case where an equal division is demanded in Court, proof of local custom should be adduced.]

(iii) A son or other male descendent who has been excomunicated by the Pārhā Panchāyat for sexual union with a non-Orāon or other similar offence against the customary rules of culpable tabu, shall be excluded from inheritance, unless previously readmitted into the tribe.

2. Where the deceased has left surviving him no son or sons but only sons of predeceased sons, the sons of each predeceased son shall together inherit the share

Grandsons.

that their father would have received if he had survived the last owner.

Sons, grandsons, and great-grandsons.

3. If the deceased has left lineal male descendants who do not all stand in the same degree of kindred to him (e. g., a son or sons, and also sons of one or more predeceased sons), and the persons through whom the more remote are descended from him are dead, the property shall be divided into as many shares as the number of sons who have either survived him or have left lineal male descendants surviving him, and one of such shares shall be allotted to each of the surviving sons, if any, of the last owner who shall take *per capita*, and one such share to the lineal descendants of each predeceased son who shall take per *stirpes*.

Explanation :—(i) The shares shall be allotted on the scale fixed in section 1 above and subject to the exceptions mentioned in that section.

(ii) The lineal male descendants entitled to a share must be born of Orāon wives.

(b). Where the Last owner has left no Lineal Male Descendants.

Where the last owner has left no lineal male descendant, the distribution of his property shall be regulated as follows :—

(1) If the last owner has left a duly adopted son born of one of his bhāyāds or agnates, he shall, if he was duly adopted with the consent of the other bhāyāds, inherit all the property left by the deceased after deducting a suitable portion for the maintenance of the widow or widows, if any, of the deceased.

Adopted son belonging to the same clan.

(2) If the last owner has left an adopted son belonging to a clan different from his own, he shall inherit the non-Bhūinhāri lands left by the deceased. The Bhūinhāri lands of the deceased shall, in such a case, remain in the possession of the widow or widows during their life-time, and on their death shall revert intact to such member or members of the *Khunt* of the last male owner as stand nearest to him in agnatic relation.

Son Adopted from a different clan.

(3) If the last male owner has left a sonless widow but no adopted son,—although she may have a *ghardamad*, adopted into the house as a prospective son-in-law either by the deceased male owner or on his death by his widow,—the widow shall be entitled to the administration and usufruct of the property so long as she lives in the house and does not remarry, and any surrender of the lands by her in favour of the landlord or any transfer of real

Sonless widow.

property made shall be void as against her reversioners.

Explanation.—On a widow remarrying she shall forthwith lose all interest in her late husband's property. The fact that she goes to her parents and does not return is ordinarily sufficient indication of her intention of marrying again, and no questions are generally asked. Should a widow be found in intrigue with any man except a younger brother of her deceased husband,the *Panch* on being appealed to by the reversioner shall on being satisfied of the truth of the allegations * forthwith expel her from the house of her late husband and make over the house and other property to the next reversioner. If there is a *ghar-damad* of the class referred to above he shall receive the rājhas lands.†

* Sexual intercourse by a widow with a man of her own tribe practically amounts to a marriage with that man. We know of an instance in which in such a case the widow complained in the Courts that her house was looted by the reversioners and their partisans and some of the latter were punished.

† Although now-a-days moveable property is ordinarily taken by the 'ghar-damad,' yet should any illness or other calamity befal him soon after he steps into the property he often makes over the moveable property to the last male owner's nearest male agnates.

Ghardamad.

(3) If there he no male issue or adopted son, but only a *Ghar-damad* duly adopted into the house as a 'prospective son-in-law' by the last male owner or even by his widow and since married to a daughter of the deceased and living in the house,—the rājhas lands left by the deceased male owner shall on the death of the widow go to such 'ghar-dāmād', and the bhūinhāri lands shall go to the nearest male agnate or agnates.

Agnates.

(4) If an Orāon owner of property dies leaving neither a son (either born of him or duly adopted) nor any lineal male descendant of such a son nor a 'ghar-dāmād' adopted into the house as a prospective son-in-law, the property shall go to the nearest male agnate or agnates in the following order :—

(i) If the father of the last male owner is alive, he shall inherit the property.

(ii) In the absence of a father, the last owner's brother or brothers together with the sons, if any, of a predeceased brother or brothers, shall inherit the property,—the sons of a predeceased brother taking between themselves the share that their father would have received if he had been alive.

Explanation : The brothers of the deceased in such a case are entitled to equal shares. If, however, the deceased owner lived joint in mess and property with one or more brothers and separate from his father, such brother or brothers succeed to the property in preference to the separated father.

(iii) In the absence of a father or brothers or brother's sons, the deceased owner's father's brothers together with the sons, if any, of a predeceased brother of the father, shall inherit the property, the sons of a predeceased uncle taking between themselves the share that their father would have received if he had been alive.

(iv) In the absence of father's brothers, the sons of the father's brothers shall inherit the property *per stirpes*; and in the absence of father's brother's sons, the property shall be divided in equal shares amongst those of the surviving agnates who are in the nearest degree of kindred to him and the sons of any of the predeceased brothers of such agnates,—provided always that the sons of such a predeceased kindred shall receive between themselves the share that their father would have received if he had been alive.

[*Note* :—According to Orāon custom the inheritance is not limited to agnates up to any particular degree of relationship. When all relatives with whom any agnatic relationship can be traced are exhausted; and, in the case of a deceased Bhũinhār, it is only when all his fellow-Bhũinhārs of the same village and belonging to the same clan (whether actually living in the village or elsewhere) are extinct,—only then is the landlord of the village properly entitled by local custom to the lands. In practice, however, the landlord now-a-days generally manages to take possession of the lands when there are no members of the deceased's *Khunt* surviving him. In the case of Rājhas lands, the landlords even go further and often resume such lands when the deceased tenant has left no near male agnate. This is, however, an innovation. Formerly, when no agnate of the deceased tenant survived him, such land used to be settled by the village-headmen to a tenant whose lands were not sufficient, and the landlord used to receive only a goat and the Māhtō and the Pahan used to receive each a fowl and a pot of rice-beer by way of 'salāmi.']

(5) An unmarried daughter of a deceased Orāon owner shall be entitled from her father's heirs, out of her father's assets, to a suitable maintenance until her marriage, and to the necessary expenses for her marriage. Such heir or heirs of her father as maintain her up to her marriage and bear her marriage-expenses shall be entitled to the bride-price paid by the bride-groom.

[Note : Usually her brothers or the other

heirs of her deceased father agree to maintain her by turns until her marriage].

Such are the main features of the Orāon law of intestate succession to property.

Will.

The Orāons never attained that stage of legal development in which the will of an owner of property is permitted to override the claims of his kindred in blood. The only contrivances hitherto employed to deflect the ordinary course of devolution of property are adoption of a son or, in the alternative, of a 'prospective son-in-law.' And even these devices, as we have seen, are not extensively resorted to. But at the present day there appears to be a growing desire to change the customary course of devolution of property when an Orāon owner has no male issue. Such an Orāon generally seeks to make a will or a gift of his lands to his daughters or daughter's sons, but when he is told that this is not allowed by the law, he seeks the advice of 'people who know.' And he readily follows their advice, and seeks to defeat the law by making a 'surrender' of his rāyati lands to the landlord, and the latter is induced to make a fresh settlement of the land with the man's daughter or son-in-law or daughter's sons as may be desired. The landlord of course sees his chance and generally drives a hard bargain in such a case.

IV. The Village Brotherhood and Artificial Kinship.

We have seen that the present social system of the Orāons is a product of totemism, exogamy, and father-right. The Orāons in time came also to recognise an artificial form of relationship which they termed village-relationship (gāō nātā).

With the establishment of agricultural villages and the expansion of population, the solidarity of the totemic clan was gradually impaired and ultimately lost, each clan came to be scattered over a large area, and villages established by different branches of the same clan came to be separated from one another by intervening villages founded by members of other clans. Communication gradually ceased between different villages of the same clan that were thus separated from one another by great distances, dangerous jungles and settlements of other clans often hostile. Necessarily, therefore, the local group of the village came in time to be practically all in all, although the clan group continued to be recognised as the marriage-regulating agency. The settlers of an Orāon village, as we have seen in a previous chapter, in time came to be arranged in two social grades—the Bhūinhārs or original settlers and the Gairōs or later settlers not belonging to the original village-family. The Bhũinhãrs, in their turn, came to be subdivided into two and sometimes three functional sub-divisions known as khũnts. The Gairõs or non-Bhũinhãrs were divided into two sub-classes now called respectively the jeṭh-rāiyats and the ordinary rāiyats. No difference in social status or rank is recognized as between the different Bhũinhãr khũnts; but amongst the Gairõs, the Jeṭh-rāiyats would seem to occupy a slightly higher position than the ordinary raiyats: Whereas, in important politico-social gatherings, the presence of some representatives of the Jeṭh-rāiyats of the village is usually considered essential, it is of no consequence if the ordinary raiyats go unrepresented. These different sections of the Orãon inhabitants of a village together form an organized community with its own Panch or administrative council of villages-elders •

• The Samskritik names applied by the Oraons to their village-officials might seem to indicate that although the dominant ethnic element remained Dravidian, Hindu culture with which they came in contact during their migrations had an important influence on their village organization and Parha organization. But the democratic character of the organization was determined by the tribal temperament. The Oraon term for the village-priest (Naegas or Baiga) looks like a corruption of the Sámskrit word 'Nayak,' leader, the term 'Mahato' is apparently derived from Samskrit 'mahat,' great, and the term 'Munda' from Samskrit 'Munda,' head.

and its own staff of village-officials and village servants.

It is to the village elders and the village officials that ancient Orāon custom entrusted the protection of the village against natural and supernatural evils, the maintenance of civil rights, the preservation of social order, and, generally, the administration of the public affairs of the village. The authority of the village elders was and is to this day unquestioned. The Māhātō's insignias of office are his turban with which he is ceremonially invested and, as may be still seen in a few villages, a bamboo staff sometimes crowned with a small 'Jhūnki' consisting of three or four curved iron spires joined at the top and having small iron rings fitted into them. These rings make a chiming sound when the stick is moved. In case the Māhāto has to attend ceremonial feasts at two houses on the same day and he cannot be present throughout at one of the houses he leaves his staff planted on the ground before the assembly, to represent him.* The Pāhāṇ's insignia of office is a peculiar knife which he does not however carry about. The young men of the village with their own staff of officers formed (and in many villages still form) an orga-

* This custom is now dying out.

nized body under the general control of the village headmen and the council of village-elders. Besides their magico-religious and economic functions, these young men formed the fighting force of the community. Thus, the village-elders may be said to form the head of the social organism,—the able-bodied young men its arms,—the Goṛāit, the Lohrā and other village-servants its legs,—and the general body of cultivators—Bhūinhārs and Gairōs—its trunk. Complete social integration was (and is to this day) secured to the village-community not only by common joys and sorrows or merely by co-operation in resisting common enemies and common dangers and by common subordination to the authority of the same village-elders, but also by participation in common worship, common sacrifices, ceremonial feasts, ceremonial dancing, and ceremonial hunting. Besides the common ties that bind together the village-community as a whole, each different section of the village-community seeks at stated intervals to cement the bond of union between its members by particular ceremonies. Thus, the Bhūinhars of each Khūnt of a village hold an annual ceremonial reunion known as 'parpūj'; and the Gairōs or non-Bhūinhārs of an Orāon village join once in twelve years in a common sacrificial feast of their own on the occasion of the 'Bar-pāhāṛi' pūjā and the bond of union between the wives of the Orāons—Bhūinhārs as well as Gairōs—of each village is sought to be cemented periodically by the interesting friendship ceremony known as the 'Sahiārō'.

Parpuj or the Annual Social Reunion of the Bhuinhars.

The bond between the members of each Bhūinhar Khūnt is both social and religious. Descendants of a common ancestor, they deposit the bones of their deceased members under a common *Kundi*-stone where, on the annual bone-burial (hāṛ-bōrā) day, the bones of the deceased members of each Bhūinhār Khūnt having been gathered with the left hand by women after cremation are ceremonially deposited, and where food is laid out that evening for the manes of all the dead members of the Khūnt. Even the bones of such members of the Khūnt as may have died away from the village are brought to the village and ceremonially deposited at the Kūndi of the Khūnt on the annual bone-burial day. Thus do the Orāons of the same Khūnt emphasise the solidarity of the Khūnt of which both the living and the departed members are believed to form a compact whole. Again, in the periodical sacrifices offered by the eldest member of the Khūnt, even those who have migrated to other villages come together, contribute their share of the expenses and partake of the sacrificial meat together. But the most interesting ceremony is that known as 'Parpūj'. This is held once every year in the month of Jeṭh (June-July) generally on the morning of the day on which the Jeṭh-Jātrā is held in the village or its neighbourhood. A week beforehand information as to the date and place where the 'parpūj' of a particular khūnt is to be held, is given at the village-markets to all non-resident members of the Khūnt. The person in whose house 'Parpūj' is to be held brews a few big jars of rice-beer for the occasion. On the appointed day all the members of the khūnt assemble, each bringing with him a jar of rice-beer, a handful of *arua* rice, four or five *seers* or more of *usna* rice, and some pulse. Those who do not bring their pots of rice-beer pay for them in cash. As the the guests arrive, some member of the house in which 'parpūj' is held washes their feet. Then the guests are seated on a palm-leaf mat spread out on the court-yard (āngan), and rice-beer is served to them in leaf-cups. A Bhūinhar of another Khūnt of the village now draws on the floor of the courtyard a mystic diagram consisting of an oval figure with some resemblance to the form of an egg fringed round with seven smaller figures each resembling the half of an egg. Every member of the Khūnt puts a small quantity of *arua* rice in the centre of the diagram, and even for each absent member of the Khūnt a little *arua* rice is put there. Over this rice the officiating man places a hen's egg which is inserted into the fork of a *bhelwa* twig which has been forked at one end. The egg is offered to Dharmes or the Supreme Deity represented by the Sun, a red fowl is sacrificed to the guardian spirit of the Khūnṭ, a grey fowl to the ancestor-spirits of the Khūnṭ, and a black fowl to the spirit called Dārhā-goisāli.

The non-Bhūinhars or Gairōs of the village attend as witnesses to this 'bhelwā-phāri' or 'dāndā-kāttā' ceremony, and, when the sacrifices have been offered, take away the sacrificed fowls to some distance, and boil the rice and flesh together and eat the 'ṭahari' thus perpared. No members of the khūnṭ concerned may partake of these offerings. The sacrificer takes up in a leaf-cup a little of the the *arua* rice placed over the diagram, mixes up this rice with the yolk of the egg offered to Dharmes, puts the leaf-cup over a fire, and, when the contents of the leaf-cup are sufficiently baked, offers it in small bits to the different gods to whom libations of cold water are also given at the same time. The shell of the egg is filled with water, and with this water the diagram on the floor is washed clean,—the remnants of rice-flour, pounded charcoal, red earth, rice, *etc.*, being taken up by the sacrificer in a leaf-cup. The sacrificer now takes this leaf-cup outside the house and throws it away. On his return to the house, he waits at the entrance, and, pretending to be a stranger, asks "Is this A's (so-and-so's) house ?" Some one from within asks him —"Who are you ? Where do you come from ?" The man says in reply, "I have been to such-and-such (names) a village. I have been searching for A's house all the time." The man from within says, "Who knows that you are not a thief or an out-caste ?" "No," he replies, "I am A's kinsman. I met him at such-and-such a village. He invited me to come here." "Come then," says the man from within, "You are really a kinsman. Take your seat, and drink a cup of rice-beer." The man enters the house, salutes every one present, and takes his seat. In the meanwhile, ever since the Bhelwā-phāri ceremony had begun, the assembled members of the Khũnṭ were agreeably engaged in brotherly conversation, renewing their acquaintance with such members of the Khũnṭ as have been living away from the village, and discussing the genealogy and marital relations, history and migrations of the different families of the Khũnṭ. The day's rejoicings are concluded by feasting and drinking, after which the guests take leave of one another.

This annual gathering of each Khũnṭ-brotherhood is held for three successive years at the residence of each family of the Khũnṭ by turns. In the third year, after the ceremony is over, the person at whose house the 'parpũj' has been held for these three years, gives a 'dhōti' (loin-cloth) to the person who officiated as sacrificer; and the person at whose house the 'Parpũj' will be held for the next three years is selected in the following manner. All the members of the Khũnṭ stand in a row, and a clod of earth representing each absent member of the Khũnṭ is also placed in the same row. The person who officiated as sacrificer rolls on the ground a curry-stone, and the man at whose feet the stone stops has to arrange for the Khũnṭ-reunion at his house for the three years following. Should the stone stop at a clod of earth representing an absent member of the Khũnṭ, it will be his turn to celebrate the 'parpũj' for the next three years.

Sahiaro or the Ceremonial Alliance between married women.

The Orāoṅ has an aversion to marriages between a young man and a girl of the same village; and such a marriage is generally believed to bode ill for one or both of the married pair.* Necessarily therefore the

* As for the Bhuinhars, the rule of exogamy ordinarily necessitates marriages of their sons or daughters to girls or boys of other villages.

wives of the Orāons of a village generally hail from different villages and belong to different gōtrās; and they are not therefore expected to be naturally friendly to one another. Apparently to make up for the absence of any natural bond of union between the wives of the Orāons of a village, the ancient organizers of Orāon society devised an interesting mode of effecting an artificial but sufficiently strong bond of union between the wives of the Orāons of each village and, derivatively, between their respective families.* This ceremonial mode of union is the artificial friendship of married women known as 'Sahiārō'. Once in three years or so, after the lowland paddy has been harvested, married Orāon women in every village have to select their 'sahiās.' The idea starts with the elders of one or more neighbouring villages; and information is sent round by proclamation at the different village-markets that 'sahiā' alliances have to be formed

* Another possible reason for these artificial unions is to secure strength (by union) against the hostile attentions of evil spirits and indefinite spiritual influences of a harmful nature. I have heard some Oraons classing these 'Friendship' ceremonies of their women with the periodical 'disease-driving' and 'calamity-driving' ceremonies. Persons hailing from outside the village may have some alien evil spirits at their beck and call, and it may therefore be considered desirable to secure the good will of such persons by these 'Sahiaro' alliences.

that year all over the Orāon country. The information is taken from one village-market to another and thus the news spreads all over the district. Each village fixes its own day—usually a Tuesday—for the ceremony. Each village-Goṛāit proclaims the message in his village, saying,—"Select ye your sahiās, for Tuesday next is the day fixed by the village elders for the celebration of sahiārō ceremonies." In view of the coming ceremonies at least one Orāon woman of each family in the village has to choose a Sahiā from amongst the women of another Orāon family. She either elects a new Sahiā or decides to ceremonially renew her relationship with an old one. In the former case, however, her relationship with her old sahiā or sahiās does not cease to subsist. Early in the morning of the day appointed for the Sahiāro celebration, the courtyard of every Orāon house in the village is cleaned with cowdung and water by some female members of the house. An hour or two after sunrise you see groups of married women walking in ceremonial procession along the dirty lanes and alleys of the village. The woman at the head of each group carries on her head a bamboo-basket, and in her hands a brass jug (lôtā). The basket holds some paddy and a small leaf-cup containing a little rice-flour (āripan) and the brass jug is filled with water from which you see sticking out a small leafy mango twig. This woman carrying the brass-jug and bamboo-basket is going to greet her Sahiā-elect. The latter, on the approach of the party, shuts herself up in her hut; and the former, on reaching the doors of the hut, besmears the fingers of her own right hand with moistened rice-flour and makes finger-marks on the door-plank. Over these rice-flour marks on the door-plank she next puts vermilion finger-marks. Then she takes up in the joined palms of her hands some rice from her basket and places the rice at three spots on the door-sill, and sometimes fastens selected sheaves of paddy to the door-frame. Now she takes out the mango-twig from her brass-jug, and, with this, sprinkles water all over the door-planks. The water of the jug is now thrown on the roof of the hut. At the sound of this water striking against the roof of her hut, her Sahiā-elect hastens to open the door and, rushing out of the hut, spreads a portion of her wearing cloth underneath the eaves of the hut so as to receive a few drops of the water dripping down the eaves. Now the two women address each other by the sweet name of 'Sahiā' and salute each other by each bowing her head down to the knees and touching the forehead with the fingers of her right hand which is supported at the elbow by the left hand. These ceremonies over, the party return to the house from which they came ; and then the woman who carried the basket and the brass-jug sends word to her newly-made 'Sahiā' that she is ready to receive her at her house. Thereupon the latter, at the head of a party of female companions, returns the visit and goes through the same cremonies as the other 'Sahiā' did.

About a fortnight later, the village-Goṛāit again goes about in the village and proclaims the day on which the feasting in celebration of all these sahiā alliances is to take place. "Prepare ye your *chiura* (flattened rice) and *dahi* (curdled milk), and brew your rice-beer, for on Tuesday fortnight comes on the sahiārô feast." Thus shouts the village crier, and every Orāon family in the village takes note of the message. On the morning of the appointed day, the "Sahiās" all bathe at the village spring, tank, or stream, change their clothes, and proceed to the 'Devi-āsthān' or shrine of the goddess 'Devi.' Each 'Sahiā' carries on her head a basket containing some flattened rice, a cup of curdled milk, a small quantity of vermilion, a little clarified butter (*ghee*), a little milk, molasses, incense, and leaf-plates. Little girls follow their mothers carrying a little fire in a fragment of earthen pottery. On her arrival at the shrine, each woman pours a little milk on each of the seven rounded lumps of earth that represent the goddess.

The fire is placed in front of the 'goddess' and into it incense, *ghee*, and molasses are thrown as burnt offerings.* The religious part of the ceremonies being thus over, the women proceed to an open space close by. There each pair of 'Sahiās' sit down by themselves, each woman exchanges her leaf-plates and *dahi-chiura* with her Sahiā's, and each eats the food brought by her Sahiā. Then all return to their respective houses, each pair of Sahiās walking together and deciding on the way which of the two will entertain the other that day. Shortly afterwards, a formal invitation to dinner is sent, as agreed upon, by one of the Sahiās to the other. The other members of the latter's family are also invited and all respond with alacrity. Those who can afford to do so also send out invitations to other friends and relatives as well. As the guests arrive, a mat is spread out on the courtyard for them to sit upon and two or three pots of rice-beer are placed before them. The '*Sahia*', on her arrival, is taken

* In some vilages, however, only the Pahan and his wife go to the Devi-asthan. The *sahias* clean the court-yards of their respective houses with cowdung diluted in water, and the sweepings of the courtyard and the broken broom with which the courtyard is swept and the rag with which the cowdung is besmeared on the ground are taken up on a broken tile (*khapra*) and deposited on the borders of the next village. Then they bathe themselves, exchange presents and go to some selected site for eating *dahi-chiura*

inside the house, and is presented with a new cloth which she now puts on. At one end of this cloth is tied up a cash present of a rupee or so. After this, the Sahiās sit together and drink rice-beer. Then follows a feast of boiled rice and pulses, and, if possible, of fowl-curry or even pork. After the feast, all salute one another and the guests return home. On the following day a feast is provided in return in the same way by the family of the other Sahiā, and a similar present of cloth and cash is made in return. And thus the bond of Sahiāro is finally sealed. Thenceforth the families of the two Sahiās may not enter into matrimonial relations with each other. Although only presents of food, garments, and money are exchanged and not blood,—unless the vermilion marks made on the door plank be taken as the substitute for an earlier employment of blood,—the relationship thus created is practically regarded as blood-relationship, so far as the two families are concerned, and an 'unification,' so to say, of the two friends themselves.

Goi' and 'Karam-dair' friendship.

In this connexion we may notice that besides the 'Sahiā' form of friendship, which appears to be considered by the Orāons as a matter of tribal necessity, there are a few minor forms of friendship entered into by young Orāon girls with one another as a matter of individual choice. The more common amongst these are the 'gōi' and the 'Karam-dāir' forms. In the 'gōi' form, when two girls perceive a growing attachment for each other, they address each other as 'gōi,' swear eternal friendship, inform their parents of their attachment, and, on the parents' approval which is seldom withheld, exchange presents of cloth and a few *annas* in cash, and each invites the other to a feast in celebration of the new relationship. Ever afterwards, at every festival the two 'gōis' (so long as they are unmarried and live in their parents' village) entertain each other at their respective houses. If a particular festival is celebrated in both the families on the same day, each 'gōi' takes to the other gōi's house from her own some cakes and other delicacies for her 'gōi'; When the 'gōis' get married, the husband of one 'gōi' calls the husband of the other his own 'gōi', and, so far as circumstances permit, interchange of tokens of friendship is continued as before between the families of the two 'gōis'. The ceremonies observed in the 'Karamdāir' form of friendship and the duties and responsibilities that follow are the same as in the 'gōi' form. While entering into this alliance the two friends address each other as 'Karam-dāirs', and after their marriage the husband of the one girl becomes related as

'Karam-dāir' to the husband of the other girl.

'Iar' and 'Sangi' forms of friendship.

Of the same class as the 'gōi' and the 'Karam-dāir' forms of friendship of the Orāon girls, are the 'Iār' and 'Sangī' forms of friendship of Orāon boys. Like an Orāon girl, an Orāon boy informs his parents of his desire to enter into the 'Iār' or the 'Sangī' form of friendship with another Orāon companion. If the parents see no objection to such alliance, they tell the boy, "you should bear in mind that you will have to remain friends to the end of your days." On the boy's agreeing to do so, each boy invites the other to a feast at his house where other guests too are, if possible, invited for the occasion. The boy makes a present of a cloth (*dhoti*) with some cash (ordinarily one rupee and four annas) tied up at one end of the cloth. A few pots of rice-beer are always prepared for such an occasion, and if possible a pig is killed. After drinking and feasting, all salute one another and the guests depart. On a subsequent day a return-feast is provided and presents made in the same way by the other 'Iār' or 'Sangī.' Thenceforth at every festival the two 'Iārs' or 'Sangīs' must entertain each other at their respective houses. At all festivities, the two Iārs or Sangīs keep together. When they are married, their wives call each other 'Iārins' or 'Sangīns,' as the case may be. It is important to note that no matrimonial connexion is permitted between the families of two 'Sangīs' or 'Iārs,' although they may belong to different clans. If, however, a branch of the family of one friend has migrated to another village there is no objection to a marriage of a member of the other friend's family with a member of such non resident branch of his friend's family.

Such are some of the devices by which the different sections of an Orāon village-community are welded into one united whole.

V. The village Panchayat.

(a) Its Constitution and jurisdiction.

The common will of the community is, when required, expressed by the village *Panch*, which in theory includes the entire village community but in practice is represented by the village-elders. The authority of the Panch in all matters of public interest or private right was up till recently considered supreme. And to this day the orthdox formula for an oath amongst the Orāons, as amongst the Mundās, is,—"I swear by Dharmes (God) in heaven, and the Panch on earth." Disputes about partition of family property, certain offences against marriage, suspected cases of witchcraft, and sometimes even cases of assault and theft, are still submitted to the Panch for its decision.

(b) Procedure of the Panch.

The procedure adopted by the Panch in such cases is as follows. The aggrieved person verbally complains to the village Māhāto and village Pāhān. The elders of the village assemble at the village ākhrā or some other appointed place. The village Goṛāit summons the disputing parties before the assembly. The Pāhān or the Māhātō informs the defendant of the substance of the complaint against him and hears his answer, and, if necessary, takes evidence. In a dispute regarding partition of property, the Panch divide the property in accordance with tribal custom, and each party pays two or three rupees to the Panch for their trouble. This money is spent in liquor.

(c) Torts and Crimes.

In cases of tort or crime, fine and excommunication are the only penalties that the Panch may now-a-days inflict. In cases of alleged witch-craft however, persons adjudged guilty have been known to have been severly thrashed and driven out, bag and baggage, from the village, and sometimes even beaten to death. Before the British courts were firmly established, a modified form of 'blood-revenge,' it is said, was formally sanctioned by the Panch in cases of murder, grievous hurt, and the like. Thus, when a man killed another or broke another's arm or leg, the Panch would hand him over to the Khũnṭ-brethren of the murdered or injured person to be killed or his arm or a leg broken, as the case might be. In cases of theft, the thief is beaten as well as fined. Adultery is regarded as a form of theft, * and the adulterer is severely

* We know of a case in which during the trial by the panch of a married young man who was caught eloping with a married girl of his village, the young men of the village were present in a body and taunted the offender by asking

thrashed, and fined as well. If the adulterer belongs to a different village, the thrashing is generally severe (and occasionally fatal) ; and the *Panch* of the offender's village, on being complained to by the other village, usually impose a fine on the adulterer. Fines imposed on a culprit are spent in a feast with plenty of liquor. Except cases relating to witchcraft and certain social or other tabus, all offences are regarded as private wrongs and not offences against the community.

(d) Contracts.

In cases relating to contracts, specific performance, is, when possible, enforced, or damages awarded. But the orders of the Panch in such cases are now-a-days often disregarded. Contracts, amongst the Orāons, are, even to this day, generally not written but acted. Thus, a lease of land is made by the lessor handing over a clod of earth (which symbolizes land) to the lessee ; a contract of sale of cattle is entered into by handing over to the buyer a few blades of grass (which symbolize so many heads of cattle) ; a contract of payment of bride-price

him "Could we not seduce your wife or sister like this, if we liked ?" In this case the *panch* demanded Rs. 25, and finally reduced it to Rs. 20,—of which Rs. 15 was spent in the feast and Rs. 5 in liquor. The *panch* finally warned all present that in future such an offence would be punished with a fine of thirty rupees.

is made by the bridegroom's father or other relative handing over a number of *baris** (which symbolize so many rupees) to the bride's father or other relative; and a contract of service is made by the mistress of the house anointing the head of the intended servant with oil and making a present of a few pice and entertaining him to a feast and thus signifying that he would receive food, lodging and some pay. Such contracts are naturally difficult to prove in a regular court of law. In case of desertion by a wife without sufficient reason, Orāon custom allows the aggrieved husband to seize and carry away one or two buffaloes or bullocks from the house of the wife's parents unless the latter return the bride-price paid by the husband on the occasion of his marriage with their daughter.

(e) Breach of tabus.

Cases against sexual tabu or 'caste'-tabu which require to be punished with excommunication are decided by the Pārhā Panch to which we shall refer later on. But offences against other tabus are decided by the village Panch. Thus when a female drives the plough, or thatches the roof of a house, the village Panch inflict such punishment as they think proper. Breaches of certain tabus such as those against touching a 'baenāli' are expiated for in

* Tiny white cakes made of the *urid* pulse.

the family circle as it concerns only the family in question. And breaches of certain other tabus such as uttering the name of a certain person, place or thing considered of bad omen are not punished at all as they affect only the offender himself.

(f) Ordeals.

We shall conclude this section by a reference to certain methods occasionally employed by the Panch or by private individuals to determine the guilt or innocence of an accused person. When a person is suspected of theft, cow-dung is sometimes boiled in water and the suspect is made to dip one of his arms into this boiling-hot liquid. It is believed that if the man is guilty his arm will get scalded, otherwise it will come out unscathed. Another ordeal sometimes employed is to put successively three small ladlefuls of burning charcoal on the palm of the suspect's hand. If the hand burns or if the suspect throws down the live charcoal as soon as it is placed on his hand, his guilt is taken as established. We met two such suspects—one a boy and the other a girl both suspected of theft of a few rupees—whose hands had been scalded in this way. The boy got off with a slight injury, as, after the first ladleful, which he had quickly thrown away, he refused to submit to the ordeal again, but the girl stoically underwent the ordeal to the end (or rather was made to do so by force) and got her hand permanently injured.* An Orāon whose money, cattle or goods are stolen, does indeed sometimes resort to some superstitious method or other to detect and also to punish the culprit. An orthodox method is the following: As soon as the loss is discovered, the owner of the lost money or other thing goes from house to house in his village with a pumkin-gourd (tūmbā) in his hand. He asks for a little water from each neighbour's house and puts the water into his gourd. With this gourd, as well as with a little āruā rice and a black fowl, the man goes to the village smithy, and there puts the rice on the ground; and as the fowl feeds on this rice its throat is cut with a knife, and the blood of the fowl and also the water in the gourd are poured into the black-smith's bellows. Now, as the black-smith begins to work at his bellows; it is believed, that the real culprit's belly begins

* When we saw the girl, gangrene had set in and the girl had been sent to a hospital. When the case came to court, it was represented even by the complainants that it brother of the was only the woman, whose money was stolen who had made the suspects undergo the ordeal but that the Panch had nothing to do with the affair. The man was sentenced to rigorous imprisonment for a few months.

to correspondingly swell at the same-time, so that death will not be long in coming. As soon however as the owner of the lost property goes about from house to house with his gourd, the thief generally restores the stolen thing to him for fear of the supposed dire consequences of the step the owner of the stolen property is about to take.

(g) Oaths.

The most effective oath administered by the Panch to a party or a witness in a case, is to make him take up in his hands a small quantity of paddy, a little cow-dung and a clod of earth, and place these on his head. It is emphatically impressed by the Panch on the deponent, and indeed it is firmly believed, that a man deposing falsely with these things on his head is sure to suffer loss of crops or of cattle or of lands. It need hardly be pointed out that the paddy placed on the deponent's head symbolizes crops, the cowdung symbolizes cattle, and the clod of earth symbolizes land.

Such are some of the social institutions that have helped in producing a genuine social and psychological unity—a common sacramental life in all the members of an Orāon village-community.

VI. The Parha Federation, and Inter-Parha Alliances.

The Parha.

In time the villages felt the necessity of working together in larger wholes for purposes of self-protection against natural and supernatural foes. And, as a result, arose the Pārhā organization modelled on the old Orāon hunting groups though formed not upon the principle of association of kindred but upon the basis of local contiguity. The Pārhā, as it now exists, is a confederacy of a number * of neighbouring villages with a central organization known as the Pārhā Panch. In the Pārhā organization we find the ancient spirit of the clan-group clothed in a new body suited to the new environment and changed conditions of life. Although in the outer form of the organization—in the names of its different functionaries and the nature of their formal functions, we see the influence of the Aryan Hindu monarchical system —in its inner soul—in its ruling idea,—its aims

* The number of villages is generally seven, nine, twelve, twenty-one, or twenty-two. But in our days owing to partial disintegration of the system we sometimes meet with parhas consisting of five, four, or even three villages.

and objects and the methods of pursuing such objects, we recognize a characteristic institution of the Dra vidian Orāon who is essentially a democrat and an animist.

Each Orāon Pārhā, as we have said, consists of a number of villages. One of the villages is called the Rājā (King) village, another the Dewān (Prime Minister) village, a third the Pānṛey (Clerk of the Crown) village, a fourth the Kotwār (Bailiff) village, and so on. Such of the villages as have got no such denominations are known as 'Parjā' (subject) villages. The Rājā village is the head village of the Pārhā ; some headman of this village presides at meetings of the Pārhā Panch. The Pāhān of this village or, in his absence, the Māhātō may act as the Karṭāhā,and in his absence any elderly Bhūinhār of the village may be chosen to officiate as the Karṭāhā at a social or socio-religious ceremony of the Pārhā. In some Pārhās, however, there is a separate Karṭāhā village, and the Pāhān or, in his absence, the Māhātō or other elderly Bhūihār of such village officiates as Karṭāhā at a social or socio-religious gathering.The Māhātō or other headman of the Kōṭwār village officiates as the Kōṭwār of the Pārhā. An iron spear with a long bamboo handle is ordinarily carried by him to a Pārhā-meeting as his insignia of office. Now-

Constitution of the Parha.

a-days, sometimes only a thick bamboo-staff is used instead of a spear. With the exception of the Pārhā-Koṭwār, the other functionaries of a Pārhā have no particular insignia of office at the present day. It may be noticed here that some of the Orāon emblems of office appear to be considered as possessing a special virtue of the nature of *mana*. Thus, the Pārhā-Kōṭwār, as we have seen,* while distributing the game bagged during a hunt, gives a stroke of his bamboo stick to each hunter as the latter takes up his share of the game, and thereby would appear to mysteriously impart *mana* to the hunter; and the straw whip (korrā) used by the Dhāngar Koṭwār to maintain discipline amongst the young bachelors during the dances, and the whip made of *sabai* (*Ischaemum angustifolium*) grass used by the spirit-doctor to maintain discipline among his disciples and also to induce spirit-possession, would appear to have been, in their estimation, rods of occult power.† In fact, the whip of *sabai* grass used by the Orāon magician and spirit-doctor is still regarded with awe and is regularly marked with vermilion as sacred objects ordinarily are. The ascription of mystic powers to

* P. 236, ante.

† It is on the principle of homeopathic magic that a mysterious power appears to be attributed to such objects. Thus the Sal branches and mango twigs by reason of the abundant blossoms that those trees bear are naturally associated in the Oraon's mind with the fertility of man and of the Earth.

such whips and their use by the magician and the Dhāngar-Koṭwār may perhaps have been originally suggested by the report like that of a cracker produced by the similar whip made of a stem of the Kūdrūm (*hibiscus cannabinus*) plant with which an Orāon boy amuses himself by whirling it round and round over his head from the right to the left and then with a sudden arrested motion giving it a pull towards his right side. This toy-whip and the two mystic whips are all made in the same way by interweaving the strands of the particular fibre used, and making the handle thicker than the rest of the whip. The toy-whip is two yards or more in length, the magician's whip is a yard or more in length, and the Dhāngar Kōṭwār's whip is generally shorter still. The sound happens to depend on the length, the toy-whip being of the proper length and thus producing the loudest report. The startling sound thus produced may have been originally taken to signify the presence of some mystic power or rather a powerful spirit in the whip.

The Badges and other privileges of particular villages.

Although every functionary of the Pārhā no longer possesses a distinttive badge of office, every village of the Pārhā has its own distinctive flag and other badges which may not be used by any other villages unless ceremonially presented by the village whose exclusive privilege it is to use them. The following short account of the flags and other badges of a small Pārhā consisting of nine villages will give the reader an idea of their nature. The Bhūinhārs of five out of the nine villages of the Pārhā in question belong to the Crow clan, of one village to the Tortoise clan, one to the Minj fish clan, and two to the Stork clan. The 'Rājā' village, of which the Bhūinhārs belong to the Crow clan, has for its emblems flags of white cloth, one of which has a small white turban tied to its upper end like a crown and a red tassel suspended from its lower end like a tail, and the other has a red tassel for a tail and two or three feathers to serve as a crown. The 'Dewān' village, of which the Bhūinhārs also belong to the Crow clan, has two flags, viz., a red flag with a small wooden tobacco box (Kiā), a blue turban to serve as head-gear, and a red tassel to serve as its tail, and also a white flag with a white turban and a red tassel. The Koṭwār village which has also the Crow for its totem, has for its emblems a wooden tobacco-box painted red and blue and attached to the upper end of a bamboo pole, a brass spear crowned with a strip of blue cloth with pendents of small balls of red thread, and a red flag with a white turban as a crown and a red tassel as a tail. Of the other two villages which have the crow for their totem, one has a white flag as well as a red flag,—both with pendents of balls of red thread. Of the two villages which have the Stork for their totem, one village has two flags,—one with a crest of peacock feathers and a pendent of red tassel and the other with a blue turban and a pendent of red tassel; and the second village has two white flags,—one with mango twigs as a crest over a white turban and a red tassel as a tail and the other with only a crest of peacock feathers. The village which has the Minj fish for its totem, has two white flags one with a white turban and a pendent of balls of red thread, and the other only a red pendent. Besides these flags, this village has also for its emblem wooden heads of birds painted black and facing each other. These two heads of birds are set an a pole with a string attached so that when the string is pulled the two birds appear to peck at each other. The ninth village of which the Bhūinhārs belong to the Tortoise clan, has for its emblems two wooden Tortoises and one wooden pig besides two white flags—one with a white turban and red tassels and the other only with a red tassel for a pendent. Of these nine villages, jātrās are held in five villages,—in three villages, one after the other, in Kātik (October-November), in another village in Jeṭh (June-July), and in the third in Māgh (January-February). The badges of the Pārhā, as we have seen, are of the simplest. But in most Pārhās you see flags,made up of strips of cloth of various colours* sewn up together to form multi-coloureds 'bairākhis.' The flags of some villages bear on a white ground the red figure of a peacock or of the Sun or of a betel-leaf or some other device. In some villages, again, besides the flags and the wooden or brass figures, you also see garlands, made of bits of mica, or of the *Khuskhas* grass set up on the top of a long pole and used as Pārhā-emblems. In most cases it is impossible to find out whether a particular device has a symbolic or merely an ornamental and fanciful origin. Whatever may be the origin of a particular device, the unauthorised use by one Pārhā of the flag-device of another Pārhā is still regarded by the latter Pārhā as *casus belli*. Some of the Pārhās have their own distinctive method of playing on the drum, and any infringement of this exclusive privilege during a jātrā or a hunting expedition is another *casus belli* for the Pārhā whose privilege is thus invaded.

* The number of colours in such a multi-coloured parha-flag often represents the number of villages comprised in the particular parha.

The Functions of the Parha.

The Pārhā system which grouped men of several clans together, evidently marked a further advance on the former socio-political hunting clan-groups or the later village-communities. It was a larger whole with a greater complexity of structure. The establishment and maintenance of law and order, and the settlement of disputes between one village and another, naturally came to be added to the list of the recognized functions of the Pārhā council.

Each village would co-operate in the pursuit of the common objects of the federation. These common objects were, broadly speaking, the protection of the allied villages from human and non-human foes,—from natural and supernatural dangers that beset them on all sides, and, generally, securing 'luck' for themselves. Each village was allotted a special function such as that of the 'Rājā,' the 'Dewān,' the 'Kōṭwār,' *etc.*, in the common work of the Pārhā. The different villages of the Pārhā still hunt together, fight together, and on stated occasions meet together in dancing trysts, social feasts, and deliberative and judicial committees. But under present conditions, there is little room for the existence of militant or even of law-giving federations, and practically the only matters in which the authority of the Pārhā is still supreme are those relating to social and magico-religious 'tabus.' The 'luck' of the Pārhā is the main thing which the Pārhā council has always had to look after, and at the present day, it is practically their only legitimate concern. It is the breach of certain social and magico-religious tabus that are believed to affect the 'luck' of the Pārhā and even of the Tribe. Of such tabus the most important are those against sexual union between Orāons and non-Orāons or between Orāons of the same clan or of prohibited degrees of relationship, and taking cooked food at the hands of a non-Orāon.* Again, it is the proper observance of the Jātrā-dances and of the great annual hunts that ensures the 'luck' of the villages comprised in the Pārhās concerned. Besides cases of infringement of certain tabus, disputes regarding precedence at the Jātrās or regarding right to game, disputes regarding boundaries between two villages, and such other matters as the village Pānchāyats cannot decide or in which their decisions are not accepted, are laid before the Pārhā Panch for deliberation and

* An exception is often made in favour of the Mundas at whose hands an Oraon may take food cooked in a new vessel. An Oraon boy who has not yet married, or a girl who has not yet had her hair ceremonially tied into a chignon, need not observe these food tabus.

verdict. The Kōṭwār of the Pārhā has to execute the 'decrees' of the Pārhā Panch.

Change of Parha.

The tie that binds the different villages together appears to have slackened in our days. Although such instances are few and far between, we have known a few cases in which either owing to some disagreement with the other villages of its own Pārhā, or owing to its proximity to the villages of another Pārhā, a village has severed its connexion with its old Pārhā and joined another.

The Procedure of the Parha Panchayat.

The procedure followed by the Pārhā Panchāyat in the hearing and decision of disputes is as follows. On the headman of a village of the Pārhā submitting a complaint to the Pārhā Rājā or Dewān, the Kōṭwār of the Pārhā is ordered by the Rājā to inform the different villages of the Pārhā that on a particular day the Pārhā Panch will meet in the village where the cause of complaint or dispute has arisen. On the appointed day, some representatives from each, or at any rate the majority, of the villages of the Pārhā assemble at the 'hādri' or usual meeting-place of the Panch—generally under some old wide-spreading tree near the Sarnā or Sacred Grove of the village in question. The Pāhān, the Māhāto, the Pānbharā and one or two Jeṭh raiyats of most villages usually attend such a meeting. When the Panchāyat is assembled, the Kōṭwār spreads out in front of the assembled representatives a sheet of cloth—either his own *chadar* or that of any one present, which he may, if he chooses, ask for, or take by force, if necessary. On this sheet of cloth the 'Rājā' of the Pārhā takes his seat, and close to him sits the 'Kōṭwār' with his spear. Formerly, it is said, the flags of the different villages of the Pārhā used to be planted at the meeting-place, but this custom has now generally fallen into disuse. The procedure as to explaining the substance of the complaint, hearing the answer of the defendant, examining witnesses, *etc.*, is the same as in the case of a trial by the village-Panchāyat, but sometimes more elaborate. Thus, some Pārhā Panchāyats now-a-days record the deposition of the parties and their witnesses. And in one instance, we found a document written out in Hindi and duly signed by the disputants by which they agreed to abide by the decision of the Panch. The individual or village at whose instance the Panchāyat is assembled entertains with rice and pulse-soup the representatives of the other villages on their arrival; and before they disperse a more sumptuous feast is got up for them with the fine generally imposed on the party against whom verdict is passed.

The foot-burying ordeal.

Until recently an orthodox mode of settling disputes regarding the boundary-line between two adjoining villages used to be the ordeal known as the 'Kheḍḍan-sājā' or 'Gōṛ-gāṛi' in which a representative of each of the two villages is made to stand with one leg buried up to the knee in a hole dug on the boundary-line claimed by him. The hole is filled up wlth rice-flour. The Orāons, like the Mundās,* believe that white-ants, attracted to the hole by the rice-flour, will eat up the leg of the false claimant. But before that extreme consequence befalls either party, one of them gives in either through sheer exhaustion or through lack of fortitude to stand the biting of ants and other insects that are attracted to the hole by the rice-flour; and the verdict goes against his village.

In olden times, it is said, boundaries between two adjoining villages shifted from time to time in consequence of armed fights between the two villages. When a dispute arose between two such villages as to game or some other matter, and the people of one village attacked the other village, the line up to which the people of the former village could drive back their assailants would be fixed as the boundary-line between the two villages.

* Vide *The Mundas and Their Country*, Calcutta, 1912, p. 425.

Readmission into the community.

Besides its judicial and deliberative functions, the Pārhā Panch has an important socio-religious function to perform. As the Pārhā Panch may excommunicate an Orāon of the Pārhā, so also it may readmit into the tribe an Orāon who has been excommunicated. The procedure followed in readmitting into the community an Orāon excommunicated either for sexual intercourse with a non-Orāon woman, or for having eaten cooked* food at the hands of a non-Orāon, or for having been a Christian for a time, is as follows: The repentant outcast having approached the headmen of his village and promised to perform the requisite ceremonies and provide a suitable feast to the Pārhā-brethern, the Pārhā headmen are informed and a date fixed for the restoration of the man to his tribal rights. On the appointed day, some representatives from each village of the Pārhā assemble at the usual meeting-ground of the Pārhā in the village of the outcast. Almost all the adult Orāons of the village in question are also invited. The Pāhān, or in his absence, the Māhāto of the 'Rājā' village generally officiates as the 'Kartāhā' or social head of the Pārhā. In

* This tabu has to be observed only by married persons and by girls after their chignon has been ceremonially tied for the first time.

some Pārhās, there is a separate Karṭāhā village, a headman of which officiates as the 'Karṭāhā' on such occasions. Some grains of 'āruā' rice are put down on the ground, and with this the Karṭāhā feeds either a white goat or a white cock supplied by the candidate for restoration to 'caste.' As the fowl or animal begins to eat up the rice grains, it is sacrificed to Dharmes or the supreme Deity represented by the Sun. The sacrificer faces east. A drop of blood of the sacrificed animal or fowl is put into a bowl of water into which a bit of copper or, if possible, gold, and also a few leaves of the *tulsi* or sacred basil plant are dipped. And this water is then drunk by the candidate. For the social feast that follows, generally a buffalo or one or more pigs are killed. The person thus rehabilitated in his former tribal rights now serves rice-beer to all present. When dinner is ready, some relative of the man first approaches the Karṭāhā and with folded hands requests him to 'deign to partake of a little of the humble fare' prepared for the occasion, and then makes the same humble request to the other guests. At this the guests get up from their mat, wash their own mouths, hands, and feet, with water provided for the purpose, and sit down to a hearty dinner. Before the guests sit down to dinner, the Karṭāhā, as the socio-religious head of the Pārhā, receives a sum of five rupees or more, according to the circumstances of the man restored to his tribal rights and also the gravity of the offence thus atoned for.* A rupee or so has also to be paid to each of the other villages represented at the assembly.

Three leaf-plates are placed before the Karṭāhā and on these is served such rice as has been boiled first of all. Rice is next served to the other guests on one leaf-plate each. The Karṭāhā, in the meanwhile, distributes the rice from one of the plates to a few guests seated within easy reach of himself. Now, when rice has been served to all, the Karṭāhā must eat the first morsel before the other guests begin to eat. The man restored to 'Jāt' sits down to dinner with his assembled 'Pārhā-brethren'. Where there are Mundā villages included in an Orāon pārhā, the representatives of such Mundā villages attending the meeting have their food cooked separately in new earthen vessels. At the present day, it is only as occasion arises that the representatives of a Pārhā meet to decide a dispute or punish a delinquent or restore a man to his tribal rights. But people still remember the days when, at the

* In some Parhas, the Kartaha also receives a few *maunds* of rice which he takes to his house where he provides another feast for the 'Parha-brethren.'

end of the great annual hunt called 'Bisū Sikār', the Pārhā elders would hold their great annual Panchāyat in which all the undecided disputes of the year would be settled and all important matters affecting the tribe and the Pārhā would be discussed. In these annual gatherings, each village would plant its village standard at the meeting-place. The 'Raja' of the Pārhā would sit in state with the other officials of the Pārhā seated by his side in their order of precedence, and the rest of the assembled Pārhā brethren would be seated all around. After their deliberations, they would regale themselves with drink. Each village would contribute a couple of rupees or so with which liquor would be purchased and drunk; and a small portion of the game bagged at the hunt would be roasted and eaten along with the liquor. And finally the rest of the game would be divided amongst the villages of the Pārhā.

Bhayari.

Sometimes two villages of the same Pārhā may knit themselves together by a closer bond than mere Pārhā-fellowship. This is accomplished by a ceremonial present by one village to another of a flag bearing the distinctive emblem the use of which has been hitherto its exclusive privilege. The social gathering of the men of the two villages on this occasion is known as a Bhāyāri.* The bond between two such villages is sometimes made all the stronger by a nnmber of boys of the one village entering individually into the *sangi* form of friendship with individual boys of the other village. Thus, not only does the group-soul, so to say, of the one village unite in a bond of friendship with the group-soul of the other village, but there is also a communion of individual souls. *Sangis*, as we have seen, are sworn friends to each other, who sit side by side at all social gatherings, eat together on all possible occasions, and stand by each other in weal or woe. Marital relations between the families of the two *sangis* are forbidden, and the wives of the *sangis* become *sangins* to each other.

Inter-Parha Alliances.

Stronger even than the bond between the different villages of a Pārhā, is the bond between a Pārhā, and its 'Dūdh-bhāyā' village. Whereas any village of a Pārhā may now-a-days sever its connexion with the Pārhā and go over to another Pārhā, the old bond between a Pārhā and its Dūdh-bhāyā village is inalienable, A 'Dūdh-bhāyā' village of a Pārhā is a village, which, though belonging to a different Pārha, entered in the days of tradition into a ceremonial alliance with another Pārhā of which,.it thus became a 'Dūdh-

* See *ante* pp. 258-9

bhāyā' (*lit.*, milk-brother) or foster-brother. Almost every Orāon Pārhā has one, and sometimes two, 'Dūdh-bhāyā, villages, As fresh 'Dūdh-bhāyā' alliances are no longer formed, the rites and ceremonies by which the bond used to the created are no longer remembered. In fact, some of the Orāons whom we questioned about it appear to regard it as a natural and not an artificial bond. They would have us believe that in every case, some ancestor of the Bhũinhars of a 'Dūdh-bhāyā' village and an ancestor of the Bhũinhārs of some village of the Pārhā of which it is a 'Dūdh-bhāyā' were related to each other as cross-cousins, and that the mother of such ancestor of the 'Dūdh-bhāyā' village having died soon after she had given birth to him, he was nursed by the mother of his cross-cousin. This explanation is obviously a modern speculation based on the etymological signification of the term 'Dūdh-bhāyā.' But even if the relationship was in reality (as we believe) an artificial one at its inception, it is now regarded not only as a 'milk-relationship' but even as a 'blood-relationship.' By such alliance, the village comes to be regarded as 'of one blood' with all the villages of the Pārhā, and is bound to take their part in all quarrels and fights (as formerly they did in all 'blood-feuds') with other villages and Pārhās. So intimate is the bond of union between a particular Pārhā and its 'Dūdh bhāyā' village that although marital relations may be, and often are, formed between Bhūinhār families (not belonging to the same clan) of different villages of the same Pārhā, such relations are not permissible between a Bhūinhār family of the Dūdh-bhāyā village and a Bhūinhār family of any of the villages of the Pārhā of which it is a Dūdh-bhāyā, although they may belong to clans other than its own.

Thus these Dūdh-bhāyā villages form the links between two or more Pārhās. Each Dūdh-bhāyā village, while forming an integral part of its own Pārhā, has also its recognised duties and privileges in connexion with the other Pārhā of which it is a 'Dūdh-bhāyā'. Although fresh 'Dudh-bhāyā' alliances are no longer formed, the old alliances are scrupulously maintained. Such inter-pārhā alliances appear to mark the final stage in the process of social integration that the Orāons attempted. But here all further progress in that direction was arrested. Nay,—in course of time a process of disintegration set in. The solidarity of the Pārhā itself began to languish into a state of inanition when owing to the changed political situation of the country and the establishment of peace and order by the British Government, much of the Pārhā's old occupation was gone. The union gradually became less stable. Old combinations here and there got broken up and reduced in size. And the Pārhās of our days are only the *debris* of the old Pārhā federations. The association of the different Pārhās during the tribal Jātrās and hunts and the inter-tribal congress held on such occasions to discuss matters of common interest, are now mere formal gatherings which appear to lack life and virility. At the present time the fullness of co-operation for the common good of the community may be seen only in the village-brotherhood which is indeed in most parts of the Orāon country a living organism to this dāy.

Such are the main features of the social organization of the Orāons. The pressure of common danger and a consciousness of the common good appear to have suggested most of the institutions described in this chapter. The prime care of the people,—the dominant idea directing and controlling the tribal soul, has been how to live and multiply, how to maintain an independent tribal existence and solidarity, how to secure good luck and avoid ill luck in so far as tribal security, health, progeny, cattle, and agricultural interests are concerned. And the social, religious, and magico-religious customs and institutions of the people are mostly intended to serve that end.

The tribal soul early perceived that union was

strength, and in the social organization of the tribe we meet with a process of alliance and combination—resulting in a real fusion or communion of souls—all along the line. Whether the earlier steps in that process were for the most part unconscious or not, there can hardly be any doubt that in its later stages, human mind and human effort have played a considerable part. In our own days we find in almost every Orāon village one or two Bhūinhārs—sometimes comparatively younger men—who, though not always the actual village headmen,* yet exercise considerable influence over their fellow-villagers by reason of their superior intelligence and personality. Such persons appear capable of introducing a new social usage to supplement or modify older usages. This is probably the way in which a number of social usages of their neighbours, the Hindus, have been gradually grafted on the social and religious systems of the Orāons in many parts of the Orāon country, and this is how in our days certain objectionable practices are being given up, and in some villages Orāon parents are being induced to send their boys to 'Primary' and 'Secondary' schools instead of to Dhūmkūṛiās. Ordinarily, however, any inno-

* In villages, where the post of the village-Mahato is elective, such men are often elected Mahatos, if they are otherwise eligible.

vation shocks this people who by reason of their geographical situation, their tribal history, and their racial genius, have on the whole remained essentially conservative.

Ideals and Character.

Ordinarily slaves to custom, they betray no partiality for idealism. They accept the world as it presents itself to them, and do not trouble their minds about the deeper meaning of life. When not actually engaged in agricultural operations or other modes of food-quest, the majority of the Orāons generally lead the semi-conscious life of a sensuous nature. Centuries of struggle with alien peoples have indeed evolved in the tribe a remark able power of combination, but have not changed their old racial light-heartedness, carelessness, and easy-going temperament. And thus they have always been more submissive and less tenacious than their neighbours and fellow-sufferers—the Mundās. Once, indeed, in 1832, and again in 1889 and 1899, they followed in the wake of the Mundās, when—

'The brute despair of trampled centuries,
Leaped up with one hoarse yell,'—

but in their crass stupidity they sought to 'set wrong to balance wrong, and physick woe with woe,' and necessarily failed to regain their rights by such lawless methods. But for only a few such incidents in their history, the bulk of the tribe have, on the whole, adopted the line of least resistance, and generally resigned themselves to their fate in listless apathy. As in social and public life, so also in individual and family life the Orāon's main idea has always been to live on terms of good-fellowship with all around him,—with man and beast, with Nature and the gods, with spirits that hover in the air above and the souls of the dead that cling to the earth below. In fact, the social mind and the individual minds act and react upon each other, and this interaction determines the current of social life as also the conduct of the individual. The Orāon's ideal of a good man is one who does not quarrel with his neighbours nor causes them* harm,—who does not covet lands, cattle, married females, or other 'property' not his own, nor meddles in the black art,—who minds his own affairs, keeps his promises and gives in charity to beggars whatever he can,†

* It is, however, not considered wrong to deposit on cross-roads or other much-frequented places, 'niksari' (such as, sweepings of a disease-infected house, *etc.*) meant to transfer disease-spirits from a house to people who may happen to walk unawares across such 'niksari' things.

† It is worthy of note that beggars of the Ghasi or other castes and tribes going for alms to an Oraon's house are generally given a handful of paddy or other grains, so lon as the Orāon has any to give.

—who takes proper care of his own lands, cattle, and family, and conforms to the laws and usages of his forefathers,—who is hospitable to his tribe-fellows, and stands by his family, his clan, his village, and his Pārhā in resisting a common danger or pursuing a common good. The only 'rift in the lute'—the only dissonance that jars against the dominant note of harmony in his relations with his neighbours and tribe-fellows, is caused, now and again, by suspicions of witchcraft or of the evil eye in some neighbour, or by dormant passions roused by the demon of drunkenness. *

Conclusion. We have now finished our hurried survey of the social life of the Orāons,—a tribe that has suffered cruelly and long,—

"Whose chronicles are writ with iron pen,
In the crooked shoulder and the forehead low."

As we have seen, the vital impulse that has hitherto regulated their tribal life and guided their social development has been the desire to secure alliance and concord, wherever possible. In most of their institutions we have seen the social soul

* Land-disputes are not infrequent; but in most cases one or other of the contending parties acts at the instigation of some alien landlord or his creatures, so that the village panchayat cannot settle such disputes.

striving, in its own way, for union and co-operation within the clan, the village, the pārhā or the tribe. As for outsiders, Orāon tribal history, which we briefly traced in the first chapter, has naturally made this people suspicious of all aliens. Although occasionally in the past they made fitful efforts to prevent the spoliation by alien jāgirdārs and ṭhikādārs of their rights in land, the tribe, as a whole, before long resigned themselves to Fate. The iron helm of Fate which their own weak arms feebly sought to turn in vain, was, however, destined to be directed before long by a Heaven-sent agency into new and broader channels leading to a more glorious haven than any they ever dreamt of. It was reserved for their British rulers to introduce amongst them the shining light of Education to quicken their moral nature, widen their field of opportunities and give them a broader outlook on life. The more intelligent amongst the Orāons are beginning to realise that they can expect to emerge from their long social degradation and serfdom only through the ever-widening portals of Education and enlightened Co-operation and not through the blind violence of revolutions foredoomed to futility. Already a growing section of the people appear to have awakened from the slumber of ages and are bestirring themselves to take advantage of the educational facilities liberally supplied by their benevolent Government, and to remove the plague-spots in their social system. And every well-wisher of the tribe now rejoices to think that under the wise and kindly guidance of their British rulers, these younger brethren of humanity, so long lagging behind in the race of life, are being at length launched on the forward path of social, intellectual, moral and material progress. And one fancies the people joyfully exclaiming—

"Standing on what too long we bore
With shoulders bent and down-cast eyes,
We may discern—unseen before—
A PATH TO HIGHER DESTINIES."

APPENDICES.

APPENDIX I.

Some Agricultural Customs Among The Oraons.

The 'Ban-gāṛi' ceremony, as described at *pp*. 143-4 *ante*, appears to be a mutilated form of the more elaborate ceremony which may still be seen in several parts of the Orāon country. This ceremony is also known by the significant name of the 'marriage' of the corn-seedlings. Similar 'marriage' ceremonies are also in vogue with respect to certain fruit-trees and of tanks and wells. These 'marriage' ceremonies are believed by the Orāon to stimulate fecundation, and, by preventing irregular fecundation, to render the produce of the fruit-trees and rice-plants and the fish and the water of the tanks and wells fit for human use.

The ceremonies observed in the marriage of the rice-plants, annually celebrated on the day that an Orāon cultivator begins the transplantation of his paddy-fields, are as follow: The men first plough up the field and retire, leaving a plough stuck up on the field in the belief that it will avert rain during the transplantation. The female members of the cultivator's family now put up on a ridge of the field three or five lumps of earth, on each of which the cultivator's wife places a few paddy seedlings and deposits a little *arua* rice and a handful of barley, unhusked rice, mustard, *Kurthi*, *Surguja* or other grains (generally five varieties in all) and marks them with vermilion and moistened rice-flour (*aripan*). When the paddy-seedlings have been duly 'married' in this manner, the cultivator's wife first takes down these 'wedded' paddy-seedlings to the field and plants them close to the ridge. Other female labourers then enter the field and the women all proceed to transplant paddy seedlings on every part of the field with the exception of a small space at one end of it. The women next plait together a few paddy-seedlings in the form of a marriage-'kārsā' (a crown of paddy sheaves) and plant it in the middle of the space left untransplanted. Then they all dance round this 'kārsā', sing wedding-songs, and, apparently as a rain-charm, spatter one another with mud and water. Finally, they transplant this remaining portion of the field and proceed to the owner's house where they are given a jar of rice-beer to drink, and each gets a handful of 'pachāit' (āruā rice soaked in water) to eat, and a little oil to anoint herself with. The owner of the field has to observe a fast that day (although he may drink as much rice-beer as he chooses) until the transplantation is over. In the case of the first field transplanted in the village, it is the village priest (Pāhān) and not the cultivator's wife who has to perform these rites. In addition to the rites described above, the Pāhān in such a case has to offer a libation of rice-beer to Mother-Earth, saying—"O Mother-Earth, may we have plenty of rain and a bumper crop." On the spot where rice-beer is thus offered the Pāhān plants the paddy-seedings duly "married."

Another class of customs connected with the reaping and the threshing of corn and the gathering of certain fruits deserves notice. At the rice harvest, the Orāon cultivator leaves unreaped on his last harvest-field a few stalks of paddy wherein apparently the corn-soul or corn-spirit is believed to reside. The Orāon calls this clump of rice-stalks the "Field-guard" (khālkhā-pāgé), and believes that it keeps guard over the field until the next sowing or transplantation, as the case may be. Now-a-days, however, this cluster of sheaves is, in many places, subsequently taken away by anybody who chooses,—barring, of course the owner of the field or any other member of his family. Even this latter restriction is now disregarded in some places. In fact, in some Orāon villages, the owner himself subsequently brings home these sheaves on an auspicious day (preferably a Monday), and describes this proceeding as "bringing the Bride home." When the rest of the paddy (i.e., unhusked rice) has been threshed and garnered, these last-reaped sheaves are taken home and threshed, and the paddy-grains are carefully set apart to serve as the seed-grain for the next sowing.

Again, when an Orāon has threshed his rice and is carrying it home, he leaves three or five handfuls of the threshed rice on the threshing-floor. This paddy is called by the Orāon the 'Bur̤hi Khes' or Old (Mother-)Rice.' It is said that this Corn-Mother keeps guard over the threshing-floor until the following harvest. This Corn Mother is usually covered over with straw, probably to protect her from the evil eye or evil spirits. Similarly to 'keep guard' over his jack-fruit tree until the next fruiting season, the Orāon leaves on the tree the last jack-fruit of the season as *Mankha-page* or Tree Guard.

* This Appendix modifies the statements made at p. 157 *ante* as to the absence of any other superstitions about the sowing, reaping, threashing and winnowing of corn.

APPENDIX II.

The Traditional Story of the Genesis of Man and of the Spirits.

We have referred more than once to the Orāon story of the genesis of man and of the spirits. This story is recited by an Orāon spirit-doctor or by any other Orāon who may know it by heart, at the Dāṇḍā-kāṭṭā ceremony performed at every Orāon house on every possible occasion. The avowed object of this ceremony is to save men (especially, children), cattle, and crops from the 'evil-eye' and the 'evil mouth.' The bhelwā twig used in the ceremony is believed to be potent against the evil eye,—for a drop of the oil obtained from the bhelwā fruit falling into the eye is believed to cause blindness. And so too the black charcoal-powder, the white rice-flour, and the red earth of the hearth, with which a mystic figure is drawn for the ceremony,—are supposed to represent the three principal colours of the rainbow which is the largest 'bow' ever known and therefore considered the most potent weapon against the evil eye, the evil mouth and evil spirits

If the ingredients used for the ceremony—viz the bhelwā-twig, the charcoal-dust, the rice-flour and the red earth,—thus serve to ward off mischief, the recital of the story of the multiplication of the human species and of the introduction of agriculture, may not improbably have been originally meant to magically promote the increase of progeny and prosperity in agriculture.

The story is given below just as we heard it recited by an old Orāon Bhūinhār. As will be seen, it consists of two parts. The first part describes the genesis of the human race and the institution of agriculture, and the second part refers to the discovery of iron and describes the origin of the gods and spirits.

PART I.

Innā	mūndhūntā	pūrkhargāhi	kāhini-kaththā
Today	original	ancestor's	story

tengā-lāgdan.	Belāṭpūr	be'las	rāksas
[I] am telling.	Belatpur	king	demon

telā-khūṭā-nū	khūṭā-lāgias.
tela -stump-to	fasten-used.

Be'las	saikā-tikhil	chūnjtā-lāgias.	Hormār
King	*saika*-rice	threshed-was-getting.	All

saikā-ti'khil	cheṛā-lāgiar.	Rākas
saika-rice	carry-were-doing.	Demon

hormārin	mokhkhās.	Abiri ōnṭā
all	ate up.	At-that-time one

rānḍi	pāchchō-gé	tāngdas	ra'hchas.
widow	old-woman-to	her-son	lived.

As-gāhi pāli mānjā ti'khil cheṛā-gé.
His turn became rice carry-for.

Belas-gāhi ālar kerār chertā-ge.
King's men went cause-to-carry-for.

Ā chenḍās sāukāṛās-gūiā jonkh
That boy rich-man-there servant

rahchas. "Gūchā bābu, nighāé
was. "Come-along, boy, thy

pāli cheṛā-ge." Tāngiō chi'khā
turn carrying-for." His-mother cry

hellrā. "Onṭā eklā engdas,
began. "One only my-son,

mōkhō-chiō rākas." Ā kūkkōs bāchas
will-eat-up demon." That boy said

"Tikhil hō-on darā kā-on." Bārō-manna-
"Rice take-will and go-will (I)." Twelve-maunds

gāhi khānḍā tero-manna-gāhi barchhā
of sword thirteen-maunds-of spear

darā nāgṛā khāj dharchas. Ānṛiā
and black clay seized. Strong

āḍḍō-nū dunduā-ghaṭin ṭāngchas.
bull-on high-sounding-bell fastened.

Tikhlan lādchas, bārā' hellras.
Rice loaded, come began.

As tin kōs gechchhā rahchās ānnūntim
He three *kos* distance remained when

rākas bāchas,— "Ekā-lekhā bīris
demon said,— "what-like warrior

bārā-lāgdas ?" Rākas-gāhi lāddi-pōttā
come-beginning ?" Demon-of bowels

āsrā-lāggi. Ās khāpā 'bārchas.
quake-began. He await came.

Kūkkōs ānṛsias darā ānias,—
Boy reached and said,—

"Bāiān āngla. Hōrmārin mōkkāe
"Mouth open. All ate

ōndkāe : Engān-hū mōkhā." Khané
drank : Me-too eat." Then

ās ānglās. Kūkkōs barchhān ildas,
he opened. Boy spear thrust,

darā pharilan jhōlchas. Antilé
and sword brandished. Then

rākas kechchas-keras ; khané tikhlan
demon died ; then rice

khōetāchas. Antilé āḍḍō kālā
weigh-caused. Then ox go

hellrā. Kukkōs āddōn ānias,
began. Boy ox-to said

"Manukhārin khakhhōe hōlé bā'-ke,
Men wilt-meet if, will-say,

'Kerā-jhariānū bāchhranā-kālā'." Dharmes
'Plantain-grove-to to-be-saved go'." God

ghōkhchas ki rākas rājinū gamkārōs
pondered that demon country-in will-smell

holé, mankhār-ge mānḍi-amm mālā
if, men-for rice-water not

su'hā.' Khané ās chich-chep ṭiṛā-keras.

will-relish. Then he fire-rain throw-went.

Āḍḍō mukkārin k͟hākhkhiā darā āniā.

Ox women met and said

"Kālā kerā-jhariā-nu bāchhrnā-ke;

"Go Plantain-grove-to to-be-saved; for

Dharmes chich-chep ṭirā-keras."

God fire-rain throw-went."

"Em āk͟hā' bāldam; i āddo āk͟h'i.

"We know don't; this ox knows.

Pāse' k͟hāddio." Ar āddon pāssar.

Beat friends" They ox killed.

Antké Pārvati Dhạrmesin

Then Parvati God-to

āniā ki "Dūbhā tūr chich-chēpan

said that "Bowl-with fire-rain

ṭirké." Anti Halmānsin Dharmes

throw." Then Halman-to God

ānias "Bhāgnā, chhāmhe-nū

said that "Nephew, front-in

rā-'ké: chich-chep ṭiṛōn hōlé, dāmuān

remain; fire-rain throw-will (I) if, drum

ṭhōk-ké." Bhāgnās telā-mūkhnūm

beat." Nephew tela-eating

lōbhras; dāmuā mālā thokchas

was-absorbed; drum not beat.

Dharmes thārā-ti " chich-chepan

God plate-from fire-rain

ṭiḍḍās ; khané ūrmi rāji ūlliā ;
threw ; then all country burnt ;

manu-mās ūrmi ūlliā. Pārvatī
tree-fruit all burnt. Parvati

bhāiā-bahinin nūddā Sirā-sitā
brother-sister concealed Sira-sita

nālē-nn gānglā-baid Kakṛō lātānu.
field-in gangla-baid crab-hole-in.

Ond-phārā masri dāli chichchas ;
One-half masuri pulse gave ;

sāttē-ullā sāttē-mā'khā mokhkhār.
seven-day seven-night ate.

Antilē Dharmes bārchās. Tikhil
Then God came. Rice

mālā khākhri. Annū Parvatīn
not found. Then Parvati-to

āniās ki, "Dānā-khatri kheā-lāgdan."
said that, "Grain-without die-beginning."

Khané Pārvatī āniā, "Dūbhā-tūr
Then Parvati said, "Bowl-with

tundā-ge ānkān ; khané nin
throw-to said (I) ; then thou

thārā-tū tund-kāe. Manukhārin
plate-with threw. Men

eksan beddōe ?" Antilé gōṛ-mūṛ
where will get ?" Then feet-head

nānā hellras Pārvatīn.
make began Parvati-to.

"Kālā, Gānglā-bāid-nū rānār."
"Go, Gangla-baid-in are they."

Khané kōhi besrā Lili-Bhuli-Khairi-
Then kohi (bird) kite Lili-Bhuli-Kairi-

kuṭi ālla-guṭhin sonā-gahi taini
bitch dogs gold-of stick

Dharmes ōchchās-ki beddā-keras.
God took-and search-went.

Allā-guṭhhi bānrnūti kerā,
dogs scenting went,

gāngla-jhūṛ-kākṛo-lātā-nū āllā bānrchā
gangla-bush-crab-hole-in dog smelt

darā bhukā-hellrā. "Erājjō, erājjō,
and bark-began See-grandfather, see-grandfather.

dhārō." "Mālā dharo nātti; En rādan."
seize-"will" "Not seize-will, grandson: I am present."

Khané Dharmes manukhārin biddias, ki
Then God men searched-out and

ochhās; "Biddkān Pārvati," bāchas.
carried "Found, Parvati," said-he.

Annunti ārin sebā nānā hellras.
From-that-time them-to service make began.

Annunti sebā nanjas; antile manukhār
From-that-time service did; then men

bāchar "Jināpāni edā." Khané
said "Life-water show." Then

pinḍi-hebṛā-ge āniaś. Erbarim
embankment-throw-for said. They-two

pinḍi hebṛā hellrar.

embankment threw began.

Dharmes onṭā eklā ūllā kāmchas

God one only day created

Antile Dharmes ārin menjās

Then God them asked

"Idin iklā hibiṛkar ?" Ar bāchar

"This which-day prepared ?" They said

"Innā." Dharmes sāttē-ūllā-

"To-day" God seven-day-

mākha'-gāhi ullā-nū menjas,

night-of day-in asked,

"Idin iklā hibiṛkār ?" Ar bāchar

This what-day made ?" They said

"Innā." Antile Dharmes ānias

"To-day." Then God said

"Ohré ! rāji māl bānchā, ullā

"Oh ! world not completed ; day

mākhā mānan-nekā." Khané ullā

night become-may" Then day

mākhā mānjā. Nānnā pairi-biri

night became. Next morning

Dharmes menjas, "Idin iklā hibiṛkar ?"

God asked "This what-day prepared ?"

Ar bāchar "chero." Antile, biṛi puttia,

They said "yesterday" Then, [the] sun set

khané nānnā ullā Dharmes menjas

then another day God asked

"Idin ikla hibiṛkar ?" Khané ār
This what-day threw-up ?" Them they

bāchar, "Hōrobhré". Dharmes ennem sātté ullā
said "Day-before-Yesterday" God thus seven day

minnum keras. Antilé bāsarka
asking went Then remaining

kām-gahin ārin menjas, "Idin iklā nā-nor ?"
works-for them asked. "This what-day will-do ?'

Ar bāchār, "Idin innā, idin nela, idin
They said "This today ; this to-morrow this

nelbenjā ;" khané Dharmes bāchas, "Akkū
day-after-to morrow Then God said "Now

manūkhārgāhi raji ṭhik bānchā."
men's world well completed".

Antilé pindi kāmchar ki bihini
Then embankment made and seeds

neā' kerar. Onṭa nol-gōṭān chichchas,
beg-went one pumpkin-seed gave,

khané, iḍḍār ; antilé kūndiā ; larangārā ;
then planted (they) then grew ; trailed ; ;

pūi-dā, khānjā, antilè pānjā. Dharmes
blossomed ; bore-fruit, then ripened. God

khāli chholtāchas, dara egtāchas.
threshing-floor got-scraped and got-cleaned

Antilé tātar-tūr khōetāchas. Ugi-
Then sickle-with got-reaped carrying-

epṭā-tūr cheṛtātās ki khōptāchas
pole-with got-carried and got-heaped-up

khāli-nū. Antilé paṭaktā hellras.
threshing-floor-in. Then thresh-to got-commenced.

Annunṭi khes ūrkhā-hellrā ; būṭ
Then paddy come-out-began ; gram

ūrkhā ; gōhūm ūrkha ; māsi ūrkhā ;
came-out ; wheat came-out ; masi came-out ;

kōdāi ūrkhā ; masūri ūrkhā ; mānni
kodai came-out *masur* came-out sesame

māghā ūrkhā ; rahari ūrkhā, ūrmi
magha came-out *rahar* came-out all

jinis ūrkhā.
thing came out.

Antilé ōnṭā dōhār e'das uiā-
Then one stretch-of-land shewed plough-

-khōsā-gé. Antilé Pārvatī bāchā "Bhāgnā,
dig-for. Then Parvati said, "Nephew,

en ḍāmūā ṭhokā'-gé ānikān ānnū ḍāmuān
I drum beat-for said yet drum

mālā thōkchkai. Khané kālā, Bhāgnā,
not beat. Therefore go, Nephew,

toṛāngnū āṛkhān chekhlan dahūrān-patirān
jungle-in herbs leaves twigs leaves

mōkhké. Manūkhār-gāhī atri-gāḍḍi
eat Men's plough-furrow,

bhāṭro āulā mānuktān ho'é ;
level-up that-day man's-body will-take ;

tarhāt-nū chuṭṭi kūndo āulā
palm-in hair will-grow that-day

mānuktān ho'é." Annūntim ālas
human-body will-have." Then-from man

ūssas; khes chakhas. Anti ĕnd-koṛān
ploughed; rice sowed. Then one-corner

khessān bōkhkhō mōkhkhā. Ond-koṛān
paddy locusts ate-up. One-corner

ergō mōkhkhā. Ond-kōṛān khes
mice ate. One-corner paddy

hariārā. Ond-kōṛā-nū keṭkeṭrā
became-green. One-corner-in became-stunted

"Kānḍhri khessan chunjtā-ké. Boṛe' bāttāké;
Karhani rice get-unhusked. Ricebeer prepare;

nātti. Bōṛé' biō-hōlé, teng-ké." "Bichchā,
grand-son. Rice-beer ready-if tell." "Ready

ājjo bōṛé." Dharmes keras darā ānias,
grandfather rice-beer." God went and said,

"Chulhā khājjān kāstā', ānti tikhlan
'Hearth earth get-powdered, and rice

kāstā'; kūilān kāsta'; bhelōā-dahurān
get-powered; charcoal get-powdered; bheloa-twig

ōndōrtā;' ennéné lihā; bhelōā-dahurān
get-fetched; thus-thus draw; bheloa-twig

pāl-kā;' binḍō māṛābā; enné
split; straw-pad put down; thus

enné bā'. 'Innā, e Dharmé! Dānḍā-kāṭṭā
thus say. 'Today, O God! Stick-splitting

lāgdan. Nin, Dharmé, bārō-chhāeā
making-I-am Thou, God, twelve-shades

nandāi ; tero chhāiā nandāi.
makest; thirteen shades makest.

Sirā-sitā nālé-nū Dharmes sikrā- becha-keras.
Sira-sita field-in God hunt- hunt-went.

Tina-tara sonéhi ṭaiṛi, Lili
Right slde Gold-of Stick Lili

Bhuli-Khairi āllā-guṭhi, Gānglā-jhūṛan
Bhuli-Khairi dogs, Gangla-bush

jōbbūkās ittias. 'Hāṛi-ré āllā', bāḍas.
beating descended. 'Go-away dog,' says.

Kakro-lātā-erpā iām rā'dām ;
Crab-hole-house in-this remain (we);

Dharmé Panch-rūpi ḍānḍā-kāṭṭā
O God Panch-as dada-katta

bārchkan. Ninghāé tinkā ninghāé
(I) have come. Thy spoken thy

paṛighkā. Juṛi kānḍō juṛi menchi
described. Double-seat-plank pair(of) chairs

ūkkāékī ṭingkāe. Dharmé
sitting instructed. God

Belāeō, khitinū bārinū hariārki
Master, agriculture-in cultivation-in greenery (abundance)

phariār-ki rā'-neka ; pōsnu pārā-nū
fruitfulness be-may; cattle-in family-in

bārhāntri mānānnekā.' Panch-rupi
increase be-may. Panch-as

ānā-lāgdan. Ninghāé tinkā ninghāe
say-(I am) continuing. Thy said Thy

paṛikā kaththan ténga-lāgdan. Kūk
instructed words saying-am. Head
mālka kheḍḍ-mālkā ningāe-gé
not-having leg-not-having Thee-to
jiā-eṛbālāgdan. Erā, Dharmé, nekhāe
life-am-sacrificing. See, God, any-man's
bailāggō nekhāe khānlāggō hōlé
mouth-strike-will any-man's eye-strike-will if
ekāsé kher-biā-khuṭrii ānnem
as hen-egg-bursts thus
ārghi khann khoṭrān-nekā.' Ekāse
their eye burst-may. As
kirohi-ḍānḍā palikkārai annem
bhelwa-stick split-is thus
bāi pālkrān nekā." Annu ānias,
mouth burst may." Then said,
"Dhingrān mājhinū āṭṭā. Ijgō nāttis
"Log middle-in place. This-side grand-son
chū'tōs ; dhingran kāṭṭ'ké ki
will-sleep ; log pass-across and
kālké holé, ālar bāṛrho."
go if, men will-multiply."

PART II.

Bāro bhāir Asurār, tero bhāir
Twelve brothers Asurs thirteen brothers
Lodhrar, din-nā-rāiṭ pānnā dhuknār ;
Lodhars, day-night iron smelt ;

Hānk-rāj Pankh-rāj Dharmes-gāhi ghōṛō
Hank-raj Pankh-raj God's horse

dānā māl mūkhi. Antké Dhichuā
fodder not eats. Then King-crow

Mangrū Māhāto bārjā-keras, "Anā hārō
Mangru Mahto warn-went, "Oh ye

bhāiro, din-nā-rāit pānnā āmbā
brethern, day-night iron don't

dhukā." Ār āniār "Bāro bhāi
smelt" They said "Twelve brothers

Asurām tero bhāi Lodhām
Asurs [we are] thirteen brothers Lodhars [we are]

din-nā-rāit pānnā dhūkdam ; imimga
day-night iron (we) smelt (we) ourselves

Dharmem, imim bélam,......dharā-
God (we) ourselves kings,............seize-

hārō !" Dhichuā bōngā-lāgiā ; sānṛsi-
friends !" King-crow fly-began ; pincers

turu khōlān dharchār, kūilān
with tail caught, charcoal

tāpā-nanjar. Kholā-kōchā mānjā ; mokhrārā
throw-did. Tail broken became became black

Dhichuā. Antilé Dharmes Jhagṛu-
Dhichua Then God Jhagru

-Kerkettā-bhānḍāri-sin bāchas, "Nighāé
Wood-pecker-steward-to said, "Thy

kathhān mennār hōlé, bārjā" "Anā
words listen if, warn." "O

hārō, bhāiro ! Din-nā-rāit pānnā endargé
ye brethern ! day-night iron why

dhūkdār ?" "Em bāro bhāi Asurām,
smelt ?" "We twelve brothers Asurs

tero bhāi Lodhrām ; em gōllām ; em
thirteen brothers Lodhars ; we landlords ; we

bel'ām ; dharā toṭān". Sārsi-tūrū melkhān
kings. seize neck." Pincers-with throat

dharchar ; chindān tāpā nanjar chhāti-nū.
caught ; ashes throw did chest-on.

Khané ādigahi chhāti pānḍru mānjā.
Then her chest white became.

Antilé Dharmes pānnān dhuknan bāgṛāgé
Then God iron smelting spoil-to

khāsra-khūsru mānjas, darā tusā-daharé-nu
leprous became, and spring-road-on

ukkias. Anti bārō-bhāi-Asūrār-
sat. Then twelve-brothers-Asurs-

terō-bhāi-Lōdhar-gāhi tāngmukh-bāgār
thirteen-brothers-Lodhars-of their-wives

āmm hoā bārchar. Khasrā-khusru
water take came. Leprous

kūkkōs ārin ānias, "Chi, āiāng amm"
boy them said, "Give, my-mother water."

Ar-gāhi tangkhai-bāgar āniar,—
Their wives said,

"Bāro-bhāi Asūrār terō-bhāi Lodhrār ;
"Twelve-brothers Asurs thirteen-brothers Lodhars ;

ār-gāhi em tangmukh-bāgām, chich erkhdam;
their we their-wives; fire (we) evacuate;

phūngi pītdam; ārrā-phārrā ārlag-parlag
sparks (we) emit; broad-and-wide beautiful-red-coloured

kichrin kurdam, āsgé chiōm amm?"
cloth (we) wear; to-him shall-give water?"

Ar-madhé ōntā rāndi pāchcho
Them-among one widow old-woman

rahchā; ādi-gusān nechas, "Chi
was; her-to asked, "Give,

āiāng amm" "Aré betā, ekātarti
my mother, water," "O, son, wherefrom

bārch-kāi? Isan bāro bhāi Asūrār
didst come? Here twelve brothers Asurs

terō bhāi Lodhār nāmé-jagarki
thirteen brothers Lodhars notorious

rā'i, ālarin pitnār." Ad amm chichchā;
are, men kill(-they)." She water gave,

ās ōndās. "Ningūiā kaōn, āiō," bāchas.
he drank. "Thy-house shall-go-I, mother," said.

Anti ā pāchchō āni, "Bhūti-bāni nāndan,
Then that old-woman says, "Field-labour do-I,

bāṛhā nandan; tab en ujjudān;
sweeping-work do-I; then I live;

ender nālkh nānōe?" Khané ās
what work wilt-do?" Then he

āndas, "Eṛpā khāpūn; khes khāpun."
says, "House (I) will-guard; rice (I) will-guard."

Annuntim hōrmārgāhī khālī-nu
From-that-time all-men's threshing-floors-in

bāṛhānānjā. Adihi bārā-ge khessan
'barha'-paddy-made. Her coming-to rice

khāedas, chunjias. Antké pāchchō
dried, husked. Then old-woman

bārcha. "Khāiā betā? Chunjā
came. "Has-it-dried, son? To-husk

kāloé? Nekhāénim khāddkāi ender
wilt-go? From-any-one stole whether,

beṭa?" "Māl āiāo; khāṭnā-onnāsé
son?" "No mother; cook-eat-with

kām. Hormārgahi khāli chochā;
business. All-(men)-of threshing-floor (rice) carried (home);

nāigās-ghī rai. Kālā, mājhi
priest's remains. Go, middle

khālinū būsūn ondrké darā khettké."
threshing-floor-in straw bring and thresh."

Khes āur būsū barābari mānjā.
Rice and straw equal became.

Antké ā pāchchō barchā-ki āsin
Then that old-woman coming him-to

ānīā, "Nin-hō khāsra-khusru beṭā,
said, Thou-also leprous, son,

khes āur būsū barābari mānjā;
rice and straw equal become

ne chero? En-hō pāchchā āli."
who will-carry? I-too old-woman."

Ās ānias, "Kālāé pōllārin, jokhārin
He said, "Go maidens, youngmen

khānjké ; cherōr. Nin māṇḍi āmkhi
summon ; carry-will (they). Thou rice curry

khāṭāe, āiō. En khe'tā-chhoṛā ōjjā
cook, mother. I leaf-plates prepare

kādān."
go."

Antilé bārō bhāi Asūrār tero
Then twelve brothers Asurs thirteen

bhāi Lodhar-gāhi pāññā bāgṛāchas.
brothers Lodhars-of iron got-spoiled.

Antké deorā beddā-keras ; eksan
Then magician search-went ; anywhere

hū deorār mālā khākhrar. Antile
even magician not were-found. Then

ās usan bārchar. "Anā bhāi
he to came-they. "O, brother,

hūngūṛ-jūngūṛ ākhdāé ?" "Kūchh ākhdan
magic-spells know'st ? "Something know-I

kūchh bāldan." "Guchānti, bārō bhāi
something don't-know-I." "Let-us-go, twelve brothers

Asūrār eddār." "Māl kāōn. Pitōr chiōr."
Asurs call (you)." "Not go-will-I. Kill-will give-will-they"

Antilé tām-tām āniar, "Kālā hārō,
Then self-self said-they, "Go ye,

āsin dharā ondrā." Āntké ās menjas,
him seize bring." Then he asked,

"Endr mānjā, hāro bhairō?" Ar āniar,
"What happened, ye brethren?" They said,
"Pānnā emhāi bāgṛārā; hūngūṛ-jūngūṛ
Iron our spoiled; magic-spells
nānnār-chiā." "Engān kūṭhinū mānkhā,
make-give." "Me furnace-in place,
nisgar chiā, sāté ullā sāté mākhā dhūkā.
plaster give, seven days seven nights blow.
Pūnā bisālinu amm ōndrā; ṭāṭhkhā
New pitcher-in water bring; mango
dahurā-turū chhiṭkāké. Uṭhpūṛi chāri-tūrū
twig-with sprinkle. Uthpuri reed-with
bālin kōllké." Khāsra-khūsrūs ekāsé
door open." Leper as
ānias ānnem nanjar. Antké sōnā ār
said so did-they. Then gold and
rūpā-tūrū jhābrarkas ūrkhas. Ar āniar,
silver-with covered came-out. They said,
"Anā bhāi, eksan ibṛan biḍḍkāe?"
O brother, where these didst get?"
"Iam kuṭhinū biddkān. Nim bāggé
This-in furnace-in found. You many
rā'dar. Nim-gā bāggé beddōr." Antlé
are. You even more find-will." Then,
"Kōrōm kā?" "Kō-rā." Korchār hormar.
"Shall (we) enter then?" "Enter." Entered all.
Bārobhāi Asūrār 'tero bhāi Lodhrār
Twelve brothers Asurs thirteen brothers Lodhars

kōrchār. Tāngmūkh-bāgārin chhābā-ge
entered. Their-wives plaster-for

ānias. Chhābchar, mūndhchar.
told. [They] plastered, closed up.

"Dhūkā" bāchas. Dhūkchar.
"Blow away" said (the boy). [They] blew.

Kheāgé hormār āṛmūṛrar. Tāngmukh-
To die all writhed. Their-wives

bāgār menjār, "Ender mannār, bāng?"
asked, "What (they) are becoming, son?"

Ā kukkōs ānias, "Ar ānā-lāgnar
That boy said, "They are saying

'mukkā-khādd-ge bāggé hō'om'; āunge
'wives-children-for more take-shall-we;' therefore

ārba-nākhrā-lāgnar." Kechchar hormar.
(they) are-fighting." Died all.

Sabad mālā khākhri. "Tisgā, ; mōkhrō
Sound not found. "Open, black

bisālinū amm ōndrā', k̲h̲ōkhrō-dahūrān
pitcher-in water bring, sinduar-twig

ōndrā darā chhitkā; bālin kōllā."
bring and sprinkle; door open."

Ar kūlliār. Khōchōl hāṛhurri. "Anā
They opened. Bones clattered-down. "O

bāng, ender nanjkāi?" Annu ās
son, what didst (*i.e.* hast done)?" Then he

āndas, "A biri bārō bhāi Asūrār
says, "That time twelve brothers Asurs

tero-bhāi Lodhār āniar, 'chichchan
thirteen-brothers Lodhars said 'fire

he'dam, phūngi pītdam, arra-phārrā
find-we, sparks emit-we, long-flowing

kichri kūrdam." Kālā-kōé, en kā'lagdan."
clothes wear-we. Go-ye, I am going."

Ghōṛō-nu Dharmes ārgias ki challras.
Horse-on God rode and move-began.

Kerārki mūkkar jhekchar. "Emāgé
Went-and women stopped [him]. Us-to

jinā-pāni bātlārchā." Anti ās ānias
life-drink tell." Then he said

kōhān, "Nin Chālā Pāchchō manké,
eldest-to, "Thou Chala Pachcho become."

Sannirin, "Deswāri mānké, Khūt mā'nké,
Younger (ones)-to, "Deswali become, Khut become,

Chirō mānké, Rāmpāon mānké,
Chiro become, Rampaon become,

Aṣālgo mānké ; mānkhārin khokhrāké,
Asalgo become ; men way-lay,

ār bhōg ạrgōr nimāgé."
they sacrifice offer-will you-to."

TRANSLATION.

PART I.

To-day I am telling the original story of (i. e. as told by our) ancestors :" The king of Belāṭpur used to tie up a Rākṣas (monster) to a stump of *tela* (marking-nut) tree. The king was getting his *saika*-rice threshed. All (men) were carrying *sāika*-rice. The Rakṣas devoured the men. At that time (*i. e.*, in those days an old widow had a son. It was now his turn to carry rice. The king's men went to make him carry rice. The boy was a servant in a rich man's house. [They said] "Let us go, young man ; it is now your turn to carry [rice]." His mother began to weep [and said] "One only son [I have] ; the Rākṣas will devour even [him]."

The boy said, "I *will* carry rice and go." He held [in his hands] a sword weighing twelve *maunds* and a spear weighing thirteen *maunds*, and [a little] black clay. He fastened a high-sounding bell to [the neck of] a strong ox, loaded rice [on its back] and proceeded on his way. When he was three *kos* * off, the Rākṣas said [to himself], "What kind of warrior is coming [there] ?" The Rākṣas' heart began to quake. He came out to await (meet) him. The boy reached [the place], and said, "Open your mouth. You devoured [other] people. Devour me too." Then he opened his mouth. The boy thrust his spear [into his mouth], and wielded his sword ; and the Rākṣas died. Then he caused the rice to be weighed. Then the ox began to move. The boy said to the ox, "If you meet people tell

* A 'kos' is equivalent to about two miles.

[them], 'go to Kerā-jhariā * to save yourselves." Dharmes thought within Himself, 'When the [corpse of the] Rākṣas will emit foul smell, men will not relish their food and drink." † Then He went to shower down a rain of fire. The ox met [some] women, and said, "Go to Kerā-jhariā to save yourselves, Dharmes is gone to let fall a rain of fire." [They exclaimed] "We don't know, but this ox knows [i.e., this ox pretends to know more than we do]; beat him, friends." They killed the ox.

Then Pārvati‡ told [her husband] Dharmes, "Rain down fire from a [small] bowl." ** Then Dharmes told Halūmān, "Nephew, stay by me. When I rain down fire, beat the drum." The nephew became absorbed in eating the telā fruit (marking-nut) and did not sound his drum, [So] Dharmes rained down fire from a brass dish. And thus there was a general conflagration [*lit.* all coun-

* 'Kera-jharia', literally means 'the plantain-grove', but it is generally identified with Keonjhar, a tributary state of Orissa.

† *Literally*, 'their rice and water'.

‡ Some versions have 'Sita' instead of 'Parvati'. May not this Parvati or Sita, the wife of the Sun-God Dharmes, be really none other than the Earth-goddess whose marriage with the Sun is annually celebrated by the Oraon at the Sarhul ceremony?

** She in mercy asks Dharmes to pour from a smaller vessel a less quantity of fire.

tries got burnt]; [and] all vegetation was burnt up. Pārvatī concealed a man and a woman (*lit.*, a brother and a sister) in a crab-hole overgrown with gānglā shrubs in a rice-field called *sira-sita*. She gave them half a grain of *masuri* lentil (*Ervum lens*). They lived on this for seven days and nights. Then Dharmes came. He could not find rice. Then He told Pārvatī, "I am dying for want of food." Then Pārvatī said, "I told you—'throw [fire-rain] from a bowl,' but you threw [it] from a dish. Where will you find men now?"* Then he began to beseech Pārvatī [*lit.*, make with his head at Pārvatī's feet]. [But she replied] "Go, [they] are in Gānglā-bāid." Then Dharmes took a small stick of gold and with the bird *kohi*, the kite and the dogs 'Lili,' 'Bhūli,' and 'Khairi,' went out to search [for the 'Bhāyā-bhāyin']. The dogs sniffed about for a scent of them, and went on till at the crab-hole in the Gānglā-bush, they scented [them] and began to bark. [The Bhāyā-bahin exclaimed] "Look, O Grand-father, [these dogs] seize us!" [Dharmes said,] "They won't seize you, I am here." Then (thus) Dharmes found out the [two] human beings, and carried them [to Pārvatī]. From that time, He ministered to their comforts [*lit.*, served them].

* It is on the sacrifices offered by man that Dharmes and the other gods live. Hence God's need of man.

Then they said, "Reveal to us some means of livelihood." Then He directed them to make an embankment. They began to raise an embankment (preparatory to making rice-fields).

Dharmes had [then] made only one day [i.e., night was not yet created]. Then Dharmes asked them, "What day did you prepare this?" They said, "To-day." After a time equal to [what would now be] seven days and nights, Dharmes asked [them], "What day did you make this?" They said, "To-day." Then Dharmes said, "Oh! the world [is] not [yet] as it should be. Let there be Day and Night." Then Day and Night came into existence. Next morning Dharmes asked [them], "When did you make this?" They said, "yesterday." Then the sun set, and the next day Dharmes asked [them], 'What day did you make *this*?" They said, "Day before yesterday." In this way, Dharmes went on asking [them] for seven [consecutive] days. Then with regard to the work remaining to be done, He asked them, "When will you do these?" They said, "*This* [we shall do] to-day, *this* to-morrow, and *that* the day after to-morrow." Then Dharmes said, "*Now* the world of men is made as it should be."

Then they completed the embankment and went to ask [Dharmes] for seeds. He gave [them] one seed of the bottle-gourd. Then [they] planted it. It grew; it trailed; it put forth flowers; and bore fruit; and the fruit ripened. Dharmes had a threshing-floor prepared and cleaned. Then Dharmes pointed out a *dohar* (stretch of low lands) for [them] to dig and plough (*i. e.* cultivate). Paddy (rice-plants) began to come out (i.e., began to grow); grain came out; *marua* (*Eluisine Corocana*) [and] *gondli* (*panicum miliare*) came out, *makai* (maize) came out; wheat came out; *urid* (Phaseolus Roxburghii) came out; *masuri* [lentils] came out; *sorso* (mustard) came out; *surguja* (niger oil-seed) came out; *bodi* (*Vigna catiang*) came out; *kurthi* (*Dolichos biflorus*) came out; *barai* (*Phaseolus mungo*) came out; *rahar* (*Cajanus Indicus*) came out; all things came out (i. e. began to grow). Then He had the paddy (i.e., the rice crop) reaped with sickle and carried with *sika-bahingās* (primitive yokes) and piled up on the threshing-floor. Then He made them begin to thresh [grains]. Then Pārvatī said to [Halumān] "O nephew, I told you to sound the *nagera* (drum), yet you did not do so. Therefore, go there, and live on jungle-herbs, twigs and leaves. You shall assume human form only when furrows made (with the plough) on the earth by man will be levelled up to an even surface (*i. e.* when man will give up cultivation,—an event which it is assumed will never come to pass). You will assume human form only when hair will grow on the palms of man's hands (through their ceasing to drive the plough)." From that day man ploughed, and sowed paddy (rice in husk). Then locusts ate up the paddy in one part [of the fields]; in one part [*lit.*, corner] of the fields mice ate up the paddy; in one part the paddy remained green; and in another the paddy plants were stunted in growth. [Dharmes said :] "Get karhāni rice husked; prepare rice-beer, my grand-son. When the beer ferments, inform me." [When rice-beer was ready, the man told Dharmes :] "O grand-father, the rice-beer is ready." Dharmes went and said, "Make into powder some earth from the hearth; get some rice pounded, get some charcoal powdered; and bring a twig of the *bheloa* tree (marking-nut, or *semecarpus anacardium*) In this way draw a figure [on the ground]; split up the bheloā branch; place [on the ground] a straw-pad, [and] say thus :—"Today, O Dharmes, I am performing the (Bhelwā-) stick-splitting ceremony. Thou madest the twelve shades [Asurs]—the thirteen shades [of Lodhars]. On Sirā-Sitā field Dharmes goes a-hunting. [On] His right [are] a a golden staff and the dogs Lili-Bhuli-Khairi. [He] alights [on Sirā-Sitā fields] beating the Gānglā bush, and says "Go away, dog." In this crab-hole-house, we [the Orāons] remain (i.e., remained). O Dharmes, I (the sacrificer) have come as Panch to perform the 'Dāndākāṭṭā' [ceremony] as commanded by Thee,—in the manner laid down by Thee,—as instructed by Thee [whilst thou didest sit] on a pair of seat-planks—on a pair of chairs. O Dharmes, Master, in [our] cultivation, in agriculture, may [there] be abundance. In our cattle, in [our] progeny, may [there] be increase. As Panch I am saying (*i. e.* praying) this. I am speaking [these] words [as] instructed by Thee. [I am] sacrificing to Thee [a thing] without head or leg (*i. e.* an egg). See to it, O Dharmes, if the 'evil mouth' (*i. e.* malicious words) or the 'evil eye' of any one falls [on so-and-so] may the [evil] eye burst even as this hen's egg is [now] broken ; may the evil mouth burst even as this bheloā twig is split."

Then [Dharmes] said, "Place a log of wood in between [you two]. This side of the log, O Grandson, wilt thou sleep. Should'st thou pass across the log and go [over to the other side], mankind will multiply."

PART II.

[There were] Twelve brothers Asurs—thirteen brothers Lodhars : Day and night they would smelt iron. Dharmes' horse [named] Hankrāj-Pankhrāj does not eat fodder (i.e. they did not get fodder to eat). Then the Dhichuā* [otherwise known as] MangrūMāhāto went to warn [theAsurs]: "O brethren, do not smelt iron day and night." They said, "We twelve brothers Asurs—thirteen brothers Lodhrās†—smelt iron day and night. We ourselves [are] gods, we ouselves [are] kings.........Let us seize [this fellow]." [As] the Dhichuā began to fly, [they] caught [its] tail with iron-pincers [and] cast charcoal-dust [at it]. [Thus, the Dhichuā's] tail became shortened, and the Dhichuā turned black.

* The Dhichua is the king-crow and the Kerketā is the wood-pecker. These are the traditional bird-messengers of Dharmes, the Supreme God.

† The names 'Asurs' and 'Lodhars' appear to refer to one and the same people and they are reputed to have introduced the art of smelting iron into the Chota-Nagpur plateau. The numerals 'twelve' and 'thirteen' in the text appear to have been used in the sense of 'many.' The Iron Age in Chota-Nagpur appears to have been preceded, as elsewhere in India, by a Copper Age and that in its turn by the Stone Age. Ancient stone implements, chipped as well as polished, are dug up now and then in various parts of the plateau, particularly in its southern and south-eastern parts. The author has collected a number of them. Copper axe-heads are also known to have been dug up now and then. Recently twenty-one copper axe-heads were dug up at a village in *thana* Basiā. In cinerary urns attributed to the Asurs copper ornaments are now and then found.

After this Dharmes told the Kerkeṭṭā [also known as] Jhagṛu Bhāndāri (steward) "If they will listen to your words, warn [them]." [The Kerkeṭa told them,] "O ye friends! Why do you smelt iron day and night?" [They said:] "We twelve brothers Asurs—thirteen brothers Lodhars,—we [are] lords (masters of all), we [are] kings. Let us seize [the kerkeṭa] by the neck." They seize [the kerkeṭa] by the throat with princers, [and] cast ashes on [the Kerkeṭa's] chest. Then Dharmes, in order to hinder ironsmelting, became leprous (i. e. assumed the appearance of a boy full of sores) and sat on a road [leading] to a spring. Then the wives of the twelve Asūr brothers—thirteen Lodhrā brothers—came to fetch water [from the spring]. The itch-covered boy told them "Give me water, O Mother!" Their wives said, "We are the wives of the twelve Asūr brothers, thirteen Lodhār brothers. We evacuate fire*; we emit sparks of fire; we wear broad and

* It may be noted that before the introduction of lucifer matches, the Oraon, like the Munda, used to obtain fire by friction of wood. And even now when the Oraon or the Munda goes to the jungles he sometimes uses two pieces of *putri* or similar other easily inflammable wood and by steadying the one with his feet and twirling round the other fixed perpendicularly into a groove in the former, causes the sawdust thus produced to ignite and set fire to dry leaves or a rag placed underneath.

wide beautiful red clothes. Shall we give him water (*i.e.*, shall we give water to such a miserable vagabond)?" There was a widow amongst them. To her he said "Give [me] water, mother." [She said,] "Oh son, where do you come from? Here the twelve Asūr brothers—thirteen Lodhar brothers—are notorious. [They] kill people." Then (*i.e.* after saying this) she gave him water; he drank [it] [and said,] "To thy house I will go, O grand-mother." Thereupon that old woman says "I work [as] a field-labourer; [I] work [as] a sweeper * [on other people's threshing-floors]; and thus I maintain myself. What work will you do [for me]?" Then he says. "I shall guard [thy] house; guard [thy] paddy (unhusked rice) [when laid out to dry]."

From that time] [He] gathered rice from [other] people's threshing-floors. * By the time she returned [home] [the boy] got the paddy thus collected dried [in the sun] and husked. Then the old woman came [home and asked:] "Has [the paddy] dried? Will you go to husk [the rice]? Have you stolen [the rice] from anybody, O Son?"

* The reference here is to poor people gathering rice by scraping together with the broom what is left on other people's threshing-floors, when the villagers have threshed and taken home their paddy after harvest. This is called 'Bāṛhā-khes' or 'paddy gathered by sweeping'

No mother; your business is only to cook and eat. [All] People's threshing has been finished. All [men] have taken [their] rice home. Only the Naega's (village-priest's) is left [on the threshing-floor]." "Go, bring straw (i.e. rice in straw) to the middle of the threshing floor and thresh [it]." The rice and straw became equal [in quantity]. Then that old woman having come to him said, "You are an *itch-afflicted* boy [just as I am an old woman]; the rice and the straw have become equal [*i.e.* equally large in quantity]; who will carry [them home now]? (The sense is, who has strength for the work?) I too [am] an old woman." He said, "Go: Summon maidens and bachelors [as labourers]; they will carry it. [Do] You cook rice and curry. Go to sew up leaf-plates [to eat from]."

Then the iron of the twelve brothers Asūrs —thirteen brothers Lodhārs,—got spoiled. Then [they] went about in search of a spirit-doctor. Nowhere did they find a spirit-doctor. Then they came to him [and said:] "O friend! Do you know spells?" "I know a little, don't know a little." "Come then, the twelve brothers Asūrs are calling [you]." "I won't go. They will kill me". Then they (*i. e.* the messengers) said among themselves, "Go, ye seize [and] bring him." Then he asked, "What has happened, oh friend?" They said, "Our iron got spoiled;—do your spells." [He said,] "Place me [in] the iron furnace, [then] plaster it up, and blow away [with your bellows] for seven days and nights. [Then] Bring water in new earthen pitchers; [and] with mango twigs sprinkle [the water] [on the kiln]. [Then] open the door [of the kiln] with *reeds* of *utpunri* grass." They did as the itch-covered boy directed. Then he came out covered with gold and silver. They said, "O friend (lit., brother), where did you get these?" "[Even] here, in [this] kiln, I found [them]. You are many [in number]. You will find more." "Then may we enter too?" "Do enter then." All [of them] entered [the furnace]. The twelve Asūr brothers—thirteen Lodhār brothers—entered; they told their wives to plaster up [the furnace]. [He] told them "Blow away". They blew [with their bellows]. [Then] all [of them] writhed in death-agonies. Their wives asked [him], "O Son! What is happening?" He said, "They are saying, 'we shall take a good deal for [our] wives and children.' Therefore they are quarrelling amongst themselves." All of them died. [When] no sound was audible, [He said] "Open [the furnace]; bring water in black earthen jars; sprinkle [water] with *Sinduar* twigs; and open the doors." They opened [the furnace]; bones fell clattering in large numbers. [The women said]

"O son, what hast thou done?" Then He says, "At that time (*i.e.* previously) the twelve Asūr brothers —thirteen Lodhar brothers—said (used to say), 'We bind down fire, we emit sparks, we put on long and flowing clothes!' (*i.e.*, this is the punishment for their pride and disobedience.) Go away, I am going." Dharmes rode on [His] horse and began to move away. The women went [forward] and stopped Him. [They said] "Tell us [what shall be our] means of subsistence." Then He said to the oldest, "[Do thou] become Chālā Pāchchō" * To the younger ones, [He said:], "Be Deswāli, Khūnts (sept-spirits), Chirōs † Rāmpāwans † Asālgos† [Do ye] waylay men. Men will offer you sacrifices (*i.e.*, on which you will live.)"

* Chālā Pāchcho or Sarnā Buṛhiā is the 'Old Lady of the Grove,' the most popular Orāon Spirit, who appears to represent the Spirit of Vegetation.

† Chiros, Asalgos and Rāmpāwans are thorny creepers which hurt the jungle-going Orāons unawares, and make their feet bleed. They are accordingly believed to be animated by blood-thirsty spirits.

APPENDIX III.

Oraon Songs.

We give below a few specimens of the different kinds of Orāon songs with literal translations:—

(A) Jadur Songs.

[1]

Chālki-binṛio bārā lāggi,
Guchā bhōngot Rohidās kila
Lahar lahar chālki-binṛiō barā-lāggi,
Dahar ḍahar guché bhōngōt Rohidās kilā.

[TRANSLATION]

'Broomstick-earstick, * is coming on,
Away let us fly [to] Ruidās fort.
Flaming forth the scourge doth come,
Along the road let's fly [to] Ruidās fort.

[2]

Guch, pelō, kālōt kōé, Tiko ḍhōṛhā,
Guch, pelō, kālōt kōé, namhāe pātṛā.
Nāmhāe pātṛā, pelō, atkhā chōkhōt,
Tiko ḍhōṛā, pelo, injō piṭhot.

[TRANSLATION.]

Let us together, girl, go [to] Tiko stream;
Let us together, girl, go [to] our own woods.

* 'Broomstick-earstick' stands for the scourge of epidemic. This has reference to the magical use, in cases of disease, of the broom and, incertain cases, of the small stick usually stuck through the lobe of the ear.

[In] our jungle, girl, let us gather leaves.
[In] Tiko stream, girl, let us catch fish.

(B) Sarhul Songs.

[3]

Chānūm chānūm, Nāegāeō!
Belār-lekhā benjrā-lāgdāé!
Khāddi pairi-biri, Nāegāeō!
Belār lekhā benjrā lāgdāé!

[TRANSLATION.]

Year [after] year, Village-Priest!
Like kings are you wedded!
[On] Sarhūl morning, Village-Priest!
Like kings are you wedded!

[4]

Jāmbu ḍahurān lāoā, dādā!
Binṛiō kāmōn;
Ningūsān bhejā bechōn.
Jambu dahurān lāoā, dādā!
Binṛiō kāmōn.

[TRANSLATION.]

That Jāmun twig do bring, O friend!
Ear-stick [of it] I'll make!
With thee [then] hand-in-hand, I'll dance,—
Jāmun-twig do bring, O friend!
Ear-stick [of it] I'll make!

(C) Kharia Songs.

[5]

Sirā-Sitā-nālnū, kākṛo-lātā-eṛpā-nū;
Bhāiā-bahin rāchār, Sirā-Sitā-nālnū.
Chiro baṛūng kūndiā,
Jūṛi-jūṛi rahachkāt, bhāiāré,
Pānti-pānti rahachkāt, bhāiāré,
Kākrō-lātā-eṛpā, bhāiāré,
Séā-lātā rādāt, bhāiāré,
Dharti-nū rādat, bhāiāré.

[TRANSLATION.]

On-Sirā-Sitā-fields, in-crab-hole-house,*
Brother-sister lived,—on-Sirā-Sitā-field.
[There] *chiro*-grass also did grow.
In pairs [they] lived, my brother, O!
In rows [they] lived, my brother, O!
In crab-hole-house, my brother, O!
In-that-same-hole [they] live, my brother, O!
In-the-earth [they] live, my brother, O!

[6]

Haredār Giridār, duiō bhāiā
Lāṛkā-pariā jiā hū kerā.
Nāo jāgālé duiō bhāiā,
Laṛka-pariā jiā hū kerā.

* 'Crab-hole-house' probably refers to the cave-dwellings of the ancient Orāons.

[TRANSLATION.]

Harédār Giridār—brothers twain,—
[In] 'Laṛka'-times,—[their] lives even went
[Their] names do live,—these brothers twain:
[In] 'Lāṛkā'-times,—[their] lives even went.

[7]

Ender oṛā chikhi koé!
Khūta māiā 'chhōé-pāpā' bāi?
Pairi-biri chikhi koé!
Khūtā māiā 'chhōé-pāpā' bāi?

[TRANSLATION.]

What bird [there] cries, O girl!
Upon [the] post sounds 'chhōe-pāpā'?
[At] Morning-time [there] cries, O girl!
Upon [the] post sounds 'chhōe-pāpā'?

(D) Karam Songs.

[8]

Urbārghi tāngdā bānnā kichri, kōé,
Pāchṛi heddé ijki rai!
Rāṇḍi pāchchō tāngeda lederā kichiri,
Rājham-rajhamrā bhejā bichi!

[TRANSLATION.]

Rich-man's daughter, dear, [dressed in] coloured cloth,
Beside [the] wall is standing [there]!

Old widow's daughter [there] [in] tattered clothes,
[How] Blithely leaping joined [with boys] doth dance!

[9]

Cho'koé, rāṇdi-pāchchō tāngedā!
Chūnja lāssā ka'-dikā māla?
Komāṛ'khān mokhdi, ghōṛō lekhā khandirdi!
Cho'koe chunjā lāssa kā-dikā mālā?

[TRANSLATION.]

Awake old-widow's daughter,
To work [at] husking are [you] going [or] not?
Koinar-herb you eat; like [a] horse you sleep!
To work at husking, will you go or not?

(E) Jhumar Song.

[10]

Ekā pelo-gāhi sāmae kerā?
Ekā pelō-gāhi sāmae kerā?
Gangā-Jamunānu biṛiō bōhāil goe, sajan!
Chenṛā-pelo-gāhi sāmae kerā,
Chenṛā pelo-gāhi sāmai kerā.
Gangā Jamunānu biriō bāhāil goe sajan!

[TRANSLATION.]

What girl [is that] whose time* is gone?
What girl [is that] whose time is gone?
Down Ganges [and] Jumnā [her] binṛio is swept, my friend!

* *i. e.*, whose life is ended.

[The] Little girl's [brief] time is gone!
[The] Little girl's [brief] time is gone!
Down Ganges and Jumnā [her] biṛio is swept; my friend!

(F) Marriage Song.

[11]

Enghai ra'na guṭi, bābā hōé!
Ninghāi eṛpā jhāl-mānjūr-lekhrō,
Bābā hōé, nighāi eṛpā jhāl-mānjūr lekhrō.
Engōn bisoé hōlé, bābā hōé!
Ninghāe eṛpā rāi-sunā mānō,
Bābā hoe rāi-sunā mānō!

[TRANSLATION.]

Throughout my stay, [my] father O!
Thy house [like] peacock-feather looked; *
O father! Thy house [like] peacock-feather looked!
Should'st thou sell† me, father O!
Thy house quite desolate will become!
O father! quite desolate will become!

* The girl's meaning is that she has been an adornment to her father's house until sold in marriage.

† *i. e.*, give me away in marriage.

To face p 254.

Oraons driving cattle-disease. The man on the left is the village-Ahir with a wooden cow-bell suspended from his neck. For the sake of decency, the men were photographed with their loin-cloths on.

To face p. 216.

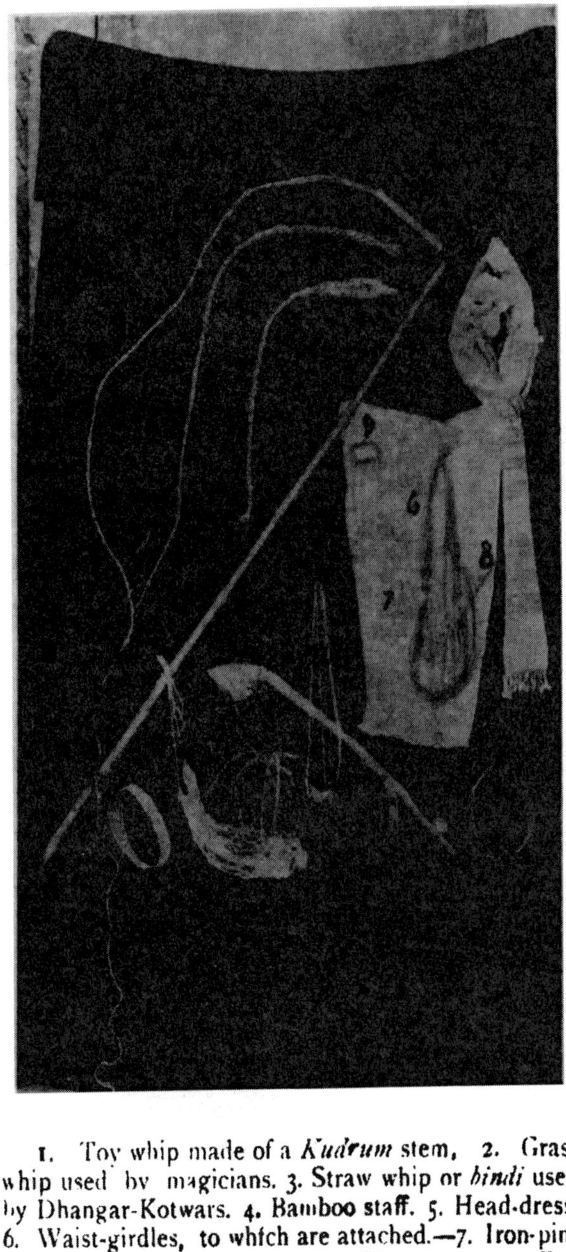

1. Toy whip made of a *Kudrum* stem, 2. Grass whip used by magicians. 3. Straw whip or *bindi* used by Dhangar-Kotwars. 4. Bamboo staff. 5. Head-dress. 6. Waist-girdles, to which are attached.—7. Iron-pincers and 8. A bamboo-flute. 9. Ear-ornament called 'bindio.' 10. The Dhebsa which looks like a non-return boomerang. 11. Sling. 12, 13, artistic crowns or hair-bands made of grass and leaves and worn by Oraon young men. 14. Jāl-khari or not-bag.

APPENDIX IV.

Oraon Population in India.

Terretorial Distribution.

The Census Report of 1911 gives the total Orāon population of the Chotā Nagpur Plateau or rather of the Rānchi district as 398,768. Their distribution *thana* by *thana* is shewn in Table (D) below. The total Orāon population in the entire province of Bihār and Orissā was found to be 587,411. Their distribution district by district is shewn in Table (A) below. Tables (B) and (C) shew the Orāon population in Bengal and Assam respectively. Besides these, the Census Reports shew in the Central Provinces a total Orāon population of 83,099, of whom 5,009 (2501 males and 2,508 females) were returned as Hindus and 78,090 (39,415 males and 38,675 females) as Animists. These do not include 36,362 Orāon Christian converts in the Jāshpur Tributary State (in the Central Provinces). Thus, the total Orāon population of India comes up to nearly nine hundred thousand.

Distribution by Language.

The total population of speakers of the Kūrukh (Orāon) language is, however, not more than 800,328 (395,530 males and 404,798 females), namely, 460,149 in Bihār and Orissā,

116,992 in Bengal, 19,813 in Assam, 2,940 in the Central Provinces and Berar, 99,346 in the Bihār and Orissā Feudatory States, 100,824 in the Central Provinces Feudatory States and 264 in the Bengal Feudatory States. It may be further noted that even of these 800,328 Kūrukh-speaking people in India, a small portion are non-Orāon neighbours of the Orāons.

Distribution by Religion.

The tables given below shew that of the nearly nine *lakhs* of Orāons in India, about a *lakh* and a half have been converted to Christianity, about a *lakh* and a half (157,134) call themselves Hindus, and the remaining six *lakhs* (or, more correctly, 594,556) have been returned as Animists. But neither Hinduism nor even Christianity has yet been able to eradicate animistic ideas and beliefs.

(A) Oraon Population in Bihar and Orissa.

DISTRICT OF STATE.	ORAON.			
	HINDU.		ANIMIST.	
	Males.	Females.	Males.	Females
Bihar and Orissa	**26,309**	**26,173**	**200,964**	**221,227**
Patna				
Gaya	14	1	19	23
Shahabad ...			802	797
Saran	1	1		
Champaran ...	1621	1,482		
Muzaffarpur ...	8	8		
Darbhanga ...	464	436		
Monghyr ...	51	75		
Bhagalpur ...	894	836	205	229
Purnea	2704	2,684	4,957	4,847
Sonthal Parganas ...	256	259	2,320	2,383
Cuttack				
Balasore	3	8	169	203
Angul			478	518
Puri				
Sambalpur ...	3036	3,236	2,064	2,033
Hazaribagh ...	1112	1,031	1,338	1,333
Ranchi	3583	3,760	141,150	161,628
Palamau... ...	5588	5,638	12,717	12,668
Manbhum ...	1318	1,156	1,020	1,078
Singhbhum ...	6	1	3,457	3,517
Orissa Feudatory States ...	5649	5,561	29,947	29,656
Chota Nagpur States..			321	314

Besides these, there are 55,594 males and 57,144 females returned as Christians, viz., in the Sāntāl Parganās (2+3), Hāzāribāg (8+6), Rānchi (43,438+45,209), Palāmau (3,680+3,660), Mānbhum (22+16), Singhbhum (212+231) and Orissa States (8,232+8,019).

(B) Oraon Population in Bengal.

DISTRICT OR STATES.	ORAON.			
	HINDU.		ANIMIST.	
	Males.	Females.	Males.	Females.
Bengal ...	45,243	39,214	43,820	37,060
(1) British Territory ...	45,080	39,057	43,820	37,060
BURDWAN DIVISION ...	3,929	1,225	3,815	721
Burdwan	208	198	59	58
Birbhum	102	117	111	103
Bankura			20	
Midnapur	170	207	109	91
Hooghly	2,239	496	2,118	352
Howrah	1,210	207	1,398	117
PRESIDENCY DIVISION	5,180	3,876	5,840	4,467
24-Parganas	3,884	2,633	3,460	2,078
Calcutta	27	25	20	7
Nadia	790	707	1,367	1,374
Murshidabad ...	477	511	795	824
Jessore			175	160
Khulna	2		23	24
RAJSHAHI DIVISION ...	35,785	33,810	34,159	31,867
Rajshahi	5,570	5,248	317	247
Dinajpur	4,117	3,827	3,408	3,529
Jalpaiguri	20,035	19,232	26,076	24,140
Darjeeling	1,057	986	2,808	2,692
Rangpur	561	337	1,443	1,190
Bogra	1,137	945	73	158
Pabna	1,246	1,091	34	11
Malda	2,062	2,136		
DACCA DIVISION ...	89	72		
Dacca	88	64		
Mymensingh ...				
Faridpur	1	8		
Backergunge ...				
CHITTAGONG DIVISION	97	74	6	5
Tippera	17	10		
Noakhali				
Chittagong	80	64	6	5
Chittagong Hill Tracts				
(2) Feudatory States	163	157		
Cooch Behar ..	3	2		
Hill Tippera ...	160	155		

N.B.—There are 314 males and 110 females in Jalpaiguri who have accepted Christianity. These are not included in the figures for Oraon in the table.

(C) Oraon Population in Assam.

District or States.	Oraon.			
	Hindu.		Animist.	
	Males.	Females	Males.	Females.
1	2	3	4	5
Assam ...	7,865	7,321	6,805	6,592
Cachar ...	1,224	1,154	147	153
Sylhet ...	974	858		
Khasi, and Jaintia Hills				
Naga Hills ...				
Lushai Hills ...	1			
Goalpara ...	38	25	43	41
Kamrup ...	114	96	70	62
Darrang ...	785	738	2,664	2,592
Nowgang ...	3		861	803
Sibsagar ...	1,993	1,874	548	548
Lakhimpur ...	2,733	2,574	2,472	2,393
Garo Hills ...		2		
Manipur State ...				

N.B.—Besides these, there are 152 males and 87 females returned as Christians, viz., Darrang (57), Sibsagar (83), and Lakhimpur (99).

(D) Statement showing the number of Oraons returned as Hindu, Animist and Christian in each thana of the Ranchi District in 1911.

…ES OF THANAS … TOTAL ORAON …OPULATION,		HINDU.			ANIMIST			CHRISTIAN.		
		Total.	Male.	Female	Total.	Male	Female.	TOTAL.	MALE.	FEMALE.
ardaga	57,219	384	173	211	54692	24813	29,879	2,143	1,002	1,141
u	17,524	1414	661	753	15031	6565	8,466	1,079	516	563
mu	2,321	66	28	38	2210	1005	1,205	45	24	21
idar	36,299	202	86	116	30471	13005	17,466	5,626	2,637	2,989
)	24,363	31	17	14	21062	8929	12,133	3,270	1,550	1,720
ung	7,748	71	32	39	7207	3477	3,730	470	236	234
chi	58,015	1916	972	944	45923	21831	24,092	10,176	4,849	5,327
ianjbi	1,632	13	5	8	1595	765	830	28	16	8
ara	2,986				2461	1273	1,188	525	244	281
	300	189	122	67	85	55	30	26	15	11
ra	8,209	31	17	14	7437	3586	3,851	741	359	382
pa	1,033	47	21	26	932	455	477	54	25	29
inti	2,101	45	23	22	1642	801	841	414	223	191
idu	2,072	86	48	38	1893	950	943	93	47	46
ahatu	218	115	61	54	101	52	49	2	2	
nar	1,170	184	97	87	943	471	472	43	21	22
hunpur	9,890	93	49	44	9511	4792	4,719	286	158	128
ainpur	33,488	255	125	130	4003	2107	1 896	29230	14,432	14,798
aghra	23,057	128	61	67	22025	10688	11337	904	440	464
ai	36,384	220	94	126	35129	16522	18,607	1,035	484	551
mla	23,307	249	118	131	20978	10198	10,780	2,080	1041	1,039
idih	11,308	101	57	44	3222	1589	1,633	7,985	3,969	4,016
lkot	5327	16	8	8	4638	2454	2,084	773	397	376
sia	6,700	1361	650	711	4100	2011	2,089	1,239	609	630
no	134	6	6		124	56	68	4	4	
lebira	908	4	1	3	591	294	297	313	161	152
chedega	13,503	31	13	18	3095	1583	1,512	10,377	5,103	5,274
ırdeg	11,552	85	38	47	1777	823	954	9,690	4,874	4,816
strict Total	398,768	7343	3583	3760	302778	141150	161,928	88,647	43,438	45,209

INDEX.

THE END.